YO-BWX-028

Rethinking Development

Henri BARTOLI

Rethinking Development

Putting an end to poverty

Management of Social Transformations (MOST) Programme

EDITIONS UNESCO

ECONOMICA

The ideas and opinions expressed in this publication are those of the author and do not necessarily represent the views of UNESCO. The designations employed and the presentation of material throughout the publication do not imply the expression of any opinion whatsoever on the part of UNESCO concerning the legal status of any country, territory, city or area or of its authorities, or concerning its frontiers or boundaries.

Original title : Repenser le développement.
First published by the United Nations Educational, Scientific and Cultural Organization (UNESCO), 7, place de Fontenoy, 75352 Paris 07 SP and Economica, 49, rue Héricart, 75015 Paris, France.
© UNESCO, 1999

ISBN UNESCO 92-3-103702-1
ISBN Economica 1-902282-07-8

© UNESCO, 2000

All rights reserved

Table of Contents

Foreword

The financial crises that routinely disrupt the economies of the developing countries and, to a lesser extent, those of the industrialized countries call into question a neo-liberal system founded on the globalized market principle. This system is incompatible with both sustainable and equitable development, as it is with genuine democracy.

Its foremost victims are the most vulnerable groups: the poor and the excluded, in the North as in the South. Violence is fuelled by social dysfunction, which is becoming increasingly acute by the day, especially in urban areas. Urgent action is therefore imperative.

The time has come for a dispassionate reassessment of the dominant thinking on economics and the type of governance imposed through the G-7, the Bretton Woods institutions and the World Trade Organization. This economic and financial system exacerbates inequalities, poverty and unemployment, imposes a debt burden on poor countries and negates development and democratization efforts.

Political leaders are, admittedly, awakening to the need to restructure and regulate globalization in an attempt to humanize it. Nonetheless, the need is still felt for new economic and social policies founded on an accurate analysis of the situation.

As a contribution to this task, UNESCO, on 30 November 1998, held an International Day of Reflection on the topic "Rethinking development: do we need a paradigm shift?" at its Headquarters in Paris, which was attended by senior economists and high-ranking international leaders. The challenge they faced was to seek innovative and practical solutions that would provide an escape from the crisis and create conditions conducive to the establishment of a balanced international economic system and sustainable development, reconciling the exigencies of economic growth, social equity, the strengthening of democracy, and environmental protection.

The aforementioned was also a fundamental concern of that great thinker and development expert Paul-Marc Henry, who died in 1998 and whose presence was greatly felt throughout the International Day of Reflection. Visionary extraordinaire that he was, in the 1980s he was already perturbed by the phenomena of social marginalization and exclusion. As early as 1986, while chairing a meeting of experts on "Poverty, progress and development" at UNESCO, he emphasized "the risks of a profound rift between the affluent and the marginalized in human society".

In view of the quality of the discussions that took place on that 30 November 1998 Day and the ensuing proposals, UNESCO invited Professor Henri Bartoli – co-author of the work "Poverty, progress and development" – to review and develop their salient points and add his own opinions.

Introduction

The United Nations was created while the Second World War was still raging. Its principal objective is the maintenance of international peace and security, the prevention of threats to peace, the suppression of acts of aggression and the settlement of international disputes by peaceful means. But these are not its only tasks. The preamble to the Charter of 26 June 1945 affirms the faith of its signatories in fundamental human rights. Its first article states that one of the aims of the Organization is to secure respect for human rights. Within the framework set by statements of that nature, the General Assembly adopted the Universal Declaration of Human Rights on 10 December 1948. That instrument adds social rights (education, social protection) and collective rights (associations, trade unions) to the individual rights enshrined in the 1789 Declaration of the Rights of Man and the Citizen.

The initial impulse had been given. The General Assembly adopted a number of international instruments on human rights. These included the Convention on the Prevention and Punishment of the Crime of Genocide (adopted in 1948), the International Covenant on Economic, Social and Cultural Rights (adopted in 1966) and the International Covenant on Civil and Political Rights (adopted in 1966). The latter provides for the establishment of a Human Rights Committee to consider reports submitted by Member States on the measures they have taken to ensure respect for human rights and the effect of those measures. In 1993, following the World Conference on Human Rights held in Vienna, the post of United Nations High Commissioner for Human Rights was established.

Member States have made abundant specific declarations benefiting women (1979), children (1989) and migrant workers (1990),
giving rise to the danger that the multiplicity of categories of human
beneficiaries will weaken the impact of instruments designed to
constitute absolute benchmarks. At the beginning of 1998 there
were 72 international conventions or covenants relating either to
the entire range of rights set out in the Universal Declaration – that
is to say, the rights of all of humankind – or to rights relating to particular categories of humans or combating discrimination of various
kinds. The dispensation of justice is a sovereign act, and the international community is moving towards the establishment of a common body of laws, even though it does not share a common
sovereignty. Guarantees of justice are being granted in increasing
numbers; even governments which commit violations of human
rights officially refer to them. Special procedures have been introduced to deal with individual violations of human rights, brought
either before the Human Rights Committee established in pursuance of article 28 of the International Covenant on Civil and
Political Rights or before the European Court of Human Rights in
Strasbourg. The concept of an international criminal tribunal is
making headway.

In the opinion of Sachs[1], the struggle for human rights, with its
dearly bought successes and failures, is a central policy feature. He
describes their evolution. The first generation consists of political,
civil and civic rights, the absolute value of which we have learnt by
experience. This is followed by a second generation – the generation of social, economic and cultural rights. The former circumscribe the extent of the power of the State; the latter impose on the
State the requirement of positive action. The third generation is
that of collective rights – rights for the child, for the environment,
for cities, and the right to development, which, as Sachs points out,
was finally recognized at the 1993 Vienna Conference. Finally,
there is a fourth generation, consisting of "republican" rights; these
guarantee the citizen access to public assets (and especially the environment[2]) and proper use thereof; it is also the generation of rights
relating to bioethics.[3]

Bobbio, in a burst of enthusiasm, uses the phrase "the age of
rights" to describe this evolution. Sachs, however, observes that
much still remains to be done to make them a reality in the every-
day lives of individuals. Even so, he is similarly inspired to describe
the second half of the 20th century as the "age of development".
He distinguishes successive generations: the simplistic (and soon

abandoned) concept that economic growth is sufficient to ensure development; the acceptance of pluridimensionality, a concept within which development is simultaneously envisaged as economic, social, cultural and political; the addition to that concept of the environmental dimension in the form of "sustainable" development; the subordination of the pursuit of economic and social objectives to ecological constraints concurrently with a search at the instrumental level for economically efficient solutions (the United Nations conference on the environment in Stockholm); and finally the use of the word "human" to qualify development in order to make it clear that the aim is not just the production of wealth, however necessary that may be, but rather the development of the human personality.

Unfortunately that burst of enthusiasm soon fades when confronted with reality. The century which has just ended was one of brutality and inhumanity. Kolko[4] has described it as a "century of war" in which the "machinery of massacre" has become ever more efficient: 8.5 million people killed in the First World War; 50 to 60 million in the Second; massacres have become a commonplace, and individual and communal violence are continually becoming more widespread. Between 1990 and 1994, over 50 domestic or international conflicts were observed – not counting the struggles of minority peoples aspiring to autonomy or independence and the conflicts between Islamic movements and incumbent governments.[5]

The ideal of democracy and human rights is not unanimously appreciated throughout the world. The achievement of solemnly proclaimed ideals is slow when interest provides an incentive to disregard them. As obligatory benchmarks, human rights have become weapons in international competition: throughout the cold war period the West made itself the champion of individual rights; the East did the same for social rights and the South for collective rights.[6] When the West obtained the inclusion of a clause concerning respect for human rights in the final act of the 1975 Helsinki conference, the Eastern-bloc countries immediately secured the introduction of the principle of non-interference in the internal affairs of the signatory countries. In the preamble to the Universal Declaration of Human Rights, the Member States of the United Nations pledged themselves "to achieve, in cooperation with the United Nations, the promotion of universal respect for and observance of human rights and fundamental freedoms"; but the United States has not yet ratified the 1966 International Covenant on

Economic, Social and Cultural Rights; China has not ratified the International Covenant on Civil and Political Rights; and France has refused to accept article 27 of the latter instrument, which concerns minorities, invoking the tradition of an indivisible people, with all the citizens enjoying exactly the same rights.

If one looks only at the resolutions in favour of human rights that have been adopted, one might think that enormous progress has been made. On the other hand, if one looks at the reports of Amnesty International and Human Rights Watch, or the records of proceedings of the United Nations Human Rights Committee, or even simply news reports on crimes and acts of genocide committed, one has the impression that the world is regressing at an unprecedented rate.[7]

"Development decades" come and go one by one. The reports on them produced by the World Bank and the International Monetary Fund (IMF) celebrate certain unquestionable successes, but at the same time are full of alarmist observations. A few items can be mentioned here.

The value of world production, calculated in 1975 US dollars, has been estimated at $ 580 billion in 1900 for a population of 1.6 billion human beings, or $ 360 per head; the figure for 1975 was almost $ 6 trillion for nearly 4 billion, or $ 1,500 per head; and that for 1994, $ 25 trillion for 5.6 billion, or approximately $ 4,500 per head. Never was there so much wealth; but never were there so many poor people. On 28 June 1996, the United Nations Economic and Social Council estimated that the numbers of the "desperately deprived" were increasing by 25 million annually. At the end of 1998 there were 57 million poor people in the European Union.

There are 1.5 billion poor people subsisting on less than one dollar per day. It is estimated that 35,000 children die of malnutrition and sickness every day throughout the world. There are 50 million individuals deprived of fundamental rights. One third of the planet's economically active population – roughly 1 billion individuals – are unemployed; of that total, 150 million have no work at all and 850 million are working much less than they would wish and are earning less than the minimum living wage. Human depreciation and destruction accumulate. Bonvin observes with sadness that "the most serious problem is that of poverty among the young". Children born into poverty are saddled with every handicap, especially in urban areas, where solidarity within the extended family is beginning to break down. They will be excluded from employment, forced to make a living from odd jobs and marginalized, and will soon find themselves shut out of society and forced into delinquency.

Racism, as stupid and repulsive as ever, is still widespread. Political hatred is a collective construction which feeds on mendacious anecdotes which no one believes, but which maintain negative feelings towards those they caricature.

Human language is inadequate. One should speak of "misdevelopment" rather than "development". Badinter writes[8]: "From the ambitious references to the right to development there emerges the requirement that the human beings living in the poorest regions of the world should at last come to enjoy the benefits of a less unequal distribution of resources and techniques. That inequality is the primary cause of the evil afflicting the world. It is in fact the most hateful inequality of all; for it makes the States which have wealth ever wealthier and relegates the others to poverty, social injustice and dictatorships. Thus the struggle for respect for human rights is inseparable from that for a new international order based on the right of nations to fair economic development and a less unequal distribution of the world's wealth."

Notwithstanding all the setbacks encountered and the false trails followed, the themes of human rights and the right to development have gradually secured acceptance as a kind of corpus of principles to which all agents in international society must now subscribe; and at that level, as Merle has written[9], the conventional discussions on whether or not those principles have the status of law are quite pointless. What matters is the strength of the consensus with which States agree to comply, even if the opinions they express are no guarantee of the faithfulness of their compliance with the values enunciated.

How could one fail to hear the appeal launched by the non-governmental organizations at the end of their congress conducted in parallel with the official celebrations of the anniversary of the Universal Declaration of Human Rights, on 10 December 1998, testifying that disregard and contempt for human rights were still a day-to-day reality for many, and violations of human rights were taking on increasingly varied and complex forms, implicating an increasing number of agents (particularly economic agents) in a context of globalization? How can one fail to denounce together with them the widening gulf between the speeches and the realities and the pseudo-justifications of violations of human rights advanced in the name of cultural, religious or historical specificities, or even of national security? How can one fail to call on States to discharge their obligations in this field and to urge enterprises, transnational companies and the United Nations institutions to adopt strategies that would allow the achievement of human rights by the peoples?

In his address to the Social Summit held in Copenhagen in March 1995, the Director-General of UNESCO stated that a new strategy should be implemented, and a new set of priorities addressed. In the Organization's position paper addressed to the same summit, he stated that development was a "human right" and called for the adoption of a "radically new approach to development policies". In its report to the same summit, UNESCO outlined, for the period 1996-2001, activities designed to promote the achievement and the exercise of human rights – conceived as a "guiding principle" for development –, the strengthening of endogenous capacities and the fostering of "human resources" through continuing education at all levels, democratic participation in governance, the incorporation of cultural factors in development strategies, the promotion of awareness of environmental problems and the adaptation of science and technology for the tasks of development. In July 1997, at the end of the regional summit known as the "Brasilia Consensus", a "Declaration for political development and democratic principles" was presented and adopted under the auspices of UNESCO's DEMOS project. It, too, enunciated the need for "a new pact, on global governability... for peace and new arrangements to make international economic flows equitable, to control financial speculation and to democratize communications so that a system of shared development may be constructed".

"At the present moment", wrote Keynes in his *General Theory*[10], "people are unusually expectant of a more fundamental diagnosis; more particularly ready to receive it: eager to try it out, if it should be even plausible". Jolly quotes this sentence, arguing that the same is true of the present day, for we need a fundamental diagnosis and a definition of new approaches, at both national and international levels, capable of upholding a new paradigm. As early as 1994 the experts of the United Nations Development Programme (UNDP), in their *Human Development Report*, affirmed the same urgent need for a new paradigm giving "absolute priority to poverty reduction, productive employment, social integration and environmental regeneration."[11]

A "new paradigm" cannot be developed solely on the basis of observation of the devastation caused by a crisis of such gravity that some people are sometimes tempted to compare it to the crisis of the 1930s, or by that of the general crisis of civilisation caused by the radical changes taking place in every aspect of life, and the resultant disorder, which we are currently experiencing. It would probably be over-ambitious to claim to offer a reply to the questions to which the formulation of the paradigm give rise solely by reference to the writings produced in connection with the international meeting, held to pay tribute to Paul-Marc Henry at UNESCO on 30 November 1998 and the informal discussions which followed that meeting on 1 December 1998. However, one may reasonably draw from those proceedings a number of useful elements for the identification of paths showing the way to an outline of a reply, as well as risk a definition of the new paradigm and deduce its implications, in terms of both governance or governability and of the required renewal of economic thinking. This is the task the author has set himself.[12]

---

[1]"Développement, droits humains, et citoyennetés", a communication to the seminar on "human rights in the 21st century" held in Rio de Janeiro at the International Relations Research Institute, Ministry of Foreign Affairs, in September 1998.

[2]L.C. Bresser Pereira: *Citizenship and Res Publica. The Emergence of Republican Rights*, Brasilia, 1998.

[3]*L'età dei diritti*, Turin, Einaudi, 1990.

[4]*Century of War. Conflicts and Society since 1914.* New York, The New Press, 1994.

[5]M. Kidron and R. Segel: *Atlas des désordres du monde,* Paris, Autrement, 1996.

[6]M. Merle: *Sociologie des relations internationales,* Paris, Dalloz, 1988, p. 289.

[7]M. Merle: *Bilan des relations économiques internationales,* Paris, Economica, 1995, p. 81.

[8]Droits de l'Homme, Cahier spécial du *Monde*, Dec.1998, No.4.

[9]*Sociologie des relations internationales, op. cit.,* p. 427.

[10]*General Theory of Employment, Interest and Money,* Cambridge University Press, 1973, p. 383.

[11]*Human development Report, 1994,* New York, Oxford University Press, p. 4.

[12]To this end recourse is had to the written texts and the oral statements by Yves Berthelot (Executive Secretary of the United Nations Economic Commission for Europe); Francis Blanchard (former Director-General of the International Labour Office); Jean Bonvin (Chairman of the

OECD Development Centre); Leandro Despouy (Human Rights Committee); Stéphane Hessel (French Ambassador); Richard Jolly (United Nations Development Programme); Ignacy Sachs (Ecole des Hautes Etudes en Sciences Sociales); Albert Tévoedjré (Minister of Planning, Benin); and Alfredo Sfeir-Younis (World Bank).

CHAPTER 1

Human rights, the basis of sustainable development

The word "paradigm" derives from the Greek *paradeigma* meaning "example". T.S. Kuhn, who was responsible for the successful revival of the concept,[1] applied it to the entire galaxy of beliefs, values and techniques shared by the members of a given scientific community, the "disciplinary matrix".[2] The "new paradigm" pursued by international experts is not exclusive to the scientific community. It calls on all actors in economic, social, political and cultural life; it requires us to rise to the challenges of our times. What is needed is not so much an "example" as a "portrayal of development"[3] centred on a guiding principle; not so much a "disciplinary" as a "pluridimensional" matrix in which all facets of development find expression.

It is neither doctrine, ideology nor "world view" in the Schumpeterian sense that should dictate the interpretation of development. It is with reference to the actual state of the world, with a view to seizing and transforming it through the creative skills of men and women, that the "new paradigm" must be considered, and economics consigned to its role as an instrument in the service of all aspects of life, with human objectives.

Development is not merely growth. It assumes a human dimension when it encompasses the enhancement of material well-being in low-income countries, be it food, health, education or the duration and dignity of life; in other words, components not inherent in development. It also assumes a human dimension[4] when, through vigorous human activity, it seeks to establish for men and women the world over the conditions essential to the maintenance and blossoming of life. It is pluridimensional when it is a "project" (François Perroux), "an historical progression" (Ignacy Sachs); far from being restricted to countries which "diplomacy by terminology" (Gunnar Myrdal) defines as "backward", "least developed", "underdeveloped" or "developing", it affects all peoples and all nations.

Articles 25 and 26 of the Universal Declaration of Human Rights proclaim that "everyone has the right to a standard of living adequate for the health and well-being of himself and his family, including food, clothing, housing and medical care and necessary social services, and the right to security in the event of unemployment, sickness, disability, widowhood, old age or other lack of livelihood in circumstances beyond his control" and that "everyone has the right to education". Sachs advocates "rethinking development as an effective appropriation of the totality of those rights". For his part, Yves Berthelot would like the United Nations – which did nothing to dampen the wave of financial enthusiasm that prevailed in the economic policy recommendations of the "Washington consensus", so called because it expressed the coalition between the political Washington of Congress and the White House on the one hand, and the technocratic Washington of the Bretton Woods institutions and the American Treasury Department on the other[5] – to become totally involved in determining the new paradigm for human development. During one of the discussions held on Paul-Marc Henry Day, Alfredo Sfeir-Younis observed that the World Bank had been focusing for two years on human rights and the equitable development it is its function to sustain, and had initiated genuine dialogue with those who, in pursuit of equitable development, need to establish the link between human rights and economic policies, and particularly with Mrs Mary Robinson, the United Nations High Commissioner for Human Rights. This augurs well.

1. HUMAN RIGHTS, THE CORNERSTONE OF SUSTAINABLE HUMAN DEVELOPMENT

It is highly desirable that the new paradigm should emerge from the United Nations' own thinking; indeed, there is much to be gleaned from the documents that emanate from the United Nations agencies and from their annual Reports.

Such is the case of the World Bank, which in 1990 addressed the "abject" poverty that affects one billion human beings, its eradication being the prime objective. There followed reports on development strategies (1991), development and environment (1992), health investment (1993), development infrastructure (1994), the world of work in an economy without borders (1995), the transition from a planned to a market economy (1996), the State in a changing world (1997) and, most recently, the evaluation of aid in a Report which was held up for several months, the subject having been deemed "too controversial".

Each of the Reports places emphasis on what are seen as "the real problems" that need to be addressed. Some examples are touched on below.

We shall look, first of all, at the Environment Report. It shows "how environmental problems can jeopardize – indeed, do jeopardize – the objectives of development". The quality of water forms part of the well-being which is the purpose of development. Damage to the environment is deleterious to future productivity. War on poverty, which is vital for sound management of the environment, is a moral imperative. Without claiming to be exhaustive, the Report identifies the most pressing problems in need of solutions: water pollution, sanitation, air pollution, natural habitats, biological diversity, greenhouse warming, the challenge posed by the all too frequent squandering and destruction of freely accessible resources with no commercial value (water, forests, air), there being no incentive to manage them in a society whose basic logic is short-term economic profit. Endorsing the conclusions of the Report of the Brundtland Commission[6] on the need for better management of the environment that meets the needs of the present without compromising the ability of future generations to meet their own needs, the Environment Report agrees on the obligation to promote the "acceleration" of "sustained and equitable" human and economic development.[7]

Then there is the Health Report. While acknowledging the undisputed improvements in the world, through expanded health service coverage and thanks to technological advances, it highlights the persistent and considerable disparities between infant mortality rates (from 1 to 10) and maternal mortality rates (from 1 to 30), depending on the wealth or poverty of the countries polled. It also points out that we face new challenges, not least the heavy toll taken by the acquired immune deficiency syndrome (AIDS), malaria's increased resistance to present-day medicines, the steep rise in deaths from tobacco-related heart disease and cancer, and the spread of tuberculosis. Millions of lives could be saved by the determination to attain the objective proclaimed at the historic Alma Ata Conference (1978): "The attainment of all peoples of the world by the year 2000 of a level of health that will permit them to lead a socially and economically productive life"[8].

The Labour Report exhorts us to invest wisely in infrastructure, health and education, so that the workers of all countries can benefit from economic growth and the achievements of the anti-poverty struggle. For that to become a reality, it tells us, we must define "minimum standards" that prevent any recourse to man's exploitation by man. The Bank's experts optimistically declare that labour policy must not contravene the laws of the market-place nor seek to give certain categories of worker precedence over those in poor countries, while acknowledging that the transition to a market economy can entail profound rifts and "temporary regression", necessitating governmental intervention in the form of appropriate assistance.

And lastly, the State. Since 1994 the World Bank has been invoking the "permanent, but different" role the State must play. In 1997 it confronted those who, going to extremes, called for a "minimum State". Throughout the world, it claimed, it was necessary to embark on new thinking on the State and to spell out its functions: maintenance of economic stability, guarantee of basic social services and infrastructure, protection of the environment and vulnerable social groups. The role of the State needs to be adapted to its capacity for action, and its limits recognized, as must be the fact that it cannot aspire to monopolies, especially in the provision of collective equipment and social services. The need was also felt to revitalize the institutions and fight corruption. There too, the result was to be enhanced economic and social well-being, but – and this is rather disturbing – for that to be achieved, the problem of State reforms must be firmly tackled by the authorities, which can take time.

The World Bank Reports discuss "development" alone, although they provide a great deal of information and make a number of proposals concerning "human" development. However, it is with human development that the reports of the United Nations Development Programme (UNDP) are concerned.

In the view of the UNDP experts, human development is simply the development "of" the people, "by" the people and "for" the people. The earliest Reports on the subject (1990-1992) deal with the development "of" the people as an investment in human potential – be it in education, health or training – the aim being to enable individuals to work productively and creatively. The 1993 Report deals with development "by" the people, with people placed at the centre of economic and political change, since people must guide both the State and the market, both of which should serve people instead of people serving markets.[9] Which raises the question of popular participation in all its forms (familial, social, cultural and political), of reflection on discrimination, violence and exclusion, and of looking at the participation of civil society and, more particularly, at the role of the non-governmental organizations.

The main topic in 1994 was "sustainable human development"; while the absolute priority of poverty reduction, productive employment and social integration were again present, they were linked more to environmental regeneration.[10] The "new paradigm" selected – "sustainable human development" – was that of the Brundtland Report, with respect for ecosystems, on which the existence of all living beings depends.

In one sense, the *Human Development Report 1995* marks a turning-point. It stresses that, in UNDP's view of the link between individuals and development, the concept transcends approaches which, prior to its invention, had focused on issues of social justice and poverty, with models of economic growth linked to increased GNP rather than to improved living conditions. To develop "human resources" is to treat human beings as "mere factors of production" and, consequently, as a means rather than an end. "Social welfare" policies treat individuals as beneficiaries of the development process and not as participants in that process. As we shall see, to emphasize "basic needs" is to be more concerned with the provision of economic goods and services to disadvantaged groups than with the expansion of human potential. Pluridimensional, the full concept of human development encompasses and transcends all those targets. "It analyses all issues in society – whether economic growth, trade, employment, political freedom or cultural values – from the perspective of people. It thus focuses on enlarging human choices – and it applies equally to developing and industrial countries".[11]

With that general framework established, the UNDP Reports of the following years endeavoured to draw its consequences. Since people's lives were very rarely enriched, what was needed, said the 1996 Report, was for policy-making bodies the world over to concentrate on strengthening the linkages between growth and the human development that is its aim. However, a dual concern was expressed: hostility to facile answers and ready-made solutions, and the fear lest achievements "should be blown apart by sudden shifts in political power or market forces".[12] Like the World Bank's 1990 Report before it, the 1997 UNDP Report attacks the "extreme poverty" under which one quarter of the inhabitants of the planet labour despite impressive progress with reducing it during the twentieth century. Expressing their condition in terms of human development rather than income criteria, it advocates "pro-poor" growth,[13] declaring that eradicating absolute poverty in the first decades of the twenty-first century is "feasible, affordable and a moral imperative."[14] Lastly, the 1998 UNDP Report describes an increasingly widespread mode of consumption that depletes renewable natural resources and even threatens their existence, pollutes the local and planetary environment, resorts to invasive advertising to cajole consumers into satisfying prefabricated needs, and distracts attention from the legitimate needs of everyone in modern societies, whereas it should be devising a different mode of consumption in the service of human development.

One cannot fail to mention the reports of the International Labour Organization (ILO), given the enormous contributions they can make to the definition of a "new paradigm" for human development.

Lebret long ago[15] described as "primary needs" – both material and spiritual – not only food, housing and clothing, but also moral support, faithful tenderness, the gift of life, hospitality, science, wisdom and art. As a delegate of the Holy See to the first United Nations Conference on Trade and Development (UNCTAD) in 1964, he called for the "establishment of a just order" that would afford all persons access to a standard of living in keeping with their dignity as human beings, so that "the basic needs of all men and women could be met".[16] Little heed was paid to his words at the time, so convinced was the economically developed West of the future success of its development decade, during which the policies followed could not fail to enable the Third World to "catch up" with the rich nations, and hunger would be a thing of the past, thanks to the action of the Food and Agriculture Organization (FAO).[17] In 1972, Robert McNamara, the new president of the World Bank, convinced that it was impossible for hundreds of millions of people to fight their way out of a situation in which they were literally trapped, explained to the Board of Governors that "since mankind's basic human needs were not being met", the prime objective of his institution's aid policies and those of the rich countries must be poverty eradication.[18] At the 1976 Tripartite World Conference on Employment, Income Distribution, Social Progress and the International Division of Labour, the Director-General of the ILO wholeheartedly endorsed that approach.

He defined "basic needs" as "the minimum standard of living which a society should set for the poorest groups of its people."[19] Covering those needs entailed fulfilling for everyone the minimum conditions of a family's consumption (food, housing and clothing), as well as the conditions of access to basic services (water, transport, health and education), enjoyment of a healthy environment, and the people's participation in the formulation of decisions affecting their existence, since "many people's work is at present demoralizing, undignified, inconvenient and even dangerous to health, if not to life".[20] It is quite remarkable – but in keeping with the nature of that institution – that the ILO saw "basic needs" as encompassing employment and the improvement of working conditions and as targeting all population groups in the developing world, not just the underprivileged. The strategy it proposed appeared to be a policy of "synthesis" concerned, at one and the same time, with increased production and distribution of essential goods and services and the creation of reasonably paid and socially satisfying jobs, raising the question of the causes of poverty and the reforms needed for its eradication.

The idea was immediately welcomed. It was adopted by the General Assembly of the United Nations at the end of 1976; the following year it fell to the Council of the Organization for Economic Co-operation and Development (OECD) to do likewise. Studies, surveys, research projects succeeded one another. When, in 1980, Gaudier established an analytical bibliography, over 1,000 works had already appeared.[21] That situation did not last, however: faced with globalization and the welcome extended to ultra-liberal or simply neo-liberal theses, "basic needs" were somewhat sidelined.

Nonetheless, the ILO did not keep silent. In 1994 Michel Hansenne expressed his fear of a possible legal vacuum and a return to the law of the jungle.[22] When, in March 1995, for the first time in the history of the United Nations, which had never held a meeting for such a purpose, 120 heads of State and government met in Copenhagen to seek recognition for the universal importance of social development and improvement of the human condition and to strive as a matter of urgency to attain those objectives by the start of the twenty-first century, the ILO's contributions to the proceedings dealt, among other things, with full employment as a key factor in the fight against exclusion. At the Wilton Park Conference on liberalization of world trade (March 1996) the Director-General of the ILO called for a "social clause" to be included in trade agreements, on the grounds that the ILO should "promote parallelism between trade liberalization and social progress",[23] failing which protectionism might well return. Once again it is the goal of full employment, linked to social justice, and the need for international co-operation to that end, which transcends the mere question of labour standards, as discussed in the World Employment Report 1996-1997.[24]

In the past, Lebret saw development as the transition, as quick and as cheap as possible, from a less human to a more human phase, with the help of solidarity among peoples.[25] Perroux, meanwhile, claimed that a "new paradigm" was required by the outcome of the divorce between the economic image and life of our time, in which the most disadvantaged strata and countries ascend the ladder, and the "paradigm – in the strict sense of the word – by which the corporation was obsessed" (the portrayal of economic life as a network of trade transactions, and its formulation as general equilibrium in market trade). As an initial approximation, he defined this new paradigm as "the economics of all men and the whole man". That involved replacing a poor-performance unidimensional economy with a high-performance multidimensional economy which took account of "forgotten" human costs and insufficiently acknowledged human contributions. Perroux concluded by supporting growth with progress, in which economic creativity disburses its achievements to the benefit of all, with a minimum of delay and at minimum human cost, and in which human relations have a meaning that is intelligible to the most disadvantaged.[26]

Following our reading of United Nations documents, we were able to draw up a list of objectives to be included in a redefinition of the development paradigm which would not only link economic development to human development, but also take into account the human costs their realization entails. We have taken as our focus peoples' full exercise of their human rights, proclaimed, but all too often flouted, so that for vast masses of human beings, humanity is only a utopia.[27] We are now free to adduce a definition of the "new paradigm" of development in keeping with our purpose: an all-out quest for the satisfaction of the human needs of everyone as they manifest themselves and increase in historic communities – along with the evolution of civilizations and cultures – and more particularly of the poorest, at the lowest human, ecological, and instrumental costs, including material and financial costs.[28]

2. ACKNOWLEDGING THE HUMAN COST OF LABOUR

Each word of this definition has myriad implications. We shall focus on those that concern poverty and the human costs of labour.

In introducing the deliberations of the symposium organized by UNESCO on "Poverty and progress",[29] Paul-Marc Henry wondered whether poverty was only the other inevitable face of development. In similar vein, the Copenhagen Social Summit saw poverty eradication as the cornerstone of development. Extreme poverty jeopardizes all human rights, averred Leandro Despouy, who, to demonstrate the horror of abject poverty, used the examples of slavery, apartheid and dire poverty, noting that the deprivation of human rights is common to all three. He pointed out that when slavery was generally practised it was widely opposed by "humanists", that apartheid was vigorously condemned by the international organizations, but that the dire poverty that prevails today with its innumerable faces "can take its ease" – which is "agonizing, to say the least".

Poverty, like economics, is multidimensional. When, in 1997, United Nations experts undertook to define it from the standpoint of human development,[30] they immediately recognized that it did not merely denote an absence of income or a low income level, or the failure to have one's basic requirements (first and foremost, biological requirements) met. They observed that a truly comprehensive definition of poverty must include the lack of real potential, for individual or social reasons, to benefit from the opportunities most basic to human development: a long healthy life, creativity, a decent standard of living and working conditions, self-respect and the respect of others, and access to what is considered "worthy".

The definition of poverty embraces various aspects of the failure to defray the costs of a genuinely human life:[31] hunger, substandard housing that keeps individuals and families in situations of vulnerability, disease, greater or lesser long-term disadvantage, inability to read or write or (most frequently) inadequate instruction and training, inability to participate freely in the life of the community because of the accumulate burden of handicaps. Also part of the universe of poverty are the abundant affective wounds of childhood, old humiliations and exploitation, abandonment of any idea of a future, owing to the inability to build one or to repeated failures. Poverty may be caused by unconnected or recurrent events; but it can also derive from a fragile social position in which legacy plays a part. This may have many causes: impediments rooted in infant and adolescent malnutrition; the poor health of forebears or descendants; the daily spectacle of ugliness and misery; the rough, unsettled life of the family or neighbourhood; the cultural privation of a life which does not provide role models and examples conducive to intellectual development; hatred and violence against individuals and institutions; and parental shirking of responsibilities to offspring.

The paradigm of development, as rethought in these terms, also holds worthwhile implications for labour. Any production, and more generally any economic activity, creates human "values" that entail human costs. As Clark[32] put it, production is not merely the marketing of goods that can be sold at or above their "economic" cost price, but also the "management", in the broadest sense of the term, of objects, services, people themselves, and human relations. Defence of the "human factor", as Friedman[33] termed it, postulates a "compromise", in which maximum production involves minimum physical and mental wear and tear on the workers; or, to put it another way, the quest among the workers, and with them, to maintain a high potential of long-term yield without damage to their person. The idea of "sustainable" development was thus applied to human resources long before it was applied to natural resources.

But we are far from the goal, and it is worthwhile pondering the subject, since the human costs of labour deserve an important place in the definition of poverty.

Labour is not doing well in the rich countries.

We are told that instead of being made of factories and machines, the new enterprise is an association of persons and relationships in perpetual evolution, with the "manager" of the new era devising and implementing complex strategies, seeking to exploit the resources available within and outside the enterprise, like a true "master thinker" for employees with greater autonomy than before and a clear, motivating vision of the future.[34] Which takes us – although with a lot more road to travel – from the three Ss model (strategy, structure, system) to the three Ps model (purpose, process, people), involving the emergence of an organization that does not guarantee employees a job, but promises to make them more "effective" by putting their skills to advantage, delegating them responsibilities, offering them training and ensuring that they sub-scribe to the same goals.

Surveys portray quite a different reality. Taylorism is on the way out, even though the changes particularly affect all the internal workings of the enterprise[35] and social relationships, but the division of labour or the objective of optimum efficiency hardly at all.[36] Taylorism called for nothing more than physical subjection, ignoring the mental aspects of labour; the new organization of labour adds control of the psyche to that of the body.[37] It no longer focuses on the apparent job-by-job productivity of labour, but on the global productivity of the entire process, including the enterprise, its subcontractors and its other partners established as a network. What goes for industry also goes for the service sector: the performance of each category of employee is measured in terms of quality, flexibility, reactivity and, once again, productivity.[38]

From whatever angle it is viewed, wage-earning employment is today more intense and more complex and, in addition, demands involvement. True, this is a source of progress in that it calls for intelligence and creativity; but the price of that progress is enormous dependence on the flow of activity and market pressure, with the onus on the employee for what cannot – or can no longer – be measured by management control, so vast is the gap between Taylorism's analytical cost-accounting systems and the complex processes that hold the key to the performance of an enterprise.[39]

Management continues to mould human relationships and behaviour in a pitiless market economy.[40] Hence, work under pressure and mounting anxiety-making factors such as stress, have become one of the most acute problems facing our societies.[41] Contributory factors are constant changes of technology, a temporality explosion caused by a succession of actions entailing mental dispersion, tense-flow labour, the three-zeros imperative (zero breakdown, zero error and zero stock), the hunting-out of "dead" time, atypical work-scheduling and irregular hours due to the spectacular rise of "flexitime", the brusque acceleration and de-synchronization of pace imputable to information technologies, the discourse on the hyperactive enterprise and labour "by hate", the transition from a logic of discipline to a logic of belonging, recourse to internal competition, evaluation procedures, "presenteeism", the use of new technologies (badges, video-surveillance, automatic switches, etc.) to monitor all aspects of professional life (methods, movements, etc.), personalization of earnings, and the carving up of firms into "profit centres".

Actual time worked gives way to individual performance: what workers must attain is a "quantum", making them (especially executives) feel constrained to extend their own working hours which, at the same time, develop in different directions.[42] The paradox is that in the midst of an employment crisis, labour's hold over people increases, dilemma piles up on dilemma: team work, but individual evaluation; skills recognition, but a necessary mobility that can impair those skills; the requirement of personal commitment, but less job security; rejection of authoritarian red-tape, but nostalgia for the protection it provided. Peters called it "chaos management";[43] others have described it as a "psychic organizational system", a veritable cultural and intellectual lamination that imposes an "organizational ideal" on the employee and captures his or her "ideal self".[44]

Stress spills over to other more traditional dimensions of the human costs of labour and aggravates their impact. A case in point: even when noise is well within tolerable levels, in conditions of stress it disrupts cognitive activity and greatly impairs vigilance, thus significantly increasing risks. Such pathologies lead to almost complete loss of points of reference; the person no longer knows what is most important: quality of work, performance, economic viability or results. The ineluctable human costs of labour[45] develop into perceived oppression. We should not, then, be surprised if some 2,000 French doctors, specialists in occupational medicine, meeting in Strasbourg to celebrate their 25th National Congress (June 1998), almost unanimously reported not only debilitation, feelings of disparagement, psychological and psychosomatic problems, hypertension, muscular-skeletal disorders, vindictive acts (theft, vandalism, embezzlement), but also despair accompanied by phenomena hitherto unknown in their country, such as suicide in the workplace.

Against that backdrop, the health of workers in precarious employment, of those threatened by unemployment and of the actual unemployed gives particular cause for alarm.

Whether it is employment or working conditions, each situation described by the doctors in an attempt to gauge the impact of the various forms of precariousness on employees and the self-employed leads to the same conclusion: precarious employment makes for precarious health.[46] The resultant assaults on physical integrity are the business of doctors, just as they must be the business of economists and politicians. Consequently, the doctors affirm the urgency of top-to-bottom surveys to identify the risk factors of the origin and continuation of each precarious situation, of the transition from one precarious situation to another, of escape from those situations, and the combined impact that those factors and types of precariousness have on health[47] and, we should add, on poverty through human denigration. How could one fail to react to the findings of a survey by the French National Research and Safety Institute that in France twice as many workers in precarious employment as those in stable employment are victims of industrial accidents and that those accidents are twice as serious?[48] How could one fail to acknowledge the violence of precarious situations when they affect certain categories of people: women, young people, immigrants and the disabled?[49]

Even before they become unemployed, workers whose jobs are threatened show signs of ill-health, aggravated during the social measures that accompany lay-offs. Their problems are not only physical, but digestive, dermatological, cardiovascular and behavioural. They feel "betrayed" and destroyed, and endeavour to escape through conflict, illness and flight.[50] When the period of unemployment is brief they may be able to maintain their standard of living to some extent by digging into savings made during the good years, seeking help from family or friends, contracting debts, deferring payments or cutting down on consumption; but health problems become apparent. If the unemployment continues, the jobless must confront the complex task of finding a new job and obtaining alternative institutional assistance, added to which they feel tired, useless, anxious about the future, and abandon personal or family projects; sometimes they must even deal with break-up of the family, loss of friends, increased morbidity, all of which may in extreme cases take the form of "social autism" from which it is difficult to escape.[51]

On 20 February 1998, the French Public Health Commission (*Haut Comité français de la santé publique*) sounded the alarm in a publicized ruling. It described "suffering" as the "major symptom" of an insecurity to which casual insecure employment, deterioration of working conditions and health in the workplace, exclusion and pauperization all contribute. Dejours[52] also speaks of suffering. He affirms that it is through the medium of "suffering" that "consent" is obtained to participation in the system which, when it works, engenders suffering in return. Work, says Philippe Davezies,[53] is "a health operator", in that it permits access to the recognition of others; where this is not so, the suffering inevitably linked to any work experience takes centre stage, bringing with it an economy of suf-

fering and an economy of protection from suffering. This takes the
form of strategies all of which are capable of engendering social
violence: strategies of "virile cynicism", strategies of "voluntary
blinkers" (denial of reality in the guise of ignorance, reduced awareness of matter peripheral to the activity) and "survival techniques"
(alcohol, psychotropic substances).

That being so, one should not be surprised by the results of the
surveys the ILO conducted in 32 countries on the way in which
workers perceive what they endure in the workplace (no easy task
given the differences in culture – either physical or psychological)
which showed that violence was raging throughout the world, in all
contexts and for all professional categories.[54] In the United States
between 1992 and 1996, there were more than two million victims
of violence in the workplace per year.[55] In the Philippines, many
women employed in the chain of industry, as maids or in the leisure
sector, complain of ill-treatment by their employers. In Sweden 10
per cent to 15 per cent of suicides are reportedly due to psychological harassment at work. In the context of increasingly insecure
employment, the sexual division of labour would seem to be so large
a source of violence that the organizers of one survey[56] denounced
the transition of women from "service jobs to servile jobs".

Many factors pertaining exclusively to the developing countries
also aggravate the human costs of labour: users' ignorance of the
risks inherent in imported technologies and processes; poor maintenance of machinery; designers' disregard for different peoples'
anthropometric norms; signals, indicators and symbols unsuited to
local culture;[57] buildings and offices unsuited to the climate or environment; lack of protection measures or failure to observe safety
instructions, when they exist. This occurs at every stage of the
industrialization process, with huge numbers of industrial accidents,
work-related disorders and human degradation, all of which beset
people who are being integrated into a new universe of work and
life. The scandal erupts with practices the ILO describes as "export
of hazards":[58] when enterprises in the highly industrialized countries transfer to the developing countries dangerous or unhealthy
manufacturing processes that are strictly regulated, if not banned,
in their own countries;[59] negligence with regard to prevention in
countries where the labour force is composed mainly of unskilled
workers who are easily replaceable owing to the abundance of job
seekers; pressure on the local governments; and corruption.[60]

Free zones are extremely important for the developing countries' labour markets; given the volume of investments and transfers

of technology, they form an essential bridge to the global economy. The 1998 ILO Report on the subject, while considering them to be the vehicle of globalization, calls attention to sometimes very long working hours, the compartmentalization of largely female workers into unskilled low-income jobs, and to the fact that while sometimes, under pressure from international public opinion, some attempt is made to upgrade human resources, more often than not "labour is exploited to the maximum in a bid to satisfy production requirements".[61] The same Report points to the extreme rarity, in these zones, of the classical model of labour legislation which provides a threshold or a series of minimum standards, and the negotiation of binding agreements between employers and often non-existent independent trade unions.

To that should be added the ultimate link between poverty and work and the ultimate implication of the definition of the new paradigm we have selected: that is to say the particularly heavy human costs to some 250 million working children in the world – forced into that situation by family poverty, over-population and a deficient education system who would be less so but for the presence of individuals eager to exploit them;[62] and the grave violations of, or new threats to, human rights. It then becomes all too clear that there is an urgent need for people to exercise their fundamental rights and that ethics cannot be divorced from economics.

3. INTEGRATION OF ECOLOGICAL COSTS

Since the concept of "sustainable" development was popularized by the Brundtland Report, it has become an article of faith with development economists. The ecological costs cannot be ignored, consequently they appear in our definition of the "new paradigm".

It can be taken as established that development is only "sustainable" (viable) if it does not threaten the resilience of the economy or the biosphere; in other words, their capacity to rebuild and regenerate their potential, once previously stocked materials have been exhausted.[63] A safe and rational environment can, consequently, be interpreted in terms of resilience: the less a technology threatens the provision of essential ecological services by overstepping the ecosystem's resilience threshold, the greater the viability of the system.

The essence is, therefore, to be found in the interaction between the system of production and consumption and the environment from which it obtains its resources and where it discards its waste, with a feedback effect, all of which renders the environment more fragile.[64] This interaction is not limited to the economy and the natural environment; given the complexity of development, it also extends to its other dimensions: social, technological and cultural, each clarified in accordance with its special characteristics.

Sfeir-Younis considers that, in those conditions, the old paradigm whereby people as joint owners of the planet must enhance it, and the more recent paradigm whereby they must act as good stewards of any form of life, should both be replaced by a "new paradigm" in which "human evolution and nature are governed by exactly the same laws", so that "it is not only respect for life – albeit essential – that counts, but also that which is really required for living together: mutual coexistence and shared evolution". Without endorsing the theory of "co-evolution", Berthelot sees the environment as an issue that calls for an "integrating" approach. The concerns of both coincide with those expressed by Tinbergen in his preoccupation with the "threats of disruption of the natural balance, also known as ecological balance", caused by man's increased capacity for intervention.[65]

There can be no "viable" human development if the ecological costs of economic development are such that essential ecological services are not preserved. Hence, attention must be paid not only to air or water pollution, destruction of soils, forests or species, and the greenhouse effect, but also to climatic and hydrological cycles in their dependence on human interventions, to the capacity for waste assimilation and recycling of nutrients, to the pollenization of crops, to the maintenance of genetic diversity, to all transformations that have repercussions on the ecosystems' internal control mechanisms and on functional diversity, since any decline in the latter signifies less regeneration capacity.

Everyone is aware of the conditions for a possible "new alliance"[66] between humans and nature, while their increasing power takes their dependence on the environment to an infinitely higher level of stakes and risks: maintaining the social value that estimates have attributed to the heritage, and protecting the ecosystems' resilience threshold in order to maintain potential biophysical productivity.

The environment can no longer be perceived as a luxury product of interest to the rich countries and affluent social strata. It must be seen as one of the vital dimensions of the existential milieu and as a potential asset. The requirements of the type of management that ensures that the natural heritage and resilience are protected and transmitted to future generations are subject to ethical constraints which limit the quest for the type of efficiency called for by market criteria and mechanisms. One thing is undeniable: there is a variety of approaches to environmental policy, considering the uncertainties that exist. Furthermore there is a need to focus reflection on development itself. How can we combat the ecological ravages of economic development if we persist in devising it using the very methods that give rise to those ravages?[67] Undefined growth and accumulation, through the over-rapid consumption of flows of energy-matter and stocks of non-renewable resources, and the already visible destruction they reveal at a time when four-fifths of the world's population neither indulges in those practices nor contributes to those costs, make in-depth rethinking of the outlook for development an imperative.[68]

Nor must we accept the postulate that there is a mechanical link between growth rates and the rate at which nature is exploited, between economic development and the destruction of the environment. The issue concerns methods and mechanisms of growth compatible with social progress, and judicious management of resources and environment, not a cessation of growth. The question is one of "ecological prudence"[69] and the discovery of appropriate forms of global, international and local governance. This calls for a gargantuan task of "social construction", in which the economy has its place, which consists in "putting a price and cost on living things"; but it can fulfil its role only if, seeing natural resources for what they are – actual physical and biological objects – it remains within the bounds established by ecological laws and the elementary laws of physics, thermodynamics and biology, so that ecosystems are preserved and, should some be exhausted, account is taken of the time needed for new ones to replace them.[70] As Passet aptly put it, "only the logic of a living factor, likely to inscribe on its consciousness the requirements of living things, is capable of reproducing a living thing".[71]

The link between the ecological costs and the human costs of labour is a close one. The ILO has shown that the social and human repercussions of the distribution of potential costs and profits, within society and among nations, can, from that point of view, be as important as measures on behalf of the environment: unequal distribution of costs and advantages can never lead to "sustainable" development.

Environmental programmes must therefore be integrated into general policy aimed at improving living and working conditions. Employers must use production techniques and forms of organization that do not generate ecological costs which, in turn, increase human costs. Workers must demand protective measures and a fair share of the benefits, and governments must realize that ecology is now a key component of political life and labour relations.[72]

[1]"The Structure of Scientific Revolutions", in *International Encyclopedia of United Sciences*, II, 2, Phoenix, University of Chicago Press, 1962.

[2]M. Blaug: "Kuhn versus Lakatos, or Paradigm versus Research Programs in the History of Economics", *History of Political Economy*, Winter 1975.

[3]G. de Bernis: Le sous-développement, analyses ou représentations, *Tiers Monde*, Jan.-Mar. 1974.

[4]E.E. Hagen: *The Economics of Development*, Homewood, R.D. Irwin, 1968.

[5]J. Williamson: *What Washington Means by Policy Reform*, Washington, Institute for International Economics, November 1989.

[6]*Our Common Future*, World Commission on Environment and Development. Montreal, Fleuve, 1987.

[7]*World Development Report 1992*, Washington, World Bank, 1992, p. 7.

[8]*Ibid.*, 1993, p. 15.

[9]*Human Development Report 1993*, New York, Oxford, Oxford University Press, p. 4.

[10]*Ibid.*, 1994, p. 4.

[11]*Ibid.*, 1995, p. 12.

[12]*Ibid.*, 1996, p. 10. See also all of Chapter 3.

[13]*Ibid.*, 1997, p. 7.

[14]*Ibid.*, 1997, p. 12 and Chapter 6.

[15]L.J. Lebret and J.M. Gatheron: *Principe et perspective d'une économie humaine*, Paris, Editions Economie et humanisme, 1942.

[16]Father Lebret's address to the Conference. *La Documentation Catholique*, 3 May 1964.

[17]O. De Solages: "Les besoins essentiels : une notion encore neuve", *Mélanges en l'honneur de René Gendarme*, Metz, Editions Serpenoise, 1996. pp. 356-7.

[18]O. De Solages, *op. cit.*, pp. 358-9.

[19]Report of the Director-General of the ILO. *Employment, Growth and Basic Needs*, Geneva, ILO, 1976, p.7.

[20]*Ibid.*, p. 25.

[21]*Basic Needs*, Geneva, International Institute for Labour Studies, 1980.

[22]"Standards: a broader approach", *Report of the Director-General*, ILO, Geneva, ILO, 1994.

[23]"International trade and labour standards: the Director-General reports", *International Labour Review*, 1996, No. 2.

[24]"National policies in a global context", *World Employment 1996*, ILO, Geneva, 1996.

[25]*Dynamique concrète du développement*, Paris, Albin Michel, 1993.

[26]"L'économie de la Ressource humaine", *Monde en développement*, 1974, No. 7, pp. 36-47.

[27]C. Chalier: *Lévinas, l'utopie de l'humain*, Paris, Albin Michel, 1993.

[28]Similarly, H. Bartoli: *Economie et création collective*, Paris, Economica, 1997, pp.168-174, and *L'économie, service de la Vie*, Grenoble, Presses universitaires, 1996, pp. 151-184.

[29]*Poverty, progress and development 1997, op. cit.*

[30]*Human Development Report 1997, op. cit.*, p. 15.

[31]F. Perroux, the originator of the concept, places them in three categories: those that prevent human beings from dying (the struggle against death in the workplace and outside it), those that enable all human beings to enjoy a minimum of physical and mental life (preventive health care, medical treatment, disability, and old age and unemployment benefits) and those that afford them a specifically human existence marked by a minimum of knowledge and leisure. Cf. "Les coûts de l'homme", *Economie appliquée*, January-March 1952, p. 146.

[32]"Produktion als Organisation von Nutzen und Kosten", *Wirtschaftstheorie der Gegenwart*, II, pp. 269 et seq. – *The Social Control of Business*, Chicago, University of Chicago Press, 1926.

[33]*Problèmes humains du machinisme industriel*, Paris, Gallimard, 1949, p. 350.

[34]Fondation P. Drucker, *L'entreprise de demain*, Village mondial, 1999.

[35]Decompartmentalization or transversality of functions, interaction and flexibility of structures or divisions, etc.

[36]D. Linhart: *La modernisation de l'entreprise*, Paris, La Découverte, 1994.

[37]L. Bagla-Gökalp: *Sociologie des organisations*, Paris, La Découverte, 1999.

[38]M. Bartoli: "Productivité et performance", in *Les savoirs sur le travail. Recherche, Société, Syndicalisme*, Paris, La Découverte, 1999.

[39]In more than one case, data-processing programmes impose organization of labour in services which were previously self-organized. The result is a "formidable extension of subdivided and prescribed labour", even for "white-collar workers". Cf. G. Duval: *L'entreprise efficace à l'heure du Swatch and McDonald's. La seconde vie du taylorisme*,

Paris, Syros, 1998. See also V. Acquain, J. Bué, L. Vinck: *L'évolution en deux ans de l'organisation du travail : plus de contraintes, mais aussi plus d'autonomie pour les salariés*, Ministère de l'emploi et de la solidarité, DERES, Premières synthèses, June 1994.

[40]J. Kergoat, J. Boutet, H. Jacot, D. Linhart (eds.): *Le monde du travail*, Paris, La Découverte, 1998.

[41]"Stress at Work", in *World Labour Report*, ILO, Geneva, 1993, Chapter 5.

[42]If J.B. Schor is to be believed, Americans devoted more time to work in the 1980s than they did just after the Second World War (*The overworked American. The unexpected decline of leisure*, New York, Basic Book, 1991). Corroborated by R.G. Ehrenberg and P.L. Schumann, who claim that average overtime followed an upward curve ("Longer hours or more jobs? An investigation of amending hours legislation to create employment", Ithaca, Cornell University, *Cornell Studies in Industrial and Labor Relations,* 1982, No. 22), while T.D. Greis speaks, on the contrary, of a drop in annual working time (The decline of annual hours worked in the United States since 1947, Philadelphia, University of Pennsylvania, *Manpower and Human Resources Studies*, 1984, No. 10).

[43]Paris, Interéditions, 1988.

[44]N. Aubert, V. de Gaulejac: *Le coût de l'excellence*, Paris, Seuil, 1991.

[45]Creative praxis, all labour involves such costs; while they are not all caused by pathology, they all need to be contained. Hence our definition: human costs of labour are any energy a worker expends on his task or its accomplishment (e.g. cost in travel); any pathological effect (temporary or permanent) on his physical, moral or social being directly or indirectly stemming from work or unemployment; any related hindrance to the worker's development even if it is not immediately felt to be detrimental to health.

[46]*Souffrances et précarités au travail. Paroles des médecins du travail*, Paris, Syros, 1994.

[47]*Op. cit.,* pp. 301 et seq.

[48]"Le dossier du travail précaire", in *Santé et travail*, April 1994.

[49]*Souffrances et précarités, op. cit.,* pp. 211-282.

[50]M.O. Achard, V. Chastel, P. Dell'Accio: "Perte d'emploi et santé", *Le concours médical*, October 1998.

[51]P. Boulte: *Individus en friche. Essai sur l'exclusion*, Paris, Desclée de Brouwer, 1992.

[52]*Souffrance en France. La banalisation de l'injustice sociale*, Paris, Seuil, 1998.

[53]"Réflexions sur la santé au travail", *Informations et commentaires,* April-June 1998, pp. 25-26.

[54]D. Chappell, V. di Martino: *Violence at Work*, ILO, Geneva, 1998.

[55]"When work becomes hazardous", *The World of Work,* ILO Magazine, Sep.-Oct. 1998, pp. 6-9.

[56]N. Lancien, J. Machefer, D. Parent: "La précarisation du travail comme source de violence accrue dans les rapports de travail", in *Médecine et Travail*, Dec. 1997.

[57]Red denotes danger in the West, joy in the Far East.

[58]*World Labour Report*, ILO, Geneva, Vol.2, p. 147.

[59]The manufacture of trichlorophenol is banned in the United States on account of the high toxicity of the dioxin residue emitted on synthesis; it has therefore been transferred to the new industrial countries. The use of carbon disulphide, particularly dangerous owing to its effect on the nervous system, has declined significantly in the advanced industrial countries but is increasing in the developing countries.

[60]H. Bartoli: "La maîtrise des coûts humains du travail, condition de la maîtrise des transformations technologiques dans les pays du Tiers Monde", *Economies et sociétés*, November 1987, and "Coûts humains du travail et développement", *Informations et commentaires*, Jul.-Sep. 1988.

[61]*Labour and social issues relating to export processing zones*, ILO, Geneva, 1998.

[62]*Annual Report of UNICEF*, 1998 – "Child labour: targeting the intolerable". International Labour Conference, Geneva, 86th session, 1998.

[63]F. Dietz, J. Van der Straeten: "Rethinking environmental economics: missing links between economic theory and environmental policy", *Journal of Economic issues,* 1992, No. 1.

[64]I. Sachs: *L'Ecodéveloppement*, Paris, Syros, 1993.

[65]*Pour une terre vivable, notre dernière chance de survie*, Paris, Sequoia, 1976.

[66]I. Prigogine, I. Stengers: *La Nouvelle Alliance, métaphore de la science,* Paris, Gallimard, 1979.

[67]S. Latouche: "Développement durable : un concept alibi. Main invisible et mainmise sur la nature", *Tiers Monde*, Jan.-Mar. 1994.

[68]H. Daly: "Sustainable growth. No thank you", in J. Mander and E. Goldsmith (eds.): *The Case against the global economy and for a turn toward the local*, San Francisco, Sierra Club books, 1996.

[69]I. Sachs: *Stratégies de l'écodéveloppement*, Paris, Editions ouvrières, 1980, p. 29.

[70]*L'économique et le vivant*, Paris, Economica, 1996, pp. 210 et seq.

[71]*Ibid.*, p. 215.

[72]*Environment and the World of Work*, 77th Session of the International Labour Conference, Report of the Director-General, Part I, Geneva, ILO, 1990.

CHAPTER 2

Failure of strategies based primarily on economic and financial considerations. A multidimensional strategy interlinking economic, social and environmental factors

The idea of a new world order has been surfacing continually since 1948. The international community in its economic, political and legal manifestations has clamoured constantly for such an order. The idea underlay the bargaining rounds which eventually led to the conclusion of the final Uruguay Round agreement in 1993. It also underlies the rules borrowed from the old theories of the balance of power which, throughout the cold war years 1945-1989, although they could not ensure an ideal "peaceful order", could at least create a "situation of peace". The latter was envisaged as a far from peaceful competition between two systems in which the end of the Gulf War crisis subtended the highly optimistic celebration of the victory of right over might, and the re-establishment of the authority of the United Nations.

"Order, occasional or lasting, among humans", wrote Perroux,[1] "derives from a common vision of their destinies and a project acceptable to all." In the context of the global market, an economic order can be conceived as an enormous mechanism within which supply and demand adjust to one another under the guidance of the general price system. It can equally be envisaged as a human construction which is developed over time and in which human beings command objects and organize their universe while nevertheless remaining subject to the laws of those objects.

The economic and social order which the "new paradigm" demands cannot be conceived or defined in terms of a market mechanism. It can only be based on political choices. As indicated by the UNDP experts, these choices should, on the one hand, be

designed to meet directly the needs of populations rather than satisfy the preferences of States,[2] and, on the other hand, see growth
as "a means, not an end".[3]

The 1996 international covenant on economic, social and cultural rights and the one on civil and political rights both contain, in
their first section, a declaration that "all peoples have the right of
self-determination" and, by virtue of that right, freely to determine
their political status and "freely pursue their economic, social and
cultural development". The same article stipulates that all peoples
may freely dispose of their wealth and natural resources.[4] In 1961,
the United Nations declared a first Development Decade. In the light
of the results obtained, this was followed by a second Decade for
which the Economic and Social Council was made co-ordinator.
The developing countries, which previously had not reacted or had
confined themselves to expressing a measure of misgiving, then
formulated – initially within the Group of 77[5] and later in the Non-
aligned Movement[6] – a programme which they set out for the first
time at the special session of the United Nations on raw materials
and development held in April-May 1974. The outcome was the
adoption by the United Nations General Assembly of a Declaration
on the establishment of a new economic order (Resolution 3201 S
VI), together with a programme of action for its implementation
(Resolution 3202 S VI) – a short text setting out the fundamental
principles which should underlie the relations between all peoples
and all nations, namely: sovereign equality, international co-operation, transfers of technology, priority to be given to developing
countries with a legal system of compensatory inequality biased in
their favour and the establishment of just and equitable relationships
between the prices of their exports and those of their imports. Since
then practically every United Nations conference has repeated that
development is simultaneously economic, social, ecological and cultural. At the end of the 1970s it was redefined with reference to
poverty – a factor which had previously been somewhat neglected.[7]
Throughout the 1980s numerous seminars on human development
were held within the framework of the North-South Round Table. In
1987 UNICEF issued a publication on the subject of "adjustment
with a human face", and the protection of vulnerable groups and
growth promotion.[8]

Time passed. Despouy tells us that in 1987, when Father
Wresinski put to the United Nations the question of extreme
poverty in the context of human rights, people understood that
they had been almost totally "off the mark". But he goes on to

recount that several years passed before the problem was referred to the Human Rights Committee; the West feared that the poverty existing in their respective countries would be denounced by the communist countries; the "Marxist" countries feared that the capitalists would "steal their issues"; and the Third World countries were afraid that they would be branded as violators of human rights because they were poor!

Recently Gourou warned those who were envisaging a new phase in the history of the African countries that "it is no use curing people if their economic condition is not improved and no use improving techniques if their health is not better ensured... the problem is no longer a scientific one: it is political".[9] Sachs, for his part, writes that the challenge at the turn of the century is one of "escaping from policies of providing care where poverty exists and embracing proactive policies for development".

The new paradigm as defined here requires us to devote ourselves to the search for a form of organization within which all the agents in economic and social life will be at the service of all people in all nations and throughout the world. At the same time we must seek tools which will provide effective economic solutions and also ensure adequate protection of the environment. In that context the choice of a development strategy becomes essential. When considering what that strategy might be, it is useful to undertake a critical analysis of the dominant strategies of earlier years.

1. LIMITATIONS OF STRATEGIES BASED ON SELF-RELIANCE AND IMPORT SUBSTITUTION

The strategies devised by a large number of countries in Latin America, Africa and Asia between the beginning of the 1950s and the end of the 1970s were based on the idea of "in-depth industrialization". The idea emerged in the wake of the national liberation movements, followed by the Bandoeng Conference (1955), at which the Third World countries affirmed their right to existence and their determination to escape from tutelage and play a role in world affairs. Whether they sought to base development on import substitution or on self-reliance, they all considered that any solutions envisaged should emerge from within the nation itself and that the population should take responsibility for framing them. Both approaches marked a breakaway, to a greater or lesser degree, from the spontaneous trend towards international division of labour and the machinery of immediate comparative advantage. Mamadou Dia described development as "turning the entire nation towards its future, constantly surpassing itself".[10]

Prebisch[11] and Singer[12] asserted that the terms of trade were unfavourable to Third World countries both in the long term and in the short term. In the long term, this is on account of the deterioration caused by the influence of the income distribution mechanism in the absence of intermediary groups or middle classes, the substitution effects of innovations, and the relative inelasticity of demand for primary products. In the short term, it is due to the instability of terms of trade coupled with the non-diversification of exports and the inelasticity of domestic supply or demand, which is worsened by the demonstration effect. They argued that the outcome is the "strangulation" of growth by external trade. And yet import-substitution strategy relies on external dynamics.

That strategy consists of rejecting development based on forces external to the country concerned and reflected in the balance of payments, and replacing imports by home-produced goods (provided that their cost is fairly close to world prices), resorting if necessary to a measure of protectionism, at least during an initial period. In a strategy of this kind, investment should be directed to the least capitalistic sectors, promoting employment growth; the State would play its part by mobilizing national and international capital, financing infrastructure and establishing health and education standards on a par with the project as a whole. The outcome should be the emergence of a domestic market which will stimulate national production of intermediate and capital goods and thus expand the field in which import substitution is feasible.

There is nothing automatic about the results of such a strategy. If it is implemented from the bottom upwards, beginning with industries producing consumer goods and requiring little capital investment, using simple technologies and a relatively unskilled labour force, it can prove successful at the price of a slight increase in customs duties, since costs are very low. Implementation from the top downwards meets with more difficulties: the apex industries generally require higher levels of capital investment, use more complex technologies and need a more highly skilled labour force; the amount of capital required may exceed the amount which can be raised by local saving. Here customs protection is not enough; the country must also receive income from external sources which will enable it to import the capital goods essential for its industrialization (oil revenues).[13]

On the supply side, import substitution takes the form of new opportunities for industry to the detriment of the flow of imports of manufactured goods. It is difficult to explain industrialization entirely in terms of the dynamics of demand, the causes and limitations of which are difficult to discern – how and why are opportunities for substitution taken up; how and why do changes in the structure of demand and in the conditions of industrial production take place; how and why does this not always occur? Changes in the structure of imports (a sharp fall in imports of consumer goods, a sharp rise in those of raw materials and intermediate goods, rises followed by pauses – or even falls – in those of capital goods) are parallelled by an increase in qualitative dependency. The latter is due to the fact that industrialization itself precludes a reduction in certain types of imports; to the increased investment by multinational corporations; and above all to the increase in foreign indebtedness, since the resources obtained from commercial transactions and the entry of foreign capital are in part absorbed by the deficit on invisible transactions, the repatriation of dividends and the emigration of domestic capital. In real terms, the economy will continue to depend on its ability to obtain in foreign markets the production goods it will need at each stage in its industrialization – particularly as it intends the latter to advance as quickly as possible while depending on its foreign markets to finance it. Interest charges and the repayment of principal will absorb an increasing proportion of the foreign currency earned or borrowed.[14] Within such a strategy, human development is not a major consideration and benefits but little.

A self-reliant (endogenous) strategy does not neglect the opportunities offered by international trade; but it does rely on internal dynamics. Self-reliant development is based on the domestic (endogenous) resources and strengths of the nation concerned and seeks to develop them in a coherent fashion. It embraces every dimension of the economic and social elements which make up the nation and is thus "integrated".

The old structures have to be replaced by new ones; agriculture, handicrafts and industry must be improved so as better to meet needs for consumer, intermediate and capital goods. The broadening of the accumulation base is expected to make available sufficient capital for production and processing for export in order to ensure the financing of essential imports. Foreign trade, it is deemed, must contribute to the accumulation of an unobligated surplus that can be mobilized either for consumption or for investment. Foreign inputs in the form of capital, techniques and skilled personnel are all considered means of modernizing the economy.

After a long period during which economic considerations (in the narrow sense) predominated and development was envisaged solely in terms of quantitative growth, human considerations are resuming their central place as the agent and the end-purpose of development.[15] This means that no longer will material production be overrated in relation to other values; and that no longer will societies deemed to be "peripheral" be subjected to dependence on other societies, seen as "central" or "models". Instead, since no development model can claim to be the only one possible, the task now is to start with the real societal contexts and ensure, in accordance with the 1974 United Nations resolution, "the right of every country to adopt the economic and social system it deems the most appropriate to its own development and not to be subjected to discrimination of any kind as a result".[16]

These strategies are sometimes categorized as "industrializing industries" with the capacity to bring about changes in the inter-industrial matrix and in production functions by making available to the national economy machinery which increases the latter's productivity;[17] in other cases they are perceived as "poles of growth" characterized by the presence of a "locomotive" industry that can improve output (and purchases of services) in one or more other industries when it increases its own output (and its own purchases of services)[18]. In either case, the strategies all require the State to be the principal agent for the regulation of the process and of ongoing restructuring. All of them lay emphasis on import-substitution; all of them seek to promote an alliance between the authorities and part of the working classes and the lower and middle bourgeoisie against the landowning oligarchies or the groups connected with colonization. The results they obtain will depend primarily on the ability of those concerned to propagate the impetus arising from the interplay of the vertical or horizontal complementarities between industries and branches of activity; they will also depend on their ability to secure predominance over the braking or even paralysing effects of the movement of the most dynamic elements of the population and of capital towards the expanding sectors and zones, where earnings are higher, to the detriment of the other sectors and zones.

In the circumstances, it is only logical that the supporters of a development strategy based on self-reliance should not dissociate "economic" development from the mental and social behaviour patterns of the population, and above all from their culture. Gannagé[19] is one of these. He argues that social and cultural conditions are determining factors and that a prerequisite for development based on self-reliance is the creation of a favourable environment for propagation. Perroux[20] is of the same view; he considers that growth and development can be obtained only by the deliberate development of an environment making for the propagation of the locomotive effect of the poles, and that cultures play a fundamental role, since it is they which regulate economic activity at the price of continuing exchanges between the living environment and values.

The limitations of such a strategy based on self-reliance began to appear during the mid-1970s. The major Third World economies managed to reap benefit from it, and, since their economies were not based exclusively on the exploitation of their primary, agricultural or mineral resources, they were able to introduce considerable structural changes. In contrast, most of the countries that resorted to this strategy did not succeed in establishing a basis for autonomous accumulation. The dilemma of whether to give priority to agriculture "or" to industry, which seemed to be surmountable, resulted in the establishment of industries with a seriously under-utilized production capacity and excessive production costs. Vertical integration did not take place spontaneously. Recourse to highly capital-intensive techniques gave rise to dependencies – particularly for the supply of spare parts and services – which are difficult to remedy in the absence of local subcontractors and skilled labour. The unavoidable recourse to borrowing abroad to finance investments gave rise to increasing financial dependency. It had been hoped that creating imbalances between the urban and rural masses would be avoided; but the drift to the towns accelerated, while the desired alliance between the different strata of society tended to break down with the appearance of social strata favourable to restructuring based on closer participation in the world economy, and of a State technocracy isolated to a greater or lesser degree from the population.

Throughout the 1970s, UNESCO continually appealed for a "new kind of development" and propagated the idea that it should be endogenous, sustainable and above all "human".[21] By the end of the 1980s, generally speaking, UNESCO considered that hardly any of the elements of the "developmentalist" models were in application in the Third World countries or were being used as standards – either at the level of State intervention or at that of class alliances.

The countries which were most vociferous in proclaiming their "endogenist" beliefs were not the ones best able to safeguard their autonomy. *Ramsès 83-84* observed that "Ujamaa Tanzania" was one of the countries receiving the highest levels of aid per head in the world. Algeria created, at great expense, heavy industries and a petrochemical industry which, for many years, were to be heavily dependent on its suppliers and customers. Mexico, together with a number of oil-producing countries, applied the theory of "development" of national resources to a degree such that "development" generated levels of indebtedness and dependency considerably higher than those of countries "without national resources".[22]

Underlying the strategies of import-substitution and self-reliance lay the idea of a rediscovery of identity, the development of each country's particular resources and the orientation of national production towards the satisfaction of the essential needs of the population. This had given rise to challenges to internal and external structures hindering development and to the launching of a programme of demands in line, in its essentials, with the project for a new international economic order adopted by the United Nations General Assembly. The XIth special session, held in August 1980, had on its agenda a discussion of the conditions for the opening of global negotiations designed to break the deadlock reached on the subject; it proved a resounding failure. The summit meeting of heads of State which followed (Cancun, 1981) was equally unsuccessful. A draft compromise, produced by ten countries of the European Economic Community, failed in the face of American opposition. "At the beginning of 1982", observed *Ramsès 82*, "the negotiations were concentrated on the subtle distinction between the "preparatory negotiations" which the United States wished to undertake before beginning the Global Negotiations as such and the "preparatory phase" which the developing countries were prepared to accept provided that it took place within the framework of the Global Negotiations".[23]

In these circumstances, the campaign for a major world-wide "readjustment" to reconcile economic development with human development had clearly got away to a bad start. A completely new form of "adjustment" emerged as part of a totally different strategy in which there was little or no place for human development.

2. THE SOCIAL FAILURE OF STRUCTURAL ADJUSTMENT STRATEGIES

Beginning in the mid-1970s, while autonomous development strategies were still fashionable, the indebtedness of Third World countries was giving rise to increasing concern. In 1981 it amounted in all to over 520 billion dollars, as compared with $ 71 billion in 1971. During the same period the cost of debt servicing leapt from $ 11 billion to $ 110 billion, or 20 per cent of the export earnings of the countries concerned. In January 1992, 25 of them were behind in their payments to Western banks. A vicious spiral developed; the refinancing of maturing debts absorbed approximately half of the Euro-credits extended to developing countries in 1982 as against one quarter two years earlier. In 1982, debt servicing absorbed 80 per cent of Brazil's export earnings, even though the latter had quadrupled since 1973!

The principal borrowers – such as Brazil and Mexico, each of which owes $ 50 billion – know that nobody can refuse them the necessary refinancing without endangering the whole of the international monetary and financial system. The smaller debtors, whose deficits are equally persistent, are more threatened, since there is a temptation to make up at their expense for difficulties encountered elsewhere. The principal international banks, and particularly the American banks, are becoming increasingly unwilling to augment their loans to developing countries and are always selective in their lending.

The 1980s were a decade of finding responses to the large-scale external shocks (raw material and oil prices, interest and exchange rates) and the growing threats to economic, monetary and financial stability arising from the deterioration of the world economic context, as evidenced by the rise and persistence of unemployment in all the OECD member countries. For the developing countries it was a period during which the watchword was no longer "development based on self-reliance" but "adjustment".

During the 1970s the International Monetary Fund (IMF), whose customers had initially been advanced industrialized countries with balance-of-payments problems, turned to the provision of aid to the developing countries. Its initial mechanisms were designed to meet balance-of-payments difficulties which were thought to be short-term in nature; it now created new mechanisms of a longer-term nature, including, in 1986, the "extended structural adjustment facility", and, a year later, the "enhanced structural adjustment facility", to provide assistance on favourable terms to low-income countries undertaking comprehensive adjustment programmes. It eased its conditions, adding a number of factors which were to be taken into consideration by member countries in their adjustment programmes: national political and social objectives, economic priorities, current situations, the specific structural measures envisaged and the outline adjustment period for the negotiated financial reorganization programme, corresponding to the period during which the borrowing country was expected to improve its condition. In 1993 the "system transformation facility" was devised to facilitate the transition of planned-economy countries to a market economy. Having realized that it was gripping the assisted countries in a monetary and financial vice and thereby stunting their development, the IMF eased somewhat the conditions attached to its aid; from then on, the aid was to be made available to countries endeavouring to improve the supply of resources and to broaden the real base of their economies.

During the 1980s the World Bank became a very different organization from what it had been during the 1960s. Having been brought into the complex world of development by Robert McNamara, it designed strategies to combat poverty based on the acquired experience of developing countries in every region of the world. It drew up targeted intervention programmes to support projects which, to be accepted, had to include measures specifically aimed at the poor or in which the proportion benefiting the poor was higher than the proportion of poor people in the total population; it prepared human resources development projects (education, health, women); and it sought to ensure the compatibility of the projects it supported with ecologically viable development. To support the changes in the economic behaviour of the member countries hardest hit by the debt crisis – such as the Latin American countries reopening their borders and returning to the markets after decades of large-scale intervention by the authorities, import substitution, foredoomed attempts at regional economic integration and recurring financial crises – it had to replace a substantial proportion of its project loans by programme loans. It negotiated programmes in co-operation with the IMF and granted "structural adjustment loans" to assist with balance-of-payments problems and consequently, like the IMF, it introduced a more macroeconomic dimension into its terms and conditions.

In practice, loans to governments cannot be secured by real assets such as pledges, mortgages, distrainable assets, etc. The criterion justifying a loan is that of "conditionality".

In a macroeconomic context conditionality takes the form of a right to scrutinize the conduct of the economy of the borrowing country; the greater the amount of funds requested, the closer the scrutiny. The larger tranches of credit carry conditions relating to the fundamental macroeconomic objectives which the State receiving the loan has to undertake to pursue. Short-term, financial and monetary constraints take precedence over the requirements of material production and of medium- and long-term investment. The growth objectives of the final maturities are entirely subordinated to debt repayment and maintenance of the major equilibria (budget, balance of payments),[24] the achievement of which presupposes reductions in operating expenditure (subsidies, salaries of officials) and in expenditure on infrastructure and social expenditure (health, education, social protection) concurrently with an increase in revenue (increases in charges for public services, and sometimes in indirect taxation as well, since direct taxation is rarely the subject of reforms). Even where there is no debt problem, a country receiving a loan is not allowed actively to resort to budget deficits or indebtedness and is thus debarred from adopting policies based on Keynesian theories. To obtain "true" prices, subsidies to consumers are reduced or abolished. In the name of market freedom, public corporations and enterprises, and even in some cases public services, are privatized or broken up. In contrast, recourse to capital inflows from abroad is promoted and exports are highly encouraged.

On the microeconomic side conditionality relates to the use of World Bank credits for specific operations. Since the end of the 1970s the Bank has become more pragmatic and endeavours to promote lasting improvements in the financial and economic management of the sectors assisted, and loans associated with investment programmes comprise a substantial amount of technical assistance. Their award and payment is subject to protracted technical studies on the preparation of projects, the launching of international invitations to tender for civil engineering projects and the provision of consultants, reforms in structures (creation of agencies for the orientation of projects) and in financial management (charges), and also acceptance of the right of the Bank to monitor the actual execution of the programmes.

The developing countries find these provisions unsatisfactory. In their eyes the IMF and the World Bank are symbols of the Western economic order; they harshly criticize both in the United Nations, and even more harshly in UNCTAD, even though the reforms they demand are more of a financial nature than a political challenge to the existing system.

What significance, they object, can be attached to an increase in the money supply when the most developed countries have difficulty in determining what constitutes it? What validity can be accorded to short-term criteria of sound management of the national economy when the flaws in the latter are of a lasting nature and demand long-term development criteria? Can one require developing countries to adopt austere recovery policies demanding political authoritarianism while at the same time demanding a contraction of the State and making the adoption of an imported and unstable model of democracy a criterion of judgement?

The developing countries consider interventions in the form of mandatory advice to be an excessive intrusion in their strategies which raises genuine problems of interference[25] and at the same time a disavowal of the policy followed previously, which gave rise to destabilizing internal debates. They accuse the "experts" of lack of knowledge and understanding of the realities in the field. They ask whether budgetary and monetary measures designed in past years to solve problems arising in Latin America have not been transposed to economies in Asia which are not suffering from the same problems at all. They attack the denunciation of management practices – which are products of the socio-cultural environment with a past history – by experts who are unaware that current conditions make it difficult to introduce the imported practices they wish to see adopted. They reject the accusations of lack of political courage directed at them by experts to whom criticism comes easily since they assume no direct responsibility.

The main opposition to the protests and demands of the developing countries stems from the hostility of the United States which, since the Philadelphia Conference of 1982, has unceasingly proclaimed that free enterprise should take precedence over State intervention and trade over aid, as well as wishing to have control over the United Nations institutions and wanting loans to be granted preferentially to "friendly" countries.[26]

The standards for structural adjustment, by giving first priority to world market mechanisms and the opening of borders, together with intermediate budgetary and financial objectives, contradict almost point by point the objectives and the instruments recommended in the strategies followed in previous decades. The result has been a new orthodoxy and a new development paradigm.[27]

The former objective of industrialization has been replaced by an objective of adaptation to the requirements of international capitalist accumulation. Dependency is increasing. The imbalances and asymetries which under the earlier approach were considered as a starting-point for positive locomotive effects have become "deficits" to be reduced or eliminated.

The aim of the IMF through adjustment is to secure a dominating influence over the developing countries which will lead to a "normalization" of economic and social structures, in order to "bring them into line with the dictates of the functioning of the world economy"; the definition of "normal" is not what is encountered in the great majority of cases but, in the optic of IMF doctrine, what "should be".[28] It is for the world economy to validate the economic activity of each country; external constraints should bring about the construction of "a set of economic and social relationships meeting the internationally predominant criteria in the areas of productivity, return on capital and, finally, the balance between earnings and profits".[29]

The most serious aspect of the situation, and one which runs completely counter to any linkage between economic and human development, is that, whereas an adjustment strategy should ensure the establishment of a measure of social justice, the one followed by the Bretton Woods institutions does not seem to be the best way of stimulating economic growth while at the same time ensuring that the fruits of that growth are correctly distributed. Governments and international organizations have observed that in Latin America a decade of structural adjustment has, admittedly, led to a rehabilitation of the economies in the light of the monetary and financial criteria adopted; but it has also, and "above all", given rise to the impoverishment of their populations.[30] This remark can be applied in a more general context. In many countries the consequences of adjustment programmes are the worsening of inequalities in income distribution, the accentuation of poverty (in contradiction to the affirmation that the primary objective is its eradication), reductions in the resources devoted to education and health (with the poor being the principal sufferers therefrom), the expansion of the role of the private sector and, with it, the strengthening of the power of money for the benefit of a minority.[31] "Conditions" such as the reduction of subsidies in order to limit public expenditure, the abolition of price controls on staple goods, payment by users for public services and the alignment of domestic prices on world prices without other precautions certainly do not contribute to the campaign against poverty.[32]

The social difficulties to which structural adjustment programmes have given rise have been one of the principal concerns of the ILO since the beginning of the 1980s, international labour standards being one of the affirmations and defences of fundamental human rights. When measures allowing work flexibility are introduced, measures should equally be taken to protect working conditions and to provide methods of income distribution; but in the strategy imposed there are practically none.[33] The rigidities caused by the provisions of labour and social legislation are attacked as hindering the free operation of the labour market; occasionally greater flexibility is imposed as a condition for the granting of international adjustment assistance (Côte d'Ivoire), whereas silence is the rule concerning those due to the presence of multinational firms and the effect of incessant megamergers. This explains the concern which the ILO is continually expressing over the risks of the gradual whittling away of the acquired social rights of which it is the guardian; evidence of this is found, for example, in the concern of its Committee of Experts on the Application of Conventions and Recommendations at the possibility that structural adjustment programmes introduced without the intervention of the ILO may run counter to the pursuit of certain objectives such as those of the Employment Policy Convention of 1964.

The seriousness of the situation is exemplified by the "IMF riots", as they were known, which took place at the beginning of the 1990s in Tunisia, the Dominican Republic, Argentina and Venezuela; they were expressions of spontaneous social resistance, but were sometimes organised – as in Brazil; and by the "IMF suicides" of Thai workers dismissed from their jobs and without resources, who killed their wives and children before killing themselves because they could not provide for them. The weakness of the State, deprived of certain instruments of intervention under the "conditions" imposed on it and unable to solve social problems, makes emerging democracies difficult to govern, and even exposes them to the danger of *coups d'état* (Honduras, Indonesia, Congo, etc.) and at the same time – as Despouy observes – to a fragmentation of the nation, which is the forerunner of clashes between ethnic groups.

It gradually became apparent to the organizations in the United Nations family that relief of the "social suffering" inflicted on the assisted countries was a task that they must undertake as a complement to the action taken by individual States. As early as 1987 UNICEF had become aware of the urgent need for a change in direction and strategy and was recommending "adjustment with a human face". During the same year the World Bank launched the programme entitled "the social dimension of adjustment"; as a specific programme it was discontinued in 1992, but the good intentions remained. At the October 1998 session of the General Assembly J. Wolfensohn, its President, stated: "If we are not capable of facing up to urgent social needs, if we do not work for more social justice, then there will be no political stability; and without political stability no amount of money will be able to obtain financial stability".[34] He had thus come to share the views of the Director-General of the IMF, Michel Camdessus, who had affirmed in Rome in 1995 that the directors of the Fund had identified the challenges of globalization and were doing everything they could to put in place the key elements of a globalized economy, even though, he admitted, much remained to be done to introduce a broader dimension of responsibility, co-operation and solidarity into the Fund's strategies. He ended by recommending a maximum of humanization in structural adjustment; in his view that was the only possible way forward, and no credible alternative had been proposed.[35]

Richard Jolly does not share that view. He contends that human development contains all the elements necessary – democracy, civil and political rights, the obligation on the State to develop the human potential within it, equity – for the formulation of a new paradigm to replace that of economic liberalism. By the emphasis it lays on human priorities, such a paradigm offers a reference framework for all the objectives of economic development.

3. A PROPOSED STRATEGY BASED ON EDUCATION, LAW, EMPLOYMENT AND SHARING

When discussing the linkages which economists establish between wealth creation and capital accumulation, Sfeir-Younis describes the "durability" of development as "closely dependent on the securing of equilibrium between all the forms of capital participating in the development process". He divides those forms into two principal categories, one category comprising physical, human, financial and natural (environment) capital, the other containing institutional and spiritual (cultural) capital. While not denying the importance of material growth – for he is convinced that the higher forms of development, and the excellence of their results, can only stem from the accumulation of the lower forms of capital (i.e., physical and financial capital) – he considers that the gains in well-being result rather from the interactions between human, institutional and spiritual (cultural) capital, that is to say, the rules of social interplay, the organization of society, governance, participation and justice.

Following on from this assertion, Sfeir-Younis argues that the variety of forms of globalization should also be taken into account. Globalization is not only "economic" or "financial". It must also be "human", placing the peoples in the front rank of a development process which for the moment is still dehumanizing. It must also be "social", providing a basis for interactions in the "global village" which seeks to promote participation, equality of the sexes, respect for human rights and the future of democracy. Finally, it must be "cultural and spiritual"; in a context of peace (assuming that progress is being made in that direction) it offers the coherence and the space essential for human diversity.

The writings of Jolly and Sachs reflect the same conviction that the only possible strategy for development is a multidimensional one. They argue that primacy must go to social considerations; that ecological considerations must impose a new set of conditions; and that economic considerations, however important, must be confined to their role as an instrument. Once these premises are accepted, it becomes clear what should be the main guiding principles underlying the strategy to be designed. The first of those guiding principles relates to education and culture.

To live is to act in accordance with the reasons for living which one accepts and considers as the right ones. To achieve that end one must be able to mobilize one's energies, broaden one's capacities and identify and translate into deeds the values one has recognized. Without this apprenticeship neither economic nor human development are possible. Bonvin, for instance, describes the generalization of education as the "essential act" which will enable the poor to take advantage of the new opportunities which politics offers them; to participate in projects; and to control their fertility. It is essential to look beyond the contribution of education to economics and to examine very carefully the role it plays in the areas of social practices, international relations, integration within a culture and the renewal of cultures.

Globalization weakens the points of reference of the individual – family, job, nation – which used to enable him to face up to the difficulties of life, and with them his faith in society and in the future. As Hallak[36] writes, "questioning of the finalities of life, which could adress these challenges, is blurred and biased by purely economic concerns". He recognizes that education must continue to be a provider of knowledge and competencies and of an ability to learn; but in a continually changing world producing short-lived values it must also help individuals to behave autonomously, while at the same time teaching them to listen to one another, and enable them to understand not only their economic environment but above all their "social and political environment." It should be "the catalyst for the desire to live together".[37] Its ultimate objectives must relate primarily to adaptation to life in society and the possibility of changing it in order to achieve greater well-being. That implies that the institutions of the educational system must act in conjunction with other social institutions in order to attain those objectives. He goes on to state: "It is only when education is regarded as an integral part of the social system that the goals proposed for education – identified as social goals – become meaningful."[38]

The Mexico Congress, adopting a multidimensional approach, reached general agreement on a concept of "human resources" comprising education, health, culture, employment, sciences and technology; thus human resources development must be understood as implying "the full development of the individual in his entirety".[39] It linked human and economic development and declared that the economic dimension should not be approached exclusively from a quantitative perspective but also as a process of transformation of human resources management into potential for development.[40] Thence derives the importance attached to preparation for employment, the necessity of co-operation by enterprises in vocational training, the complementarity of the different modes of teaching, the establishment of global and regional co-operation networks in liaison with non-governmental and intergovernmental organizations, the pioneering role of the universities and the inclusion of the different types of non-formal education within the scope of educational "planning".

The second guiding principle relates to law and institutions.

In order to establish the securing of human rights as the raw material of development, adequate legal instruments must be created and set in an ordered framework. The task is a heavy one. Admittedly, the ILO has succeeded in establishing a world-wide system of international labour standards. It has designated as "fundamental" the conventions relating to freedom of association (1948), the right of collective bargaining (1949), the minimum age of admission to employment (1973), the prohibition of all forms of forced labour (1930 and 1957) and discrimination in employment (1958); its views are shared by the OECD.[41] Admittedly, too, the World Bank has since 1994 added to its function as a regulator of international investment flows a function of regulator of the relations between the population and the national authorities responsible for executing the projects it finances, and consequently new procedures have been designed to ensure that the people can claim their rights.[42] Admittedly, too, a number of reports on international trade draw distinctions between "licit" comparative advantages and those which are based on failure to adopt a genuinely human system of work organization; and there are increasing numbers of "social quality marks" guaranteeing the absence of recourse to child labour, the existence of decent working conditions, fair remuneration of small producers or the use of environment-friendly techniques.[43]

While all this is true, the complexity of the problems to be solved requires much more.

Since the end of the 1970s, in response to the thrust of neo-liberalism, economic and social policies have been challenging labour standards generally. The idea that deregulation is beneficial is gaining ground in both developed and developing countries; structural adjustment programmes are reinforcing that trend. The fear that poor working conditions and the removal of protection will result in strikes and social disorders has gone; the contractual strength of the unions has been weakened by unemployment and threats of delocalization, and a justification is found in the need for international competitiveness. Freedom and the interests of enterprises are the primary objects of care at both national and international levels, while the "rights" of the poor are considered as "poor rights" which can be sacrificed.[44]

At the same time there has been a revival of interest in international labour standards as a result of the broadening of the concept of the economic and social rights of the citizens and the raising of the level of expectations relating to them; the increasing awareness in public opinion of the worst forms of exploitation of child labour, or of women in customs-free zones; and the fears for jobs caused by imports of manufactured goods from low-wage countries and threats of delocalization.[45]

Also at the same time, in every part of the world, and in developing as well as developed countries, the employer-employee relationship is undergoing radical changes. New technologies, changes in the organization of work, the rapid expansion of network enterprises, externalization and subcontracting have brought with them the development of new forms of employment, which were initially termed "atypical" but are becoming generalized. Work time, work results and salaries are becoming increasingly individualized. In view of the growing complexity of the different temporalities of life, there is a tendency to resort more and more to a whole series of negotiations in order to structure them, since the regulation of working time can no longer be envisaged from the sole standpoint of the enterprise or the individual employee; the interests of the family or of the community as a whole must also be taken into account.

Employment relationships are becoming dependent on cross-frontier commercial transactions, and people working for the same firm may be covered by the laws of different countries with occasionally mutually hostile cultural foundations. The "fragmentation" of the labour force within the enterprise is compounded by "fragmentation" on the international plane. The universal predominance of full-time wage-earning employment contracts, standardized and of indeterminate duration, based on a trade-off between high degrees of subordination and disciplinary control exercised by the employer, on the one hand, and a high level of stability and compensation in the form of social benefits and guarantees of employment on the other, is coming to an end. The boundaries of wage-earning employment are continually fading; "self-employment" is once again emerging, if not always in quantitative, then certainly in qualitative, terms. It takes either the form of genuinely autonomous and highly skilled work of a service nature in enterprises, or, at the other extreme, of precarious work of an unskilled nature, which those who have lost their places among the regular wage earners must accept. Labour law has to cover every form of work, even forms which do not match up to earlier standards.[46]

If human development is to be interlinked with economic development, new rights, deriving from the fundamental rights already recognized, must be identified. The strategy required by the new paradigm calls for "reinstitutionalization", namely the fixing of rules, and the determination of areas open to bargaining, so that the agent groups can act effectively; and the invention of a new occupational status based on a comprehensive approach to work within which the imperatives of freedom and security can be apprehended.[47] The idea that any worker, wherever he or she is working and whatever the form of the work, has a certain number of fundamental rights which must be protected vis-à-vis the interests of capital must be further pursued. The emerging common rights of humankind can adapt to a plurality of legislations. But for these rights to become established certain challenges must be met: the instrumentalization of the law to serve the market, and the socio-economic pseudo-rationality which seeks to drain the rights of their nature as general principles for the benefit of obscure and complex regulations. So must the challenges of the Utopia of a universal legal community which might, if differences in value systems were neglected, lead to the discarding of the "fundamental", leaving only the "minimum".[48]

The third guiding principle concerns employment. Sachs considers that the logic which makes employment the result of a growth process led by market forces should be reversed; for him, it is "the entry point into the strategy of development". Albert Tévoédjré sees it as the real response to poverty.

The ideal of full employment has been adopted by both developed and developing countries. The operative part of the 1964 ILO Convention concerning employment policy states that "a major goal" is the declaring and pursuance of an active policy designed to promote employment and aiming at ensuring that "there is work for all who are available for and seeking work". By the beginning of the 1980s, 66 countries with different levels of development and different socio-political systems had ratified it. If one takes into account the "White Paper" produced by the Commission of the European Communities,[49] the commitments entered into by heads of State and government at the Copenhagen World Summit for Social Development,[50] and even the "Charter to combat unemployment and exclusion" adopted by the G-8 in February 1998,[51] one can without exaggeration state that full employment is still an objective on which a very large measure of consensus can be secured.

According to the ILO,[52] neither unemployment nor underemployment are "inevitable or irreversible". The OECD considers "unfounded"[53] the fears that a period of "growth without employment" is about to begin. Notwithstanding the "computer revolution", the volume of labour devoted to the production of goods and services has not decreased; the increase in employment in services has more than made up for the fall in industry and the reduction in working hours. During the years 1960-1995 North America had the highest rate of employment growth (1.8 per cent annually), followed by Oceania (1.7 per cent); the European Communities came last (0.3 per cent), while Japan came in an intermediate position (1.2 per cent). The low rate of increase in Europe coincided with a fall in the rate of population growth and a long-term decline in the proportion of economically active persons employed. In the United States the "job stock" has more than doubled, rising from about 60 million at the end of the 1940s to 124.9 million in 1995; between 1993 and 1998, 13.5 million new jobs were created, the record year being 1997, with 3.2 million new jobs. In Western Europe, between 1975 and 1990, when the new technologies were spreading rapidly and employment in industry was falling (- 5 million), overall employment increased by some 10 million; some two thirds of the new jobs were created in the public sector, but private-sector employment also increased slightly after falling for some years. The increase in employment in the developed countries can be attributed primarily to the fact that the supply of and demand for services increased much more rapidly than output per unit of labour. Estimates in the United States indicate a rate of growth in the production of services for the market of the order of 2.6 per cent annually up to the year 2005 (3.5 per cent for private services), as against 2.4 per cent for production overall; the result should be the creation of 25 million jobs, which should more than make up for losses in the goods production sector.

In the developing countries the situation is much more complex; most of them are far from having attained full employment, whatever the definition given to the term. The elasticity of employment is in inverse ratio to labour productivity; a fall means that growth is creating comparatively fewer jobs. This is not necessarily a negative indicator; everything depends on the initial value of employment elasticity. In countries such as Guatemala, Kenya and the Philippines, where it was higher than 1 during the years 1975-1980 (1.31, 2.68 and 3.66 respectively) the falls (to 0.73, 1.12 and 0.39 respectively in 1986-1992) may be considered as useful corrections, since employment rose (6.47, 2.83 and 6.4) faster than the growth of the economically active population (3.4 per cent, 2.7 per cent and 2.7 per cent respectively). In countries such as the Republic of Korea and Thailand, in which production had increased sharply but the elasticity of employment was initially low (0.53 and 0.61) and declined further (0.30 and 0.38), employment growth remained high (3.7 per cent and 3.76 per cent) – a rate much higher than that of the growth of the economically active population (1.9 per cent and 1.5 per cent). On the other hand, in a country like India, where employment elasticity fell to a very low level (0.2), employment growth slowed down sharply (from 4.6 per cent to 1.41 per cent) – less than the rate of growth of the economically active population (2 per cent). In a number of developing countries severely affected by the crisis of the early 1980s and which adopted structural adjustment programmes, the return to rapid and sustained growth has proved difficult, since the essential cumulative preconditions (a minimum of social and macroeconomic stability) were absent.[54]

There is no question of "discarding" the concept of full employment. There are too many unsatisfied needs of a nature to provide jobs, in both developed and developing countries. Rather, the concept should be "updated",[55] and its definition should include the notion of "acceptable" employment, i.e., employment which is in accordance with fundamental rights, and primarily "conventional" employment – full-time jobs held by one person – without, however, ignoring the changes in the nature of work currently taking place, and the "reinstitutionalization" they demand, which were mentioned earlier.

From this standpoint, the inclusion of employment as an obligatory element of a development strategy evidences concern at the danger that, in the medium term, it may not grow fast enough to keep pace with the growth in the active population. It also indicates concern at the many contradictions between the quantitative and qualitative structures of labour supply and demand arising from the changes currently taking place. Questions of adaptation of training to the new technologies and forms of work organization become interlinked with the reconciliation of aspirations of the workers (whose primary concerns are working conditions and pay and, to an increasing degree, the relationship between those factors and living conditions) with those of employers (whose primary concerns are labour productivity and return on capital). It also implies taking seriously the hypothesis advanced by the International Labour Conference at its 78th session, in 1991, namely that the pursuit of technical advance might in the near future lead to a sharp rise in unemployment and underemployment in the developing countries, particularly in urban areas. This would bring the developed countries under tremendous pressure from the possible inflow of an enormous potential of manpower fleeing from recurring conflicts and attracted by a higher standard of living.

The authors of the report entitled *World Employment in 1995*[56] assert that defeatism of any kind is unacceptable. They argue that, instead of merely drawing up a plan of action, institutional arrangements must be made to keep under continuous and unified review the global economic and social problems which affect employment. One cannot but agree with them when they assert that the return to full employment is, admittedly, a necessity in most countries, but is at the same time a "formidable enterprise".

The fourth guiding principle is expressed by the word "sharing".

Since the beginning of the 1980s the world's wealth has increased at an unprecedented rate. However, the poor countries have fallen far behind the rich countries in terms of economic performance, with the result that the world is now divided into two economic and social universes which are becoming ever more polarized. Moreover, inequalities are widening sharply in individual countries, developed as well as developing.

In 1995, world-wide GDP was of the order of $ 27,846 billion, as compared with $ 4,000 billion in 1960. Of that total, $ 22,788 billion (81.8 per cent) went to the industrialized countries, which contained 20 per cent of the world's population. The share of world GDP taken by the OECD member countries increased from 68.2 per cent in 1965 to 71.1 per cent in 1990 and 82.4 per cent in 1995. Assuming an average rate of growth of income per head of 3 per cent annually – the equivalent of doubling in a generation – it can be calculated that the proportion of men and women enjoying an adequate growth rate fell from 54 per cent in 1965-80 to 37 per cent in 1980-93. During the same period the percentage of persons living in countries in which income per head increased on the average by more than 5 per cent annually rose from 12 per cent to 27 per cent, while the percentage of persons living in countries experiencing negative growth increased from 6 to 18 per cent. Between 1980 and 1995 some 15 countries, mainly in Asia, experienced much more rapid economic growth rates than the Western countries had known at any time during two centuries of industrialization; but in 90 countries the situation deteriorated – although in some of them there was a slight improvement in 1994-95.

The ratio of GDP growth per head in industrialized countries to that in developing countries improved, falling from 21.5:1 in 1960 to 16.3:1 in 1980 and 14.71:1 in 1995; but as far as the least developed countries were concerned, the trend was the opposite: the ratios for the same years were 28.9:1, 43.5:1 and 54.8:1. The 20 per cent of human beings living in the richest countries accounted for 86 per cent of all private consumption, leaving only 1.3 per cent for the poorest 20 per cent. The provision of drinking water for the 1.3 billion persons who do not have access to it would cost less than the amount Europeans spend annually on ice cream and Americans on cosmetics!

During the second half of the 1980s the gap between the incomes of the richest and the poorest 20 per cent of the population was of the order of 9.6:1 in the United Kingdom, 8.9:1 in the United States, 7.5:1 in France, 7.1:1 in Denmark, 5.8:1 in Germany and 4.3:1 in Japan; but in Brazil it was 32.1:1, in Lesotho 21.5:1, in South Africa 19.2:1, in Kenya 18.3:1, in Venezuela 16.2:1 and in Colombia 15.5:1. The human poverty indicators[57] give poverty rates of over 40 per cent in Bangladesh, Burundi, Côte d'Ivoire, Guinea, Haiti, Malawi, Mauritania, Mozambique, Senegal, Sudan and Uganda; over 50 per cent in Burkina Faso, Ethiopia, Mali and Sierra Leone; and over 60 per cent in Niger; while in the United States the rate is 16.5 per cent, in Ireland 15.2 per cent, in the United Kingdom 15.0 per cent, in Spain 13.1 per cent, in Belgium 12.45 per cent, in Canada, Denmark and Japan 12 per cent, in France 11.8 per cent, in Italy 11.6 per cent, in Germany 10.5 per cent, in the Netherlands 8.2 per cent and in Sweden 6.8 per cent.

Throughout the 1980s and the 1990s disparities in earnings widened sharply in the United States, the United Kingdom and Japan; a similar trend emerged during the mid-1980s in Australia, France, New Zealand and Sweden. In some countries workers in the lowest income groups saw their earnings decline, not only in relative terms, but also in absolute value. In the United States, where low wages are much more common than in most of the other OECD countries, more than one quarter of all workers in full-time employment earn less than two-thirds of the median wage, and one fifth of them receive earnings on or below the monetary poverty line.

In the Anglo-Saxon countries, the differentials between the earnings of relatively unskilled and highly skilled workers has been widening since the beginning of the 1980s, whereas in the countries of continental Europe those differentials have remained unchanged or have widened slightly after having narrowed during earlier decades. In Australia, Canada and, above all, the United States the widening of the earnings gap has been paralleled by a fall in the real earnings of relatively unskilled male workers, whereas in the United Kingdom, although the gap has widened, the real earnings of the unskilled have improved on account of the rises in the general level of earnings during the 1980s. Inasmuch as earnings from work constitute practically the whole of household incomes, an increase in earnings disparities increases social inequalities, the effects of which transfer-incomes are not sufficient to counterbalance.

Eradication of severe poverty in the first decades of the 21st century is possible.[58] Almost all the countries in the world committed themselves to that goal at the Copenhagen summit. In view of the complexity and multidimensionality of the problem, the origins of which are national as well as international, they considered that specific anti-poverty programmes should be drawn up for each country and that national plans should be supported by efforts at the international level. In 1994 the UNDP made a proposal for a compact for human development with a 20:20 formula: the assisted countries were to devote 20 per cent of their budgets to basic social services, while the donor countries were to allocate 20 per cent of their financial assistance for the same purpose.[59] In April 1996, at the invitation of Norway and the Netherlands, the representatives of 40 countries met in Oslo, together with NGOs and the United Nations and Bretton Woods institutions, to discuss the proposal. During the same year the donor countries undertook to reduce by half, by the year 2015, the proportion of individuals suffering from monetary poverty; to ensure primary education for all by the same year; to reduce infant mortality by two thirds and maternal mortality by three quarters; etc.

When one considers the shrinking of public transfers which has occurred in nearly all the donor countries, one may well have misgivings concerning the worth of those commitments.[60] For the first time since the beginning of the 1990s, public aid from OECD member countries to the developing countries fell in 1997 ($ 49.8 billion, as against $ 57.9 billion in 1996). The United States aid budget for 1997 was the lowest in the country's history. In 1997, too, notwithstanding the commitments entered into at one world conference after another, only 30 countries had set themselves goals for the eradication of poverty, and even fewer had drawn up proper strategies for the attainment of that goal.

Admittedly, private aid flows have increased; and this fact might lead one to conclude that public aid is less needed than previously. But that conclusion would disregard the fact that shrinking public aid is primarily a sign of the failure of aid policies. The World Bank report *Assessing Aid,* published in 1998, demonstrated that there is no automatic correlation between public aid and growth, and that success occurs in countries where the rule of law prevails, inflation is contained, roads and infrastructure are properly maintained, fundamental reforms are undertaken, foreign trade is not distorted and aid is not "targeted" but "general" so as to leave the countries concerned free to conduct their own development policies.

Since the G-8 summit in Denver in June 1997, the United States has been relying on the private sector rather than public intervention. At that summit it advanced the theme of "partnership for growth and opportunities in Africa" designed for countries undertaking sweeping liberal reforms, showing a total lack of feeling for historical and socio-cultural factors; in its view trade should replace aid. As a rule the poorest countries are unable to benefit from private financial flows on account of their lack of solvency and the nature of the investments they need, since they are unable to produce the earnings needed to service foreign loans. If there is to be a real sharing between rich and poor countries, an increase in gifts and grants is not enough; nor is it enough to direct more of the financial flows into education, health, drinking water and food in order to ensure that the eradication of poverty and human development have really begun. At the dawn of the 21st century, wherever mass poverty exists the problem is and will remain, not so much one of producing more – for capitalist societies know how to do that – but one of "sharing" equitably – which is quite another matter.

If economic and human development are to have any chance of advancing in parallel in the poorest countries, that chance will not be best promoted through financing on market terms, from which the concept of "sharing" is absent. Concessionary aid – if necessary, granted under new rules – still offers the best hope. Already 2 billion people do not have enough to eat; when there are 8.9 billion mouths to feed instead of 6 billion, will the nations decide to implement a gigantic plan to combat poverty, the objectives of which will be selected on the basis of social instead of monetary and financial considerations? Every year, 17 million individuals die of curable infectious and parasitic diseases; in Africa, 30 per cent of the population is infected by AIDS and cannot obtain expensive treatment. Must the inequalities in the face of sickness and death increase still further before the resources essential for research and prevention in the field of public health be made available by the rich for the benefit of the poor – and for their own benefit as well, since in these times of globalization diseases travel?

Our proposal can be summarized as four guiding principles of a nature to give direction to strategies; set new tasks for the development-promotion institutions, the United Nations agencies, States and non-governmental organizations; and incite all those who are aware of the problem to form a world-wide alliance for development.

---

[1]*Dialogue des monopoles et des nations*, Grenoble, Presses universitaires, 1982, p. 44.

[2]*Human Development Report, op. cit.*

[3]*Ibid.*, 1994, p. 4.

[4]By 1998, the former Covenant had been ratified by 137 countries and the latter by 140.

[5]In 1967, at the Algiers conference organized to study the problems of staple commodities and non-reciprocal preferences, all the developing countries joined together to form the Group of 77. The result was the adoption of the Algiers Charter, which was basically a compendium of complaints by the poor countries against the rich ones. Subsequently, conference by conference, the group expanded further its platform of claims and action for the developing countries.

[6]The Group of Non-aligned Countries, consisting mainly of Third-World countries (but including Yugoslavia) was founded in Belgrade in 1961. Seventy-five countries participated in its fourth conference, held in Algiers in 1973. The term "non-aligned" stands, not for a neutral or uncommitted attitude, but one of economic liberation vis-à-vis the former colonial powers and the rich countries. It constitutes a not insignificant pressure group, but its institutions have always been extremely rudimentary.

[7]M. Todaro: *Economic development in the Third World,* New York, Longmans, 1977.

[8]By G.A. Cornia, R. Jolly and S. Stewart. Paris, Economica, 1987.

[9]"Conditions géographiques en Afrique tropicale", in *Le Travail en Afrique noire,* Présence africaine, 1952, No. 13, p. 57.

[10]"Vers une nouvelle coopération internationale", in *Développement et civilisation,* Oct.-Dec. 1962, p. 29.

[11]"Commercial policy in the underdeveloped countries", in *American Economic Review,* May 1959.

[12]"The distribution of gains between investing and borrowing countries", in *ibid.*, May 1950.

[13]G. Grellet: *Structures et stratégies du développement économique,* Paris, Presses universitaires de France, 1986, pp. 85-98.

[14]D.C. Lambert and J.M. Martin: *L'Amérique latine. Economies et sociétés,* Paris, Collin, 1972, pp. 68-72, 332-341; and G. de Bernis: *Relations économiques internationales,* Paris, Dalloz, 1977, pp. 1039-1042.

[15]Huynh Khao Tri, Le Thanh Khôi, R. Colin, Luo Yuan-Shenz: *Stratégies du développement endogène,* Paris, UNESCO, 1984.

[16]Resolution 3201 S VIn, operative paragraph 4(d).

[17]G. de Bernis: "Les industries industrialisantes et les options algériennes", in *Tiers Monde*, July-Sept. 1969.

[18]F. Perroux: "Note sur la notion de 'pôle de croissance'", in *Economie appliquée*, Jan.-June 1955.

[19]E. Ganagé: *Economie du développement*, Paris, Presses universitaires de France, 1962.

[20]"Qu'est-ce que le développement"?, in *Etudes*, Jan. 1961.

[21]Medium-term plan, 1977-1982. *Thinking ahead. UNESCO and the challenges of today and tomorrow*, Paris, UNESCO, 1977; *Suicide or survival? The challenge of the year 2000*, Paris, UNESCO, 1977; A.M. M'Bow: *Moving towards change: some thoughts on the New International Economic Order*, Paris, UNESCO, 1976.

[22]Paris, Economica, 1984, p. 227.

[23]*Ibid.*, 1982, p. 287.

[24]M.F. L'Hériteau: "Endettement et ajustement structurel; la nouvelle économie", in *Tiers Monde*, 1982, No. 91.

[25]*Ibid.*, 1982, p. 287.

[26]S. Treillet, *art. cit.*, p. 133.

[27]G. Grellet: "La politique d'ajustement orthodoxe, un point de vue critique", in *Tiers Monde*, Jan.-Mar. 1997.

[28]M.F. L'Hériteau and C. Chavagneux: *Le FMI et les pays du Tiers Monde*, Paris, Presses universitaires de France, 1990, p. 200.

[29]M.F. L'Hériteau: *Endettement et ajustement structurel,* art. cit., p. 71.

[30]*Ramsès 98*, Paris, Dunod, 1997, p. 71.

[31]F. Reimers and T. Tiburcio: *Education, adjustment and reconstruction*, Paris, UNESCO, 1993.

[32]M. Woodhall: *Education and training under conditions of economic austerity and restructuring*, UNESCO, 1991.

[33]G. Standing and V. Tokman: *Towards social adjustment. Labor market issues in structural adjustment*. Geneva, ILO, 1991.

[34]*Bilan du Monde 1999*, Paris, Le Monde, 1999, p. 26.

[35]"Habiter la cité globale. Stratégies et institutions économiques", in *Notes et documents*, Sep.-Dec. 1995, pp. 22-24. Hugon observes that practically no alternatives to adjustment policies have been proposed, which suggests that the ruling classes are finding it almost impossible to formulate an economic standard which can stand as an alternative to the international financial standard. See "Jeux économiques et enjeux des politiques orthodoxes en Afrique: le cas de Madagascar et du Nigéria", in *Tiers Monde,* Jan.-Mar. 1987.

[36]"Education and globalization", UNESCO, *Contributions of the International Institute for Educational Planning*, 1998, No. 26, p. 11.

[37]*Ibid.*, p. 13.

[38]*Ibid.*, p. 14.

[39]Mexico International Congress (March 1990) on planning and management of the development of education, *Final Report*, Paris, UNESCO, 1991.

[40]*Knowledge for development*, Washington, D.C., World Bank, 1999.

[41]*Normes de travail, commerce et emploi; une étude sur les droits fondamentaux des traavailleurs et l'échange international*, Paris, OECD, 1996.

[42]G. Carrier: *Défense des populations et développement. Un enjeu pour la Banque mondiale*, Paris, L'Harmattan, 1998.

[43]J. Hilowitz: "Social labelling and combating child labour", in *International Labour Review*, Summer 1997.

[44]P. Imbert: "Droits des pauvres, pauvres droits", in *Revue de droit public*, 1989, No. 3.

[45]E. Lee: "Globalization and labour standards", in *International Labour Review*, Summer 1997.

[46]A. Supiot, E. Mingione, P. Meadows, etc. : *Au-delà de l'emploi. Transformations du travail et devenir du travail en Europe.* Commission européenne, Rapport final, Paris, Flammarion, 1999.

[47]*Ibid.*, p. 203.

[48]M. Delmas-Marty: *Vers un droit commun de l'humanité*, Paris, Ed. Textuel, 1996, and *Trois défis pour un droit mondial*, Paris, Seuil, 1998. See also M. Bonnechère: "La reconnaissance des droits fondamentaux comme condition du progrès social", in *Droit du travail et mondialisation*, proceedings of the symposium organized in Montreuil in February 1998 by the Trade Union Centre for Economic and Social Studies and Research of the French General Confederation of Labour, pp. 379-391.

[49]"Croissance, compétitivité, emploi. Les défis et les pistes pour entrer dans le XXIᵉ siècle", in *Bulletin des Communautés européennes*, supplément 6/93.

[50]"World Summit for Social Development: impetus to concerted action", in *International Labour Review*, 1995, No. 2.

[51]Since 1997 Canada, France, Germany, Italy, Japan, the United Kingdom and the United States have been joined by the Russian Federation.

[52]"Towards full employment. Contribution by the ILO to the second session of the preparatory committee for the World Summit for Social Development", New York, 1994, Geneva, doc. WSSD/94.

[53]*OECD Jobs Study*, Paris, OECD, 1994.

[54]A summary assessment of the position was made by the ILO in *National policies in a global context. A brief overall review*, Geneva, ILO, pp. 139-157.

[55]*Ibid.*, pp. 40-42.

[56]Geneva, ILO, 1995.

[57]The HPI 1, created for developing countries, focuses on three aspects of human life: the probability of premature death; exclusion from reading and communication; and lack of access to decent living conditions (drinking water, health, nutrition). HPI 2, which is applied to industrialized countries only, covers life expectancy, the lack of education, living below the monetary poverty threshold and exclusion (long-term unemployment).

[58]*World Human Development Report 1997, op. cit.,* p. 1.
[59]*World Human Development Report 1994, op. cit.*
[60]Public aid as % of GNP:

	1960	1989	1996	1997
Canada	0.16	0.44	0.32	0.34
Denmark	0.11	0.94	1.04	0.97
France	0.21	0.54	0.48	0.45
Germany	0.38	0.41	0.33	0.28
Italy	0.19	0.42	0.20	0.11
Japan	0.22	0.32	0.20	0.22
Netherlands	0.38	0.94	0.81	0.81
Norway	0.13	1.04	0.85	0.86
Sweden	0.06	0.97	0.84	0.79
United States	0.56	0.15	0.12	0.09

CHAPTER 3

Governance on three levels: global, national and regional

In polite terms, Keynes declared that when "a country's capital development becomes the by-product of casino-type activity, it risks occurring in unsatisfactory conditions".[1] Events have proved that, left to their own momentum, the market economy and society beget a precarious livelihood, unemployment, exclusion and poverty. All the world's stumbling-blocks stem, now as before, and possibly more than in earlier years, from placing a money value on everything, from the transformation of money from a useful instrument into a fetish that dismisses or distorts all human values. Hilferding long ago announced the advent of a capitalism based on giant corporations hatching agreements across borders, in which bankers with "financial capital" would hold sway and in which, over and above the friction that the more powerful interests generate with one another, a sort of international "planning" would be established and result in the abandonment of political liberalism.[2] Financial capitalism has, so to speak, been caught in the trap of the organization and mechanisms it has built for itself, and we are witnessing today a veritable monetary and financial explosion. A world of speculators has established itself, lying in wait for the slightest difference in rates of interest or exchange, and for fluctuation of the stock market prices. Keynes spoke of enterprises reduced to the state of "bubbles in the maelstrom of speculation"; now one speaks of "financial" or "monetary bubbles" in which capital is deposited or withdrawn – even if it means bursting those bubbles – without the least thought for the victims of these intrigues, none of which are the least related to the real economy which has no connection with financial economics, but is affected by the latter's crises and operations.

On the one hand, there is the angelic vision of globalization lately in vogue and dear to the dominant liberalism and monetarism, the foundation of the dynamic of openness and deregulation of the Uruguay Round and the GATT, and, on the other hand, a perplexed, not to say accusatory, vision. Liberal he may be, but Maurice Allais fiercely rejects "a kind of internationalist *laissez-faire* havoc" that ignores the fact that the market economy could never be effective "if it is not set within an appropriate institutional and political framework", and which, in its present form, benefits a handful of privileged groups whose interests "could never be identified with those of humankind as a whole".[3] Ramonet[4] adds to the "economic horror" earlier criticized by Forrester[5] a "globalitarian horror", since civilization is slowly "sinking into fascination with chaos", faced with a "many-faced monster" in which he casts, higgledy-piggledly, population explosion, drugs, mafias, nuclear proliferation, religious fundamentalism, the greenhouse effect, States stripped of their prerogatives, the dictatorship of the financial markets and even all-out privatization. Artus[6] accuses finance –"rational in its calculations" – of causing upheavals in the markets. Soros[7] takes issue with the ideology anchored in the theory of perfect competition, the bastion of world capitalism, and with the "magic of the stock market", and thinks that "the moment of truth" in the form of collapse might be upon us if the reversal of capital flows is not brought to an end. Cotta[8] sees corruption as the major risk to capitalism today.

Camdessus acknowledges that liberalization has "in some cases been practised against common sense, or contrary to requirements", and counters the "anti-State Hayekian method" with his own "three hands" theory: the invisible hand of the market, the hand of justice (that is, of the State) and the hand of solidarity, with all three working together.[9] The answer to the advent of a "world without masters"[10] – in actual fact, subject to nebulous forces and oligarchies without mandates – cannot be to trust the shortsighted gods of the market-place. It is in "governance"[11] – that is, the capacity to choose objectives in the universe of possibilities, set priorities, determine the paths to be followed, regulate and correct the measures taken – that the response to the challenges of such a world must be sought, as well as through the possibility of doing so, that is to say, of "governability".

1. CONDITIONS OF GLOBAL GOVERNANCE

Throughout the 1980s and 1990s the idea of "global governance" has gradually gained ground in international bodies. As
early as 1976, the Club of Rome had proposed the progressive
transfer of economic powers from the national to the international
level through the creation of "authorities", genuine instruments of
"global planning" and management of the planet's main
resources.[12] Since then collective reflection on development and
security in daily life in an interdependent world has progressed from
"report" to "report".[13] In 1991 the "Stockholm initiative" also dealt
with global security and "governance".[14] In 1994 the World Bank
drew the lessons from its experience in that field and defined "governance" as the way in which a country's economic resources are
administered in support of its development.[15]

The concept of global "governance" should be applied with caution. The time is past when Tinbergen could dream of a World
Government with world ministries, a World Central Bank and a
World Treasury.[16] However, it is now time for international society
to fulfil a number of tasks which individual States will not or cannot
perform.

The integration of international society is far from comparable
to that of nations. Sfeir-Younis is certain that the translation of a
"new paradigm" into action depends first and foremost on the institutions, a view shared by Berthelot in his concern at the adverse
consequences that any negligence in that regard might incur. The
United Nations "system" is not a "prime minister" inasmuch as no
United Nations agency is capable of performing that role.
According to Blanchard, it is a "non-system" and it is high time it
underwent a thorough overhaul "if there is a sincere wish for the
three-fold victory of economic progress, social justice and environmental protection". Merle is of the same opinion: he considers that
the United Nations can only escape its internal contradictions and
its inability to master alien forces if it undertakes an "in-depth
reform of its structure, its powers, and its *modus operandi*";[17] but
it must remember from experience that the rules of the political
game cannot long resist a change in the power relations or value
systems that imposed them. Consequently, to seek once again institutional improvement in order to install a new international order
and leave it at that is to "take the easy way out".

The Bretton Woods institutions, especially the World Bank, have
been obliged to intervene in the most diverse areas. They cannot

set themselves up as "the world's conscience", declares Despouy, when the conditions they impose exacerbate situations of poverty, while other United Nations bodies strive to come to the rescue or to play a not inconsiderable role in human development: FAO's establishment of a prevention and surveillance system to ensure food security, UNESCO's support for literacy and education campaigns, WHO's promotion of world-wide vaccination campaigns and smallpox-eradication programmes, dissemination of family planning under the aegis of UNFPA, solution of labour problems by the ILO, and so on.[18] As long as the World Bank and, more specifically, the IMF gave their unreserved support to the "Washington consensus", no effective co-operation for economic and human development was possible between them and the United Nations agencies specializing in the protection of human beings and, later, of the environment. The time has come to reassign the Bretton Woods institutions to their proper role as instruments in the service of economic and human development. It is not the function of economics *strictu sensu*, let alone that of financial and monetary affairs, to lay down the law in social matters nor should the social impose its law on them. The social area is, by its very nature, one in which objectives emerge and become apparent; the economic area is one in which appear the knowledge and use of resources for attaining those objectives.

It is quite in order to advocate the fashioning of a set of new international institutions endowed with effective powers that allow them to perform their task, not independantly of national interests, but in concert with them;[19] that calls, first and foremost, for the reform and strengthening of the existing institutions.

In 1969 the Pearson Report[20] commended the World Bank's institutional innovations,[21] the diversity of its offers of financial and development assistance resources, and the expansion of its field of operations, but criticized it on several counts: for operating too hand in glove with the major powers because of its dependence on governments or large financial markets; for applying a lending policy that seemed to stray from the essential objectives of development; for assuming too many tasks, some of which it could not perform efficiently; and even for conducting missions too brief to be useful. The Report then formulated a number of proposals ranging from establishing a system of free and equitable international trade to developing external private capital inputs, rescheduling debt service, shifting the focus of technical assistance, overhauling education and research assistance and decelerating population growth.

The World Bank undertook a sweeping reform in the early 1980s. It replaced many of its project loans with programme loans to keep pace with changes in the economic performance of the countries hardest hit by the debt crisis. The new loans supported openness to the outside world, the liberalization of financial systems, privatization schemes and streamlining of public administrations. In that way it shared the ideology of the "Washington consensus". Following several decades of massive state intervention, import substitution, protected industrialization, abortive attempts at regional integration and recurrent financial crises, Latin America returned to the market-place. To confront that new situation, the Bank was obliged to renew its expertise, change its *modus operandi* and come to terms with new risks. Over the course of that period, during which development assistance and the fight against poverty were taking precedence in Africa and some parts of Asia, one-third of the Bank's operations and loans from the International Development Association under "targeted" intervention programmes were assigned to the fight against poverty – quite a significant shift. Conceived with a view to helping – together with the IMF – to instil a modicum of order into the developing countries' often poorly managed economies, the Bank announced an important turning-point that would lead it, in the 1990s, to focus much more strongly on world health and educational policies as well as on environmental protection.

Unlike the Bank, the IMF does not act as a capital intermediary for its member countries' development. Its capacity to assist those with balance-of-payments problems to lower adjustment costs relies on resources placed at its disposal, with the "conditions" it imposes on the beneficiaries serving as "guarantees". Its existence is justified by the surveillance it is supposed to exercise, its "crisis" prevention and its encouragement to member countries to open up their economies. The IMF is not a world joint development fund, but a co-operation fund that distributes members' contributions for the benefit of temporarily indebted States and strengthens international liquidity by issuing special drawing rights in the form of a special account on its books.

Whereas the World Bank is a partner, the IMF is an overseeing body which makes annual visits, negotiates financial assistance programmes and monitors fulfilment of the imposed "conditions" and is therefore in constant dialogue with members on the subject of their economic (fiscal, monetary, financial and trade) policies. When the economically advanced countries adopted a system of flexible exchange (initially, fixed parities had to be established by each Member State's monetary authorities), the IMF shifted its attention to the developing countries, necessitating a change in its *modus operandi*. So it was that in 1986, as stated above, it instituted "structural adjustment facilities", followed in 1987 by "enhanced structural adjustment facilities" (ESAF), occasional loans to countries with structural balance-of-payments problems – in exchange for which they were required to institute short-term (three-year) economic adjustment programmes – and structural reforms. Then came, in 1993, a "system transformation facility" designed to assist economies "in transition" (those on the way to a market economy[22]) which found themselves in a balance-of-payments predicament owing to their general instability and extreme fragility.

There is, by and large, broad consensus within the IMF on the formulation of adjustment programmes, notwithstanding the diversity of views concerning the appropriate start-up action and the time frames for implementing the measures imposed. This is prompted by the diametrically opposed positions of the "applicant" countries and the "granting" Fund and by the justification of politically and socially difficult measures that the Fund's intervention imposes on national authorities. In 1986 the Interim Committee of the IMF proposed the use of "objective" economic "performance" indicators to point the way to the ideal macro-economic policy that applicants must follow. In the aftermath of the 1994-95 peso crisis, the Fund set up a prevention mechanism containing information on the level of international reserves countries were required to hold, the balance of their current-account transactions, monetary aggregates, budget balance and inflation. That approach failed totally with the onset of the Asian crisis, for which the private and not the public sector was to blame, so that the "conditionality" of assistance on the aforementioned criteria did not prove dissuasive. In this case, the markets, not the governments, were bailed out by the Fund, inasmuch as the governments used the assistance it received to liquidate the private sector's debts. Subsequently, the IMF had to order the dismantling of an economic system based on collusion among State, banks and industry. While 50 billion dollars had been mobilized to deal with the Mexican crisis, the total loan amount in the case of Asia exceeded $ 100 billion.

The Bank and the Fund must now face up to the revitalization of the markets and their capacity to offer capital to an increasing number of countries. The ever closer integration of international financial markets poses a challenge that raises the following questions: For how long can the intermediation functions of the Bank's investment capital and the Fund's offers of loans to solve balance-of-payments difficulties be justified?[23] And how can the tasks of both institutions be redefined to ensure that their contribution to global economic governance is not only efficient, but simultaneously meets the requirements of economic and human development?

The Bank might come to serve as an international investment corporation selling bonds to countries in surplus and using the capital obtained for granting loans to the developing countries on terms in keeping with their level of development. More particularly, it should help job-creating small and medium-sized firms and small industries, as well as micro-credit institutions. The reference should not be purely financial; it should include human-development and human-cost indicators.

IMF reform might be reflected in the issuance of new special drawing rights for injecting liquidity into the economic system in order to ward off sudden regression and pump-prime or support the recovery of a sluggish economy, supplement poor countries' foreign-exchange reserves, improve opportunities for access to the Compensatory and Contingency Financial Facility (CCFF). International banking transactions and the international financial markets must be monitored on a regular basis and subjected to a minimum of regulation.[24] "Conditionality" criteria need to be thoroughly reviewed to ensure that they encourage economic growth, employment and human development. In that connection, the transformation of the Interim Committee of the IMF into a policy and decision-making organ that approves strategy options and takes account of the "real" consequences (not only the budgetary or monetary consequences) of adjustment is a step in the right direction. But the objective must no longer be the imposition of a world order regulated by the multinational or transnational corporations, under the guise of globalization and liberalism, enthusiastically supported by the Fund and other institutions.

In 1993, the General Conference of UNESCO cautioned against prescribing the same medicine for different diseases and cases. The Organization's Director-General, Federico Mayor, also drew attention to the differing situations of States and nations. There is no all-purpose model of economic development, let alone both economic "and" human development. Nothing could be more absurd than to try, under the guise of "conditionality", to impose privatization, deregulation and "less government" everywhere. As James Wolfensohn[25] (who was responsible for the streamlining and modernization of the World Bank's structures, its increased attention to education, health and the environment and its anti-corruption crusade) said in his Message to the 1998 Annual Meeting of the World Bank, if we cannot come to grips with social emergencies, if we do not work more on social justice, there can be no political stability; and no amount of finance can create financial stability. The conflict between the traditional neo-classical theory that still informs IMF policy, and the fundamental variables of culture, ethics and religion is such that anyone might surmise that awareness of these variables would significantly alter forecasts that rely exclusively on alleged "optimization" founded on purely formal models.[26]

If social imperatives are to form an integral part of policy-making criteria, far-reaching reforms must be made. The IMF speaks of "high-quality growth", the World Bank of "sustainable growth" and the ILO of "equitable growth"; the UNDP places the emphasis on "human development". Each and every organization must, in its own fields of competence and in concert, define and raise awareness of what is necessary (and even urgent) in the short term and desirable in the medium and long term: the ILO for labour, WHO for health, UNICEF for children, UNFPA for demography, FAO for food, UNESCO for education, the natural and social sciences, culture and communication – to cite a few.

In that regard, the Director-General of the ILO[27] advocated the establishment of two bodies, the one – a technical body – in which the IMF, the World Bank, the World Trade Organization (WTO) and the ILO would join forces in drawing up each year a set of recommendations designed to improve world economic performance, with a view to the general welfare; the other – a political body – comprising the ministers of finance, economic affairs, trade and labour, to study those recommendations and decide how they should be implemented. This idea should be espoused, and the list of United Nations agencies invited to participate in the formulation of the recommendations should be expanded, as should the list of ministers to be involved in drawing the conclusions, as well as UNDP's proposal to bring together in the more general programmes the countries' plans of action in the most diverse areas (education, health, food security, etc.).[28]

Proposal followed proposal: the appointment of a Director-General for international development and economic co-operation, as second-in-command to the Secretary-General of the United Nations, with responsibility for co-ordinating major world economic initiatives; the merging of pre-investment funds in a "fund of funds"; the reorganization of the United Nations Department of Economic and Social Affairs; the creation of a consultative committee on economic co-operation and development, composed of the heads of the main United Nations specialized agencies and the regional economic commissions; the strengthening of the role of the Economic and Social Council; the establishment of a group of independent experts to evaluate the progress of United Nations economic activities, and so on.[29]

One of those proposals warrants particular support: the 1994 proposal,[30] which is slowly gaining ground, to establish an Economic Security Council. Its task would be to review the pressing issues of world poverty, food, international migrations and unemployment. Its permanent members would represent the main industrial countries and the more populous developing countries, to which could be added an equal number of members on a rotating basis from various geographical and political constituencies. Since there would be no individual veto, the States' legitimate interests would be protected by decisions adopted by separate favourable votes of a majority of the industrialized countries and a majority of the developing countries, and of a favourable vote of a majority of all countries. Thus constituted, the Economic Security Council would co-ordinate the activities of the United Nations agencies and monitor the policy focus of all international and regional financial institutions.

According to Blanchard, the creation of such a body would be a positive development, provided it were used effectively – and not as a "hypocritical formality", as was currently the case – by the international organizations responsible either for major economic, monetary or financial decisions or for social, cultural and humanitarian solutions – a pronouncement he described as somewhat provocative, but one that should excite debate. Sfeir-Younis also advocates such a body, on condition that its rationale is to ensure economic and financial security, the key "value" being material progress in all its forms. He considers, however, that another body is needed if nations wish to progress further, and could take the form of a sort of "universal spiritual forum", for we can enter a world of total unity only if the human, social, cultural and spiritual aspects of globalization henceforth hold sway in the hierarchy adopted by nations.[31]

Much more ambitious was the Club of Rome, which, 20 years ago, devised an "integrated strategy of action"[32] defined on the basis of negotiations which are "of necessity global". It proposed a fundamental restructuring of the United Nations, conferring on that Organization economic powers and more definite responsibility in international economic decision-making, to ensure the introduction of "global planning components" that guarantee more harmonious global growth and allow poor nations to devote their scant resources to meeting their inhabitants' basic needs. A "voluntary transfer of power" from the nation-states to the world organization was necessary to bring about that "planetary planning and management system"; the ideal expedient would be "to set up a functional confederation of international organizations" based on the already existing (but restructured), and in some cases new, United Nations agencies, all linked through an integration mechanism.

To acquire legitimacy, the international order needs the restraint and approval of those for whom it is intended. Nobody is born a citizen of the world. No-one can enter into dialogue with an "other" if one does not first have a "self".[33] Human truth resides in a process in which civilizations and cultures confront and enrich one another with what is most alive and creative about them, not in unifying imperialism or in inconsistent syncretisms.[34] As Merle observes,[35] international order is a "myth", since it must reconcile the contradictory requirements of the universal and the particular, "but it is a salutary myth if it helps forge a path towards constructive solutions". The task is an arduous one.

The persistence of the debate surrounding the "social clause", the fact that it was not taken into consideration at the 1995 World Summit for Social Development and its rejection by the developing countries at the WTO Ministerial Conference in Singapore (1996) prove how difficult it is to induce the United Nations organizations to adopt a common vision; indeed, their collaboration must rely on the legitimate interests of their respective constituents and on winning their support. This implies the responsibility of States, for it is their task to promote co-ordination and dialogue between their governments and their societies.[36] Accordingly, respect for the sovereignty of all States can block decision-making capacity of the collective organs; and failure to take it into consideration, combined with the principle of equality of all States, might lead to the establishment of artificial majorities that represent only the minority of the world population and, consequently, lack all credibility.

The first faltering steps towards international co-operation for stabilizing greenhouse emissions further illustrate the difficulty of global economic governance. When the discussions on emission reduction first began, the real issue promptly emerged as the choice between quantitative rationing and price co-ordination with the adoption of harmonized taxes.[37] The United States having refused to work with a tax system, the Framework Convention on Climate Change adopted at Earth Summit (Rio, 1992) merely declared that the "Annex 1" countries (OECD member countries and countries in transition) would revert to their 1990 emission levels. Following the 1994 start-up in Berlin of a process of quota co-ordination, agreement was reached in Kyoto in 1997 on a 5.2 per cent average reduction of 1990 emission levels between 2008 and 2012. So-called "flexibility" mechanisms were devised in the form of "tradable permits", in other words, intergovernmental trade in emission quotas, procurement and transfer of emission credits linked to projects aimed at further emission reduction, provided that, when approved by the governments, they were regarded as merely complementing the measures taken for joint – as opposed to individual – fulfilment of quantified commitments, with the formation of subgroups, distributing the total aggregate quota in a manner different from that implicit in an individual quota system, with a possible reserve of unutilized emission quotas set aside against any subsequent commitments. A "clean development" mechanism was thought up for the developing countries desirous of initiating sustainable development and for the industrialized countries called upon to assist them; the latter benefit from certified emission reductions linked to the projects they implement in the former, which have a real, measurable impact on climate change.

Such rationing is clearly arbitrary (why is 1990 the reference year?) and questionable from both the efficiency and equity viewpoints (why must countries, such as France, which have already done much in that regard, agree to a greater reduction than the United States, a mammoth polluter?). The compatibility of the differing national approaches poses a problem, inasmuch as the award of emission permits is left to the discretion of the signatories: they are distributed free of charge to the United States, giving the impression of wealth that generates distortions in competition.[38] The rule of a more or less uniform reduction of a traditional emission level is incompatible with the participation of the developing countries and impedes their economic development; furthermore they can sell part of their emission budget. It is not by 5.2 per cent, but by 30 per cent, that emissions should be reduced if build-ups of greenhouse gases are to stabilize. Lastly, in the absence of non-emitting energy sources that can be immediately substituted on a large scale, and given the cost of the necessary technological transformations, one can hardly ignore the difficulty of attaining even moderate objectives.

The November 1998 Buenos Aires Conference was held in order to establish specific rules for attaining the Kyoto objectives. Already isolated in Rio, the United States had meanwhile refused to ratify the 1997 protocol, invoking the absence from it of the developing countries, especially China, India and Brazil. There followed a fortnight of heated discussion. The United States saw the marketplace as the only effective regulator and wished to create an emission-rights market at the earliest opportunity. The European Union advocated a mandatory or voluntary course of action on the part of States, and saw the rights market, as interpreted by the United States, as a way out of seriously binding measures and the necessary change in the consumption model. In the end, only a "plan for discussion" was adopted, under the jaundiced eye of the developing countries, who were quick to reject any attempt by the United States to mandate a reduction of their emissions. The plan comprised a list of topics to be addressed at a later conference. Nobody achieved anything; the participants neutralized one another almost to perfection. Six years after Rio and one year after Kyoto the international community had still failed to organize itself to confront a serious threat, while essays, symposia, research and conferences on sustainable development proliferatd. The subject is still "under discussion".[39]

2. A VITAL ACTOR: THE STATE

Neither an international order nor global governance can be envisaged without the participation of national States. It is incumbent upon them and their governments to work out something in the nature of a "political rationale", the expression of a "collective compromise" that reconciles the criteria of a broad economic formula developed through awareness of the human and ecological costs, and the criteria of values that wins the support, albeit not unanimous, of the political community.

Neither the nation nor the State is an outmoded concept. Post-nationalism cannot be decreed. It is still between States that international relations are maintained, even though non-State actors play a growing role. The rule of law still means respect for the principles of democratic and economic equality of States and for non-intervention and independence. No action of economic governance can be entertained without the involvement of the State. This is what Robert Reich meant when, rejecting the "cosmopolitanism" that "ignores States", he championed the idea that every nation's citizens should take responsibility for enhancing their compatriots' capacity to live their lives more fully and productively, not to the detriment of the rest of humankind, but quite the reverse.[40]

No development policy in keeping with the "new paradigm" is possible or viable without the existence of an active, robust State. This was precisely the approach adopted in the strategies for the first wave of development, during which the State was assigned the principal role as agent of structural change and regulation, and not driven exclusively by profit or currency, but predominantly by "real" goods. The State long remained the key actor, especially in countries (sub-Saharan Africa) where there is as yet no class able to develop a national project of industrialization and/or a service boom. It is still the case in countries integrated into the world economy because of their resources (oil), but also eager to build the nation in the economic sense of the term (Saudi Arabia, United Arab Emirates) as it is in those that aspire to autonomy (Algeria, Egypt). Elsewhere, there persists a socializing rhetoric that stalls privatization for reasons connected with the balance of power within those countries – this is true in Bolivia, for instance, where the mines have been managed at the outset entirely by a State body.

Development processes are slow and never linear. Human factors come into play. Tenets change. The international economic situation is playing a significant part. Politicization is spreading. All too often there is widespread corruption. State action has lost its legitimacy, and the State is now regarded merely as a representative and guarantor of the general interest. The decline of State power, caused by globalization, and the State's inability in many countries to come up with an effective solution to people's economic and social problems, afford demagogues – and even adherents of authoritarian regimes – opportunities they are quick to seize.

Federico Mayor sternly criticized excessive privatization that enfeebles the State, while private forces consolidate their position and band together through myriad mega-mergers, a type of concentration of powers as dangerous to the State as was their concentration in State hands in the Soviet Union. Berthelot rails against "the fear of the State" and the belief that good institutions can be engineered by privatization and deregulation alone, for, he affirms, "the economy cannot function without a strong State with laws and ground rules it can enforce". The authorities do damage when they sustain monopolies or cartels rather than small labour-intensive businesses or small farms; prohibit farmers from performing certain gainful activities in the interests of a consortium of large land-owners; distort market mechanisms (which they constantly praise) and award privileges to the highest bidder; show more concern for military spending – the forerunner of *coups d'état* – or for absurd wars, than for the people's welfare; build factories that cannot be used to full production capacity and neglect maintenance of their infrastructure. All these examples of misgovernment confirm that development is in dire need of responsible, honest, legitimate governments whose prime concern is growth and equity.

When the World Bank broaches the question and speaks of "the State in a changing world"[41], it does not merely acknowledge the collapse of Soviet-style administrative planning, the budgetary "crisis" of the welfare State in most of the industrialized countries, the important role of the State in the East Asian economic "miracle", or the reservations expressed about the functions of the State, resulting from world-scale upheavals that transform the milieu in which those functions are performed. It does not bring grist to the mill of the partisans of a minimalist conception of the State. Rather, it declares, through its President, James Wolfensohn,[42] that if State-dominated development has failed, so has State-less development – a message that comes through all too clearly in the agonies of peoples in collapsed States (Liberia, Somalia, Sierra Leone and Rwanda). The "rethinking" of development therefore implies, not the denial, but the "rethinking", of the State as well.

In the grip of neo-liberal ideology as we are, the trend is still to make the State revert to those functions over which it exercises a statutory monopoly and leave the regulation of economic activity to the market-place. Weber already observed[43] that, left to make its own laws, the market shows regard only for objects and ignores people and values. An under-regulated market economy can only beget a unidimensional market society and real, reductive "totalitarianism" that encompasses all the functions of society, in which money is both the "normal" and the "supreme" criterion.[44]

The order "of" the market and "by" the market is only a pseudo-order. In the nation, social relationships must be subject to the application of rules that resist its diktat, since the latter derive from practices and culture, and places the aspirations and the good of society on an equal footing to the point where politics and economics converge.[45]

Since the market-place is constrained by the law, the State must be restored or constructed. The "family" of States is disparate: they reveal differences in power and size, differences in nature (many countries barely meet the conditions needed for the normal functioning of a State) and differences in degree of cohesion and integration within their borders, differences in resources and differences in number. Nations, too, are diverse: witness the number of "quasi-nations" that are subject to domination or influence, and even to enslaving situations of force! Witness the great inequalities among nations which stem from economic "superiority" (productivity, specialization, salesmanship) and from the strategies of private oligopolies and the manoeuvring of public authorities! So great are the differences among nation-States that no universal model could be valid. For that reason it would be politic, as the World Bank experts recommend,[46] to outline a reform of the State that relies on the redefinition of its powers; this would be in function of the options of collective interest that must inform development strategy, increased capacity for action, greater heed of the population and, to that end, broader participation and decentralization.[47]

Then there are still the priorities and strategy options put forward earlier for guiding and enriching the actions of the State – education and culture, law and institutions, employment, sharing – with the State establishing and applying the rules and procedures vital to keeping them up-to-date.

Privatization is the key component of the "Washington consensus" and the IMF's structural adjustment programmes. It is seen by the World Bank as a "fundamental priority" in countries with "too much government", whose excessive hold on economic and social life constitutes an "enormous handicap".[48] This is an important issue. Advocating the restoration of the State in some places and its construction in others requires serious reflection.

One can easily accept the need to recognize the State's limits and – unlike the case of the developed countries which possess sound administrative capabilities and where arbitrary acts are prevented by a balance of powers enshrined in statutes – to reduce its room for manoeuvre in countries with weak institutions and unstable power relations among them and between them and civil society. One must beware, however, of overly general proposals and the confusion of cases. The public sector is, by and large, hetero-geneous throughout the world, both from the legal point of view and in terms of the economic nature (market or non-market) of its components. The end it pursues is not mainly profit, but an ulti-mate result based on "another" rationale, guided by "values"; this does not simplify the criteria. Hence the critical observer's frequent need to escape into description and resort to taxonomical research.

The State is a factor in economic policy, both an entrepreneur and a consumer, an essential component of the propagation envi-ronment. As a producer, it meets needs felt by the community as a whole (individuals, groups and businesses). As a factor in economic policy, it is concerned with essentially sectoral or specific needs in conditions which do not all fall exclusively to the public service, but are satisfied jointly with the private sector. As an entrepreneur, it often finds itself in similar circumstances: hence, not all "public ser-vices" are "categorical", as national defence or justice are; they become so only in function of the type of State and the methods of public intervention (education, health, transport, etc.). The State is a key variable of the propagation environment with its multidirec-tional activities; it influences the entire economy through legisla-tion, administration, justice and taxation and, in its role as referee, affects its direction, situation and balance, improving or reducing the efficiency of the economic system as a whole.[49]

There is no hypothetical-quantitative method that can accurately determine the space occupied by "categorial" and "non-categorial" public services and the manner in which they can coexist with the private sector. Neither economics nor sociology can provide abso-lute principles for defining the optimum quantum of public services. Neither empirical studies[50] nor recent theoretical debate[51] establish that public ownership of capital inevitably lead to reduced microe-conomic performance, measured in terms of factor productivity. However, there is proof that the performance of a business or a public service depends much more on the competitive environment than on the mode of capital ownership. The topic must be addressed from the viewpoint of "political" economics, not merely formal pat-terns. Clear-cut conclusions should not be expected, especially since changes in capital ownership usually go hand in hand with changes in type of governance, in alliance networks or in financing chains. After privatization, one sometimes gets the feeling that the share-holding structures are not as flexible as they might be and that the enterprises, whose frame of reference remains unchanged, are inadequately managed.[52] While the management is, admittedly, more "professional", it does not appear better able to reconcile the economic and the social; nor does the privatized organization's "public service" role or business culture immediately disappear.[53]

The reasons for public interventions are legion. They can be social, in which case they respond to concerns of equity in covering everyone's basic needs. They can be economic, in that they target shortcomings and malfunctions in market mechanisms and tend to confront situations in which the volume of investments initially required or the constraints implicit in the deferral of a return exceed the capacities of private enterprises. They may even endeavour to remedy defective resource allocation where the problem does not lie in situations of "free" competition, but in imperfect or oligopolistic competition; in other words, conflict and aggression.

More often than not the social and the economic intermingle. This occurs when – the choice not being between competition and monopoly, but between private monopoly and public monopoly, with the lion's share of income provided by middle- and low-income earners – public opinion in a democratic regime opts for "social" management. This also occurs, but with a different social bias, when a deficit is deemed necessary for developing a nation's capital and boosting its economic activity, since in such cases subsidies are by no means awarded as compensation for poor management, but as part of a comprehensive cost- and price-cutting policy.

The dominant characteristic of modern infrastructures is that services are provided via specialized networks devised for a large number of users (water, gas, electricity, telecommunications, etc.) and entail major investments which can only partly be reconverted or displaced, and where the scope for competition is limited.[54] It is hard to imagine reassigning to the private sector infrastructure services, such as the high-voltage electricity network, whose "optimum" coverage must encompass an entire country or even groups of countries.[55] It is hard to imagine how roads can be privately owned or how a drinking-water supply and its management can exist without any government specification or control. But it is reasonable to expect the principles of "commercial" management to be applied to manufacturing and service enterprises through long-term contracts, negotiated with the public authorities and within their economic plans, with a view to improved economic efficiency, subject to the adoption of a regulatory mechanism that determines the rules of the game and ensures that cost recovery is not detrimental to the poor.[56]

The scope of the State's activities depends on the social "values" accepted by civil society; since civil society is never entirely unanimous, it depends on the confrontation of economic, social and political forces. Political reasons predominate when the State is dealing with a sector it deems strategic (energy supply, research and its applications, cutting-edge technology). In that situation, instructive protectionism is but a step away. One example of this is "administration guidance" in the East Asian countries, which establishes guidelines for enterprises in respect of investment, technology options, task-sharing and cartel-formation for implementing specific programmes.[57]

There is yet another political mission. Private oligopolies help define and implement not only a country's economic and financial policy, but its social policy as well. They influence not only the branch or zone in which they are installed, but also, through their interaction and the relations among enterprise branches and zones, the way a nation organizes its economic system, social relations, income and wealth distribution and political life. We must not forget that the idea of "nationalization" has been gaining ground for nearly a century and a half, cultivated by the determination to subordinate the economic giants to the general interest, either by affiliating them directly to the State or by introducing a public-service rule in trade relations (equal treatment of users) and in internal relations (status of workers) or even by formulating recommendations and measures aimed at macroeconomic efficiency, management, and planning.[58] Glachant's observation that the idea of "nationalization" is now at a discount does not prevent him from concluding that it "does not diminish the actual problems arising from the power of the economic giants".[59] This is especially true of the developing countries.

The building-up of the public sector and the idea of public service, as well as their decline, are subject to a combination of economic, social, political and moral considerations. Delineation of the sector and of the idea's field of application concerns political organization and the "values" sought by economic and social activity. In eighteenth-century Europe the concept of the general interest supplanted that of the common good, its legacy from the Middle Ages. French republican tradition, espoused by other States, entrusts its definition to the law, which serves to articulate the collective will. This idea of the State and the representative system is now being called into question. "Conviction" procedures are considered capable of restoring public policy-making – a legitimacy denied "constraint" procedures – as participatory democracy fills in the gaps left by representative democracy.[60] The building-up of the public sector has been gradual and slow. It is now diminishing quickly, pressured as it is by the interplay of private interests and the liberal ideology that subtends them. We cannot afford to ignore the need for public enterprises and public services, but we must define new objectives to be pursued. Time is short, needs are enormous and pressing, and public-sector support can, indeed must, be substantial.

The World Bank is perturbed by the obstacles to the development of another sector, the private sector, which "would trigger a boom in informal activities". Rethinking development necessitates a quite different attitude or, at the very least, much more cautious judgement. Philippe Engelhard's "defence of a new economics"[61] can be helpful where the developing countries are concerned: he starts with poverty in his endeavour to propose an alternative strategy for Africa. He explodes the myth that poverty is a mere drop in the centre of a dominant modern economy, and takes the Washington institutions to task for the aloofness of their attention to the poor countries' cultural and social realities and for their disingenuousness in imputing the Asian crisis to "State capitalism" when they have themselves constantly vaunted the merits of the "new dragons".

Engelhard claims that the issue is not whether long-term growth will reduce poverty, but whether it will do so quickly enough; nor is the issue to drag poor farmers into deflation, but to undertake gradual improvement which does not reduce the domestic demand so vital for the expansion of small enterprises, which are the backbone of most of the poor countries' production apparatus and whose productivity pool is considerable.

In that regard, the developing countries possess two "levers" for escape from poverty: the one is to supply sufficient quality goods and services at prices and costs affordable by the greatest number and, therefore, to produce more and improve productivity and income (particularly those of the poor). The other is to ensure that the poor enjoy cheaper physical access to basic goods and services. This relies on the use of second-order technologies and culturally appropriate modes of organization that are different from those of the rich countries.[62]

Much of the poor countries' production originates in small urban family businesses and small farms. Thus constituted, the sector accounts for 80 per cent of jobs in Cotonou, 60 per cent in

Bombay, and 82 per cent of jobs created in Latin America between 1980 and 1993. It is neither a hold-over from the traditional sector nor the refuse of modernity nor wishful thinking on the advent of an "interdependent" economy. It is "a response to the penury and poverty" endured by people who, unable to gain a foothold in the so-called "modern" economy, invent for themselves one that is immersed in social interplay and makes trade a function more of circulation and redistribution than of accumulation, although the latter is there to some extent.[63] It costs them little because of the low level of fixed charges and the sector's insufficient liquidity, offset by rapid money circulation, with employer-employee relations more frequently dictated by family or traditional ties than by the capitalist wage-earning concept. Even though it still contains an element of the mafia and man's exploitation by man, this type of economy "affords hundreds of millions of people a better life than they would enjoy if it did not exist".[64] Accordingly, as Engelhard[65] has it, "popular economy" is a more appropriate term than the "informal" or "non-structured" sector as it is usually described by the international organizations.

Any genuine desire to avoid risks of explosion, to counter violence, to wage an effective war on the mechanisms of exclusion and the confection of poor masses requires helping the poor to organize themselves, to produce and to make themselves understood, which means strengthening and expanding the varied forms of "popular" economy throughout the developing countries and not staking all on the "modern" sector.[66] Rather than dispose of this "popular" economy or subject it to ceaseless and irksome officialdom, it would be wiser to integrate it into the national economy and trust in its creativity and ability to complement the "official" economy.

The following are clearly vital to the pursuit of that objective: reinvention of legality; establishment of the social safety nets essential for sector workers and the self-employed; discovery of a way of financing medical care (for instance, by fostering collective mutual insurance schemes); attention to the specific needs of vulnerable groups (working children, women and migrants); and caution in the transfer of international labour standards.[67] A better institutional framework must be found for micro-enterprises which, once endowed with improved infrastructure and special funding, would alone, in Bonvin's view, be capable of employing and integrating the young unemployed. A cornerstone of development policy is, therefore, to monitor access to credit and encourage experiments, like that of the South African commercial banks which provide simple banking services for the poor; India, Indonesia and Malaysia, which impose minimum quotas for small businesses in the loan portfolios of the large commercial banks; or Bangladesh's micro-credit schemes for rural area, managed by rural-development NGOs. That apart, development policy must still pay close attention to education and training, relying largely on traditional ways of transmitting knowledge and know-how, and, to that end, must promote the emergence of trainers from the very social groups in need of "skills training".

Similarly, Tévoédjré takes the view that while his country, Benin, has enormous social problems to resolve, it possesses "phenomenal" financial resources precisely and particularly because of the "informal" sector. He contends that each of the country's 6,000 villages should enjoy access to an equal social minimum comprising basic social services (care, schooling, rural development, etc.), which, in terms of jobs, would mean 6,000 nurses or doctors, 6,000 teachers, 6,000 rural extension workers and so on. Each village should also have its own income-management capacity. According to Tévoédjré, the process is already underway. It is slow in taking off, but each community is more than ever determined to solve its problems. One could cite many other on-the-ground experiments, the vast majority of which illustrate the potential for embracing and actively participating in the development of the most disadvantaged population groups.[68]

If the key role of the State in anti-poverty development policy is not acknowledged, it becomes absurd to campaign for "less government". An activity such as the Programme of support to small producers in French-speaking Africa (*Programme d'appui aux petits producteurs d'Afrique francophone* – PAPPU), conducted by the ILO with UNDP support, has shown beyond a doubt that the durability and extension of installed structures depend on macro-economic and institutional measures that encourage micro-enterprise and create a climate conducive to their advancement.[69] Dialogue must therefore be established between the State and civil society, and the lessons must be drawn from earlier relatively successful experiments in people's development,[70] in addition to participation and communication strategies that use both the mass media and the popular media (rural educational radio, extramural television, the press, etc.).

The policy issue must also be looked at in all its dimensions. It is not enough to say that the State is still alive. It must also cease to have a low profile and, as Mongin wrote, "the architectural ground-work must be laid for a new type of State, with planning that is not centred solely on world time, that of zero time, nor withdraws into local time alone",[71] and policy-makers must seriously assume their responsibilities.

3.   THE PIVOTAL ISSUES OF GOVERNMENT: THE CASE OF EUROPE

The United Nations Charter encourages the use of "regional arrangements" for extending its action to continents and subconti-nents. Progress is being made with regional integration. Agreements have succeeded one another since the end of the 1980s. Some of them continue establishing a structure and institu-tions initiated as long as 40 years ago (European Community – European Union).[72] Others renew or reactivate old agreements (the Andean Agreement replacing the Andean Pact)[73] or enlarge them (Association of South-East Asian Nations – ASEAN).[74] Yet others institute new regional constituencies: the North American Free Trade Agreement (NAFTA),[75] the Southern Common Market (MERCOSUR),[76] the Association of Caribbean States (ACS),[77] the Central European Free Trade Agreement (CEFTA),[78] the South Asian Association for Regional Cooperation (SAARC)[79] and so forth.

There are also inter-regional fora, such as the Asia-Europe Summit (ASEM),[80] a forum for European/Asian dialogue initiated by Singapore, as a manifestation of certain States' fears regarding the two major powers in the area, the United States and Japan, plus China; and another Asian forum, the Forum for Asia-Pacific Economic Cooperation (APEC),[81] the brainchild of Australia in pur-suit of greater access to Asian markets, and followed by Japan and the developing countries of Asia, a large percentage of whose exports are destined for the American market.

Nor must we forget the fora of heads of corporations and their support for liberalization and deregulation, reflecting as they do the interests of the enterprises they represent – usually multinational or on the verge of becoming so – which are increasingly dependent on external markets.

The trend is towards a three-tiered international order in which the "regional" joins the "global" (the world) and the "local" (the nation-states). The large regional areas are both symbolic and physical spaces of intensive trade among highly similar nations with social systems rooted in parallel histories and policies. Comprising tangled networks with blurred divisions and operating in a dialectic of openness and withdrawal, they enable governments and people to transcend common economic interests and lead a political life shared on several levels (including the supranational) and to be initiated into global life without relinquishing their identity.

At the time of the GATT talks, there were fears that regional agreements might impede trade liberalization. Those fears were unfounded. No "protected" zones have been formed. What we have, instead, is "open" regionalism that is compatible with multilateral commitments and the pursuit of the process *vis-à-vis* the non-member countries of the integrated area.[82] The mechanics of regional integration do not stifle inter-regional trade. They delineate "natural" zones, bringing together countries which, because of both their level of development and their geographical proximity, are destined to maintain close economic relations. As Sachwald points out,[83] agreements enable such regions to use their size as a means of integration in the global economy.

The main objectives of regional agreements are the dismantling of tariff and non-tariff barriers between member countries; the free movement of goods, services, capital and people from one to another; and the creation of a common market.[84] Some, however, include provisions that promote economic and social development;[85] the European Union, first and foremost, and, to a lesser extent, the North American Free Trade Agreement illustrate receptiveness to strategies that combine the economic with the social and the economic with the human.

While social Europe is still a vague concept, it is gradually taking shape. Although the Member States of the Treaty of Rome agreed "upon the need to promote improved working conditions and an improved standard of living for workers to make possible their harmonization while the improvement is being maintained" (art. 117, para. 11), it left most of the harmonization and, consequently, governance to the market mechanisms. It should therefore come as no surprise that the first large-scale achievement in the economic and social sphere was the codification of the principle of free movement of workers. Gradually, however, social Europe is taking shape in the form of harmonized labour legislation, actions of the European Social Fund, and shifts in its priorities and *modus operandi*, so that it is better equipped to address the challenges of unemployment (long-term and youth unemployment) and come to the aid of regions of the Community that "lag behind in development" or are experiencing economic decline, and of certain "target groups" (migrants, women and the disabled). The fight against long-neglected poverty has become increasingly imperative with the 1989 Community Charter of Fundamental Social Rights for Workers, the Oporto conference on the construction of an interdependent Europe (1992), the European Commission's "papers" on the "new development model" (1993) and the "green paper" on European social policy (1994),[86] which claims that Europe's permanent contribution to the search for a sustainable development that combines economic vitality with social progress is only possible if there is a confluence of social policies, including labour policies (employment, working conditions, training, etc.).

The close association of the struggle against exclusion with the fight against unemployment underscores actions aimed at integration or reintegration into the labour market. Wherever policies have been implemented in Europe they are in crisis, owing to vagueness as to their beneficiaries and targets (regular employment, socially useful activity, youth, long-term unemployed, etc.), or to the contradiction between the stated objectives of maintaining wage-earning employment with the benefit of its statutory attributes, and the de facto generalization of insecure contracts under the aegis of the State or of local communities. In a country such as France, although the "minimum insertion income" was devised as a virtually universal expedient for fighting poverty, guaranteeing a minimum of resources and access to basic social rights, it has become a special type of unemployment benefit.[87]

One thing is certain, and that is the need to reinvent integration policies and – if they are to succeed – to take into account the changes occurring in the world of work, especially in employment and business-organization policies.[88] There are some who rightly believe that those policies must, in no small measure, be transformed into local partnership development policies, using, inter alia, the employer-association framework. In that context, two facets of the Italian experience should be taken into consideration.

First, at the national level, in the form of subsidized job-training contracts with more flexible management of variations in employment levels and of labour policies, but also in the form of measures to help people establish their own businesses. In order to fill the gaps left by public policies, "social co-operatives" have been set up to integrate people or provide social assistance as an alternative or complement to public services. In 1991 a law qualified these "co-operatives" as instruments that served not only their members' interests, but also the general interest, through human progress and the citizens' social integration. They were awarded special facilities: tax relief, exemption from social security contributions for the disadvantaged workers they employed, direct access to public markets without the need to compete with other firms, and lastly – when that measure was challenged by the European Commission – public administrations were allowed to include in calls for tenders the obligation to employ a given percentage of underprivileged persons. These "co-operatives" have not yet been utilized to their full potential, and limits will doubtless be placed on their expansion, but it is an experiment worth thinking about.[89]

Next, and of quite different scope, are the "industrial districts"[90] which are rather like small and medium-sized enterprises located for the most part in the north-east and centre of the peninsula and are free from pre-established rules and chains of command. Many elements help them weave bonds of reciprocal technological and economic support: a well-established local manufacturing culture, a deep sense of belonging, traditions shaped by geography and history, a sense of co-operation. This enables them not only to become fully-fledged partners of large corporations, but to export, and even to dominate the world market (ceramic tiles in Sassualo) or forge a considerable niche in it for themselves (biomedical supplies in the Mirandolo district). Through endogenous development, these "districts" have succeeded in providing 800,000 jobs as well as virtually eradicating unemployment on their territories. In some cases, they are even obliged to call on outside labour.

The French anti-exclusion law (1998) provides for greater intake capacity of firms prepared to offer even temporary jobs, and financial support for them in a strengthened economic approach, in order to consolidate their development, facilitate the creation of new structures (market surveys, installation assistance, etc.) and promote their search for partners. Furthermore, the Delegation for Land-Use Management and Regional Action (*Délégation à l'aménagement du territoire et à l'action régionale* – DATAR) issues calls for tenders in France leading to projects for the formation of French-style "industrial districts" specializing particularly in luxury goods.

Since these enterprises are atypical, they can rightly be seen as the start of a new sector of the economy, situated at the junction of the competitive market and the State-subsidized public sector and, if their potential is harnessed, capable of serving as a foundation stone of a global policy in which integration is closely linked to economic development.[91] The districts, too, can promote the placement of activities so as to provide a better balance between the economic and the social.

"It is, first and foremost, into the production and distribution of know-how that the most disadvantaged must be integrated", states a preparatory document by the International Movement ATD Fourth World elaborated for the Special Council on Employment (Luxembourg, November 1997).[92] In this respect, it is not a question of "teaching" the poor, but of putting oneself in their shoes and listening to them. Their "know-how", which stems from their life experience, and ours build one upon another and expand when there is dialogue between us. One of the implications of the "new paradigm" should be, at the regional as at the national level, regular consultation of the non-governmental organizations which, operating on-the-ground, can identify with the hopes and aspirations of the poor whom they "hear" and "understand" better than "experts" closeted in their offices. The existing networks must be canvassed more extensively than they are at present by governments and by the European Commission. That, nonetheless, would not suffice, for it is also necessary to guarantee the direct expression of the disadvantaged populations and to respect the forms it takes.

The above applies not only to the definition of guidelines pertaining to financial assistance, the right to housing and access to health for all, but also to the establishment of training and skills-development programmes. Local, national and European partnerships must be organized so that can be pursued the difficult quest for balance between, on the one hand, the requirements of the workings and evolution of the economy, and, on the other, the exigencies of the fight against poverty and the defence or renewal of social achievements. This "direct democracy" is all the more desirable since the war on unemployment that generates exclusion calls for the disclosure of unmet needs and their satisfaction. Where the poor are concerned, these include construction of affordable housing, urban renewal, security, education and even the creation of new jobs,[93] promotion and solvency of local services.

Other proposals could be made, based on and extending European practice, such as the creation of a "citizenship income". Minimum income is one of the social welfare instruments in Europe. More frequent in the North than the South, these instruments are more or less universal depending on the country[94]; in most cases they require availability for work, special training schemes or even acceptance of any job on offer. The rising tide of unemployment, the emergence of newly poor and the slump into a precarious livelihood are the reasons for the negative tax conceived by the liberals to make exclusion from the labour market socially tolerable[95]; but, more importantly, and from an entirely different ideological perspective, they are at the origin of the universal partial benefit (under discussion in the Netherlands), of the diminishing differential benefit when beneficiaries are likely to occupy a post, of the social minimum income, established as a local solidarity right,[96] and of the universal benefit to which every citizen who is a permanent resident has an unconditional right.[97]

To be a citizen is to be free to live in a society as an acknowledged person who in turn acknowledges others. Hence the proponents of such reforms abound; for them the link must be maintained between the receipt of the "citizenship income" and the work or activity whenever the beneficiary is qualified to work or perform any other socially "useful" activity. That, for us, is not the essence. The essence is to be found in the quest for a new balance between productive activities and social or personal activities – the "pivot of a new project for society"[98] – and in the contribution that a subsistence income could make, on the one hand, to the development of the economy's income-producing capacity,[99] and, on the other, to the war on unemployment.

As of 1986 with the Basic Income European Network (BIEN), those proposals – dubbed utopias by the neo-liberals – have led to conferences at which all European countries are heavily represented, and to the publication of data and reports on the initiatives taken. The issue of unconditionality has not been settled in the Netherlands which, in 1995, showed the way with its guaranteed minimum income. It is also to be noted that the European Parliament's Committee for Social Affairs and Employment has considered introducing the possibility of a Community-wide universal benefit.

Human development relies on economic development, and social policy on general economic policy. It might be feared that the onus of codes of conduct imposed on the Member States by the Maastricht Treaty and, more so, the "covenant on budgetary stability and growth" issued by the Dublin (December 1996) and Amsterdam (June 1997) Summits may induce European governments to see wages, unemployment and social welfare as adjustment variables that could replace those of which they have been deprived. This would result in the establishment of a self-perpetuating system of instability and social fragility.

There is no economic "government" in the European Union that can counterbalance the European Central Bank (ECB), whose sole concern, according to the treaty by which it was established, is monetary stability. The Economic and Financial Committee – which is composed of representatives of States, the European Community and the ECB, and is responsible for monitoring the economic and financial situation of Member States and formulating decisions concerning the operation of the financial system and the financial relations with the other countries and the international organizations – has not been capable of filling the gap; nor has the Euro Council that replaced it, even though national labour-market policies are among its assigned tasks;[100] nor yet the membership (without the right to vote) of the President of the European Council and of a member of the Commission on the Board of Governors of the ECB.

As things stand, when it comes to reconciling the economic and the social from the perspective of a "new paradigm" for development, the governance of the Europe region would appear to necessitate joint social regulation by Europe and the nations. It is likely to assume one of two forms, depending on the procedural conception adopted: a "weak" form, realistic because compatible with a widely accepted subsidiarity, registering the national differences and the enterprises' reluctance to build a European space for social negotiation; and a "strong" form, with creation of common institutions and rules that would guide the evolution of the European community, involving understanding among States and the strengthening of the political union. This point is amply illustrated by the upheavals of employment policy.

We have made the war on employment one of the hallmarks of development strategy. European measures towards that end have long concentrated on training, especially for the long-term unemployed, with the assistance furnished by the European Social Fund (whose function is to promote job opportunities for workers) devoted mainly to vocational training. In 1998, at the time of the Structural Funds reform, the struggle against long-term unemployment and jobs for young people were among the prime objectives. Community action was intended to reinforce any action planned or already undertaken by the national authorities and was to be accompanied by multi-year planning, follow-up and ongoing evaluation of those measures.[101]

In 1993, the members of the Council observed that, although the Community had been economically strengthened through greater integration and cohesion, progress in respect of employment and unemployment was "less satisfactory". They proclaimed the need to enhance the Community approach to the fight against unemployment and supported the idea that the Commission should present a proposal for a solution equal to the problem. This need was reiterated by the Heads of State and Government meeting in Copenhagen, at which the Commission was asked to prepare a "white paper" on unemployment, growth and competitiveness.[102] Published in late 1993, the "white paper" suggested that substantial work should be undertaken on infrastructure, especially in the transport sector. The proposal met with opposition from some finance ministers wedded, above all, to the orthodox budgetary tradition. At the Corfu Summit (1994), France submitted a memorandum on social Europe, in which it stressed the need to give effect to earlier decisions to make employment Europe's top priority, and protested the fact that investment programmes established more than a year before were still in abeyance. All it achieved was confirmation of the commitment to start up within two years the 11 high-priority transport infrastructure projects.

The European Council meetings in Essen (December 1994) and Cannes (June 1995) again invited governments to take more spirited action to assist those worst affected by structural unemployment, and urged States to translate their priorities and recommendations into multi-year programmes that would be studied each year by the heads of State meeting in council. The chronic unemployment besetting some 18 million people induced the Commission to request that the intergovernmental conference held in Turin in March 1996, entrusted with the task of reviewing the Maastricht Treaty, should pay special attention to the problem of unemployment. In fact, it is clear that the single currency was the sole major political concern of the European Union, that governments were mainly intent on "stabilizing" their economic situations in order to satisfy the convergence criteria in the required time and be able to enter the Monetary Union due to come into effect by 1999. It is equally clear that they had reached consensus on the need to reform the welfare state and move ahead with deregulation in order to increase growth potential and put a halt to budget deficits. Although the European Council that met in Florence invited Member States to designate regions and towns for pilot projects on "territory-wide and local employment covenants", it made scant progress on employment policy.

The European Council meeting held in Amsterdam in June 1997 was accompanied by a mammoth European demonstration against unemployment, insecure livelihood and exclusion. Although it laid down the operating conditions of the "euro house" and drew up a German-inspired "covenant of budgetary stability and growth" that defined the rules to be observed by future member countries of the European Monetary Union, it adopted only a modest resolution on growth and employment, a far cry from the French proposal of a "covenant for stability, growth and employment". It did, however, insist that it is imperative to keep employment firmly at the top of the Union's political agenda, with a competent, trained and mobile work force and labour markets that react to economic changes as the target.[103] At the European Council on Employment held in Luxembourg in November 1997 on France's initiative, there was still fierce opposition to the launching of a convergence policy for employment, the most reluctant parties being Germany and Spain. It ended with acceptance of a "co-ordinated employment strategy", reduced to annual definition of common "guidelines" for national plans of action to combat,[104] which are to be as specific as possible and draw on the most noteworthy experiences – both positive and negative – of the Union's Member States.

In December 1998 signs appeared that economic and social employment regulations were about to take a quantum leap, with the 15 member countries accepting the idea of a European covenant on employment, the content of which was to be determined at a June 1999 summit in Cologne. Although the summit took place, the European Union leaders could not reach agreement. There was to be nothing in the immediate future to offset the financial stability covenant, and subsidiarity was being applied to the letter: it was up to the Member States to implement their own social policy. All that remained was the aid provided by the Structural Funds.

These moments of European construction could all be seen as signifying recourse to the technique of a "progressive" concatenation of measures that would ultimately lead to the framing of a new European employment policy, in which the tasks would be shared by the European Union and nations. In point of fact, after two decades of persistent unemployment and rising instability, an "Employment Summit" has finally been arranged, although unrelated to macroeconomic policy, that is, to monetary and budgetary matters! This is because, as Fitoussi[105] rightly points out, "logically separate from European construction, the unemployment issue, being a social issue, can only be addressed outside Europe; that is, in the context of national societies". The combination of the "covenant on budgetary stability and growth", the European Central Bank, the unofficial Euro Council, and the employment "guidelines" is only, as he points out, "an arrangement too ramshackle and disparate" to ensure, from the outset, collective capacity for action conducive to sustainable growth and to an effective employment policy;[106] and, beyond that, from the present author's viewpoint, to the type of development that combines the economic and the social. Even amended, capitalism contains a logical separation of the two that cannot be easily forgotten, for it is inherent in its structure and institutions and in the combined effects of economics, social relations, forces, law, technology, culture and values. What Europe needs is a "powerful" form of regulation shared by Europe and the member nations and comprising the establishment of common institutions and rules that could direct the course of the European economy so that it unites what is spontaneously separated by capitalism.

The Single European Act recognizes the importance of social dialogue. The "social protocol" that appears as an annex to the Maastricht Treaty affords the social partners the opportunity to sign potentially binding agreements that will most likely be confirmed by the Council's guidelines.[107] Those agreements may be implemented nationally in accordance with the social partners' and Member States' own procedures and practices; or they can also be implemented at the joint request of the signatories on a proposal from the Commission by decision of the Council taken unanimously or by a qualified majority, depending on the area being dealt with. Perhaps there is another possible route since the governments' concerted action must go hand in hand with the social partners' increased commitment in a Europe-wide social dialogue.

There is no lack of national precedents with regard to "covenants". The Netherlands showed the example with the 1982 Wassenaar agreements – renewed in 1997 – based on a wage freeze, and followed by differential wage increases and shorter working hours aimed at creating jobs. Italy followed suit with the July 1993 tripartite agreement regulating social concertation for the implementation of an incomes policy, and in December 1998 with a "covenant for employment". This covenant strengthened cooperation in contractual matters through biannual checking, and reduced the cost of labour by transferring a number of corporate charges and tax-exempting reinvested profits, and boosted development through a series of incentive measures. In Germany, Helmut Kohl's government and the social partners also concluded, in 1996, a "covenant for employment and the strengthening of competitiveness" requiring a whole range of reforms. It was soon contested by the employers and was never implemented. The new German leaders that emerged from the September 1998 elections trumpeted a new "employment covenant" in December of that year; its initial measures went no further than an emergency youth programme and the setting up of various working groups (lower retirement age and tax reduction).

Many events suggest that it is quite possible for the collective-bargaining game and power relations to serve in the elaboration of European "covenants" superimposed on national "covenants" of the same kind: the European steel workers' endorsement of co-ordination of wage claims; that of the European Trade Union Confederation for protection of public services, "the real founders of a Europe of citizens", according to its President[108]; the signing of the umbrella agreements on part-time work (1997) and on atypical work (March 1999) by the Union of Industries of the European Community (UNICE), the European Centre for Public Enterprise (ECPE) and the European Trade Union Confederation (ETUC). "Regional" governance – founded on a strategy in line with human development and uniting the economic and the social – would gain fresh impetus through the promotion of a contractual policy[109].

In that regard, the adoption by the Ninth ETUC Congress on 30 June 1999 of a specific resolution calling for, *inter alia*, a genuine European framework of collective bargaining and the inclusion of the right to strike in the forthcoming European Union treaty gives an important signal; however, the discussions have shown that the trade unions are far from unanimous on the idea of relinquishing national prerogatives in favour of bargaining on a European scale.

---

[1]*General Theory...*, *op. cit.*, p. 159.
[2]*Das Finanzkapital*, Berlin, 1910.
[3]Lecture on Jacques Rueff, *Transversale Science-culture*, May 1997.
[4]*Géopolitique du chaos*, Paris, Galilée, 1998.
[5]Paris, Fayard, 1996.
[6]*Anomalies sur les marchés financiers*, Paris, Economica, 1995.
[7]*La crise du capitalisme mondial. L'intégrisme des marchés*, Paris, Plon, 1998, pp. 179-186 and 195.

[8]*Le capitalisme dans tous ses états,* Paris, Presses Universitaires de France, 1997, Chapter 4.

[9]*Le Monde,* 27 October 1998, p. 17.

[10]J. Guelle. *Un monde sans maître. Ordre de désordre entre les nations,* Paris, Odile Jacob, 1995.

[11]On this concept, see "Governance", in *International Social Science Journal,* No. 155, March 1998.

[12]*Reshaping the International Order,* New York, E.P. Dutton, 1976.

[13]W. Brandt (1980), O. Palme (1982), G. Brundtland (1987), J. Nyerere (1990).

[14]The Stockholm Initiative on Global Security and Governance. Common Responsibility in the 1990s, Stockholm, Prime Minister's Office, April 1991.

[15]*Governance, the World Bank's Experience,* Washington, World Bank, 1994.

[16]Global governance for the 21st century, *Human Development Report 1994, op. cit.,* p. 88.

[17]"L'ordre et le désordre (A propos du nouvel ordre international)", *Mélanges G.C. Vlachos,* Brussels, Bruylant, 1995, pp. 272-6.

[18]P. Kennedy and B. Russet: "Reforming the United Nations", *Foreign Affairs,* September-October 1995.

[19]J.M. Harris: "Global Institutions for Sustainable Development", in F.J. Dietz, U.E. Simonis, J. Van Der Straaten (eds.): *Sustainability and Environmental Policy: Restraints and Advances,* Sigma, 1992.

[20]*Vers une action commune pour le développement du Tiers Monde,* Paris, Denoël, 1969.

[21]International Finance Corporation in 1956, International Development Association, 1960.

[22]Rather than "transition", the term used by the international organizations, a more appropriate term would be "mutation" or "rupture". "Transition" implies an ideological choice whereby the final destination can only be a market economy or "return to capitalism". In effect, it is a protracted and unstable process that calls for a genetic approach of evolution of economic systems towards "a number of" possible or accessible systemic futures that depend on the original constraints and obstacles encountered during the transformation. Cf. W. Andreff: *La crise des économies socialistes,* Grenoble, Presses universitaires, 1993, pp. 324-328.

[23]E. Grill: "L'economista e la pratica della politica economica: storia di città diverse", *Rivista italiana degli economisti,* 1996, No. 3, p. 463.

[24]Cf. *infra,* pp. 167-169.

[25]*Bilan du Monde,* Le Monde, Edition 1999, p. 26.

[26]M. Kapur: In M.G. Quibria and J.M. Dowling (eds.): *Current issues in economic development. An Asian perspective,* New York, Oxford University Press, 1997.

[27]*Towards full development, op. cit.*

[28]*Human Development Report 1997, op. cit.,* p. 12.

[29]*Towards a new United Nations structure for global economic cooperation*, New York, United Nations, May 1975, E/AC 62/9.

[30]*Human Development Report 1994, op. cit.*, chapter 4.

[31]Thus agreeing with Francis Perroux, proponent of a "world spiritual authority" eschewing appointment by a government in favour of designation by "social constituencies". Cf. "Nouvel ordre économique mondial", in *Mondes en développement*, 1976, No. 19.

[32]Third report, *Reshaping the international order, op. cit.*, part III, section 12.

[33]P. Ricœur: "Civilisation universelle et cultures nationales", *Esprit*, October 1961.

[34]H. Bartoli: "Faire ensemble un monde polyphonique", in *Informations et commentaires*, September 1998, pp. 5-6.

[35]"L'ordre et le désordre", *art. cit.*, p. 276.

[36]The reduction must, in principle, be 8 per cent for European Union countries, 7 per cent for the United States and 6 per cent for Japan, while Russia and New Zealand are expected to stabilize, and Australia should be permitted an increase of 8 per cent at most.

[37]J.C. Hourcade: "De quelques paradoxes autour de la fixation d'une taxe internationale sur les carbones, in *Revue économique*, 1997, No. 6.

[38]*Conseil d'analyse économique : Fiscalité de l'environnement*, Paris, La Documentation française, 1998.

[39]We have made the appropriation of human rights the kernel of this work. In the United Nations monitoring of human rights is the responsibility of the Economic and Social Council, which delegates its powers to an inter-governmental committee. It has erected many hurdles regarding the nature of collective, social, economic and cultural rights and the ambiguity of "universality". The concept of universality is disputed by those who see in the Declaration adopted by the United Nations the expression of an ideology alien to their culture, not forgetting those that spring from the invocation of the principle of mutual respect for national sovereignty and the principle of territorial integrity. Added to which there is the dispersion of centres of interest, which is not conducive to a prompt and serious examination of dossiers. At the 51st session of the Commission in 1995, over 2,000 people attended, 900 speeches were heard, 11,000 pages of documents were prepared by the secretariat and 93 resolutions and 15 decisions were adopted! Cf. M. Merle: "Au-delà du miroir ou le véritable chantier des droits de l'homme" in H. Gros Espiel, *Amicorum Liber*, Brussels, Bruylant, 1997, p. 838.

[40]*Work of Nations*, New York, A.A. Knopf, 1991.

[41]*World Development Report 1997*, Washington, World Bank.

[42]*Ibid.*, Foreword, p. III.

[43]*Economie et société*, Paris, Pocket, 1995, Vol. 2, p. 410.

[44]M. Beaud: *Le basculement du monde*, Paris, La Découverte, 1997, p. 17.

[45]F. Perroux: "Les entreprises transnationales et le nouvel ordre économique du monde", *Informations et commentaires,* Supplement to No. 29, fourth quarter, 1979, p. 76.

[46]*Op. cit.*, pp. 3-12.

[47]Special attention should be devoted to the construction of an efficient administration with a staff that is well-trained, motivated, competent, suitably and regularly paid, and assured of promotion on merit. Provision should also be made for consultative and advisory mechanisms for stating and clarifying the policies that determine the orientations, priorities and objectives. One cannot but agree with the World Bank (*op. cit.*, chapter 6) when it advocates the institutionalization of countervailing powers and, first of all, an independent judiciary.

[48]*Op. cit.*, p. 70.

[49]*Trattato di logica economica*, Padua, Cedam, 1966, Vol. II, pp. 1143-1171.

[50]For a brief synopsis, cf. J.J. Gathon and P. Pestieau: "Les performances des entreprises publiques. Une gestion de propriété ou de concurrence ?", *Revue économique*, November 1996.

[51]According to optimum-contract theory, the State may resort to a contract that enables it to control the performance of heads of enterprises so as to attain a maximum level of productivity. In addition, privatization can only have positive effects in conditions of "free" competition, thereby precluding situations of monopoly or oligopoly; the discussion then focuses on the government's capacity to regulate an enterprise's performance once it has been privatized.

[52]F. Morin: "Privatisation et distribution des pouvoirs. Le modèle français de gouvernement des entreprises", *Revue économique, ibid.*

[53]B. Sibilio Parri: *Il processo di transformazione delle imprese publiche*, Padua, Cedam, 1998, p. 253.

[54]Options exist in certain cases and, with them, a degree of openness to competition: investments in rolling stock and maintenance equipment for rail transport, provision of telephone lines, etc.

[55]Although for water distribution economies of scale can be made at the local or village level.

[56]That could require subsidies for access to public infrastructure services rather than the price of those services, experience having shown that in the latter instance the beneficiaries are less the poor than the rich. In Ecuador, electricity was subsidized at the rate of $ 0.36 per year for the 37 per cent of household consuming the least electricity and of $ 500 for the more affluent households which consumed much more.

[57]e.g., the role assumed in Japan by the Ministry of International Trade and Industry (MITI), which is said to have lost every battle when it challenges the views of industry and trade groups, but is highly effective when put at their service. Another example can be found in the Republic of Korea, where the State has opted for a proactive strategy in the country's sector choices, deliberately favouring – up to the 1980s – the establishment of large Japanese-style groups, closely controlling imports and the establishment of multinationals and protecting fledgling industries. Hong Kong would not be what it is today without its harbour, airport, equipment and communication media, which owe a great deal to State action.

[58]When the General Committee of Experts that emerged from the French Revolution clandestinely drew up, under the direction of the extremely liberal René Courtin, its *Rapport sur la politique économique de l'après-guerre*, it had no doubt that the de facto and *de jure* monopolies should "be placed under the control of the community, in the interest of the State, the workers, consumers and the entire national economy, so that the dual economic and political pressure on the nation would cease". Paris, 1943, p. 14.

[59]*Le marché et le hors marché. Une analyse économique des entreprises publiques*, Paris, Publications de la Sorbonne, 1994, pp. 154 et seq.

[60]*Rapport 1999 du Conseil d'Etat*, Paris, La Documentation française, 1999.

[61]*L'Afrique noire miroir du monde ? Plaidoyer pour une nouvelle économie*, Paris, Arléa, 1998.

[62]P. Engelhard: *op. cit.*, p. 75.

[63]D. Théry: "Biens mimétiques et *a priori* d'irréversibilité dans les stratégies de rattrapage technologique des pays en développement", in Boyer, Chavance, Godard: *Les figures de l'irréversibilité en économie*, Paris, Ecole des Hautes études en sciences sociales, 1991, pp. 173-193.

[64]P. Engelhard: *op. cit.*, p. 75.

[65]*Ibid.*, p. 31.

[66]J. Bugnicourt: "Villes d'Afrique : contrer la pauvreté. Changer et gérer l'urbain avec le plus grand nombre", *Economies et sociétés*, January 1998.

[67]*Rapport d'orientation sur l'extension de la protection sociale au secteur traditionnel*, Dakar, ILO, July 1996 – *The social impact of the Asian financial crisis. Technical report for discussion at the high-level tripartite meeting on social responses to the financial crisis in East and South African countries*, Bangkok, ILO, April 1998.

[68]*Culture, a way to fight extreme poverty; ten experiments in escaping from exclusion*, Paris, UNESCO/NGO Standing Committee, CLT 97/W/S/8, 1997.

[69]C. Maldonado: "Building networks: an experiment in support to small producers", *International Labour Review*, 1993, No. 2.

[70]Y. Goussault: "Rural "animation" and popular participation in French-speaking Africa", *ibid.*, June 1968.

[71]O. Mongin: *L'après 1789. Les nouveaux langages du politique*, Paris, Hachette, 1998.

[72]Denmark, Ireland and the United Kingdom in 1973, Greece in 1981, Spain and Portugal in 1986, Austria, Finland and Sweden in 1995, joined Belgium, France, Germany, Italy, Luxembourg and the Netherlands. The European Union was created by the 1992 Maastricht Treaty.

[73]Bolivia, Colombia, Ecuador, Peru and Venezuela, 1986.

[74]Founders: Indonesia, Malaysia, the Philippines, Singapore and Thailand, joined by Brunei (1984), Viet Nam (1995), Burma and Laos (1997).

[75]United States, Canada and Mexico (1992-1994).

[76]Argentina, Brazil, Paraguay and Uruguay (1991-1995).

[77]Comprising 15 countries of the Caribbean and Latin America, including Colombia, Cuba, Mexico and Venezuela, and 13 observer countries, including France (1994).

[78]Czech Republic, Hungary, Poland, Slovakia (1992), followed by Slovenia (1995), Romania (1997) and Bulgaria (1998).

[79]Bangladesh, Bhutan, India, Maldives, Nepal, Pakistan and Sri Lanka (1985).

[80]Member countries of the European Union and Brunei, China, Indonesia, Japan, Malaysia, the Philippines, Singapore, South Korea, Thailand and Viet Nam (1996).

[81]18 countries or territories bordering the Pacific, from the United States and Chile to China, Japan and South Korea, to Australia and New Zealand, to Indonesia and Taiwan, not forgetting Hong Kong and Singapore, etc, (1989-1994).

[82]F. Sachwald: "Les réalités de l'intégration régionale", *Ramsès 1997*, Paris, Dunod, p. 231.

[83]*Ibid.*, p. 250.

[84]Deadline of 2005 for the MERCOSUR member countries, 2020 for the APEC countries and 2005 for the industrialized countries.

[85]This is the case for the Lomé Conventions, combinations of mechanisms based on donations from the European Development Fund, preferential loans from the European Investment Bank, free non-reciprocal commercial access to European markets for the developing African, Caribbean and Pacific countries (with the exception of a few sensitive products: bananas, sugar), stabilization of their agricultural and mining export revenue, while also financing development projects and supporting structural adjustment programmes.

SAARC is devoted to speeding up member countries' economic and social development through joint actions and the co-ordination of policies of common interest.

[86]"Green paper on European policy. Options for the Union", Luxembourg, Office of official publications. Consultation document COM/93 551. See also "Contributions to the preparation of the white paper on European social policy", *ibid.*, 1995.

[87]F. Audier, Dang Ai-Thu and J.L. Outin: "Le revenu minimum d'insertion comme mode particulier d'indemnisation du chômage", *Partage*, September 1998.

[88]B. Schwartz: *Moderniser sans exclure*, Paris, La Découverte, 1994 – P. Ughetto, "Innovation, emploi et interventions institutionnelles au niveau local": Symposium "Changement institutionnel et dynamisme de l'innovation", IRIS, Université de Paris IX Dauphine, December 1998.

[89]C. Borzaga: "En Italie, l'impressionnant développement des coopératives sociales", *Partage*, July-August 1998.

[90]G. Becattini (ed.), *Mercato e forze locali : il distretto industriale*, Bologna, Il Mulino – M. Mistri: *Saggi su internazionalizzazione, piccola impresa, economie locali*, Padua, Cedam, 1998.

[91]S. Wuhl: *Insertion : les politiques en crise*, Paris, PUF, 1997. See also Progress report on the ERGO Programme, European Community, Social Europe, 1996.

[92]*Intégrer la lutte contre la grande pauvreté dans les lignes directrices pour les politiques de l'emploi dans les Etats membres en 1998*, International ATD Movement Fourth World, October 1997. See also "Cohésion sociale et prévention de l'exclusion", *Rapport préparatoire au XI*[e] *Plan français*, Paris, La Documentation française, 1993, and J. Gautié, B. Gazier, R. Silvera, D. Anxo, P. Auer, F. Lefresne, "Les subventions à l'emploi. Analyses et expériences européennes", *ibid.*, 1994.

[93]Such as that of the book "mediator" in deprived neighbourhoods, cf. X. Godinot (ed.), *On voudrait connaître le secret du travail*, Paris, Editions de l'Atelier et Quart Monde, 1996, pp. 169-181.

[94]Non-nationals of the European Community are sometimes denied access.

[95]M. Friedman: *Capitalism and Freedom*, Chicago, University Press, 1962. X. Greffe: *L'impôt des pauvres, nouvelle stratégie de la politique sociale*, Paris, Dunod, 1978.

[96]S. Milano: "Le revenu minimum social : un droit local à la solidarité", *Futuribles*, July-August 1996.

[97]*Bulletin du Mouvement anti-utilariste dans les sciences sociales*, March and December 1988, and Review of that Movement, 1st and 2nd quarters 1992.

[98]A project which, according to A. Lipietz and G. Asnar, must "favour individuals" autonomy and development" (*Partage*, March-April 1994, p. 2). We prefer to say "can permit training and development of autonomous persons, in a better controlled world, in a community in which the communication of consciences and a meeting of minds occur progressively", cf. H. Bartoli: *L'Economie, service de la Vie, op. cit.*, p. 417.

[99]From this point of view, the most exciting prospect of subsistence income is offered by Bresson, calculated as it is, not on minimum needs, but on economic development, with "time" value replacing "work" value. Cf. *L'après salariat*, Paris, Economica. 1984, and (with Philippe Guilhaume), *Le Partcipat*. Réconcilier l'économique et le social, Paris, Chotard et associés, 1986.

[100]Exchanges of information on economic evolution and public intentions that could make an impact beyond national borders, monitoring of Member States' macro-economic evolution and, first of all, their budget situation.

[101]*Employment in Europe*, Commission of the European Communities, Department of Employment, Industrial Relations and Social Affairs, 1990, chaps. 10 and 11. A programme of operational research and evaluation (ERGO) has been established to evaluate the measures taken and define possible lines of action for the future.

[102]*Employment in Europe, ibid*, 1993, chap. 8.

[103]The resolution formulated at the end of the Summit includes a cyclical component that provides for ten measures for sustaining employment,

and a structural component intended to flesh out the Maastricht Treaty on co-ordination of economic policies. The support measures include the possibility of calling upon the European Investment Bank to establish a programme of low interest loans for small and medium-sized enterprises (SMEs) specializing in advanced technologies, or to seek the mobilization of the European Coal and Steel Community's unutilized funds.

[104]For 1998: improved occupational integration, development of an entrepreneurial spirit, strengthening of equal-opportunity policies, and encouragement for firms' and workers' adaptation capacity. France vainly requested that the guidelines should be accompanied by quantified objectives that Member States would endeavour to implement in their national policies.

[105]J.P. Fitoussi (ed.): *Rapport sur l'état de l'Union européenne*, Paris, Fayard, 1999. p. 27.

[106]*Ibid.*, p. 115.

[107]G. Guéry: "European collective bargaining and the Maastricht Treaty", *International Labour Review*, 1992, No. 6.

[108]E. Gabaglio: "Public services, the real founders of a Europe of citizens". Press release 20/96 of the European Trade Union Confederation.

[109]Although well short of the European structure, the North American Free Trade Agreement might have served us as an example. Might it not be a first step on the road to a common market ranging from Alaska to Tierra del Fuego? Its main purpose is to escalate the area's internal trade by eliminating in 10 to 15 years from 1992 all customs tariffs among the three partners, without seeking liberalization in a common market protected by a common internal tariff. What is sought is the lifting on trade barriers among them, with each country remaining free to chose its trade policy towards the rest of the world.

In the face of the fiercest protests by North American trade unions, which see it as "a foul blow to American workers and consumers, to the health of the American economy and to Mexican workers, who will be exploited by American firms", measures were taken in parallel agreements. The preamble to the agreement states that, while the purpose is to expand the market and increase competitiveness, its purpose is also to create new job opportunities, improve working conditions and the standard of living on the States' respective territories, and to protect and enhance workers' fundamental rights and ensure that they are respected. A Labour Co-operation Commission was put in place, as were complaint procedures, with the possibility of sanctioning any of the partners that fail to comply with the rules in force under its law. That measure won the unions' full approval: it is the view of the AFL-CIO, the Canadian Federation of Labour and Canada's Labour Congress that nothing in the agreement is acceptable to employees. Only the Mexican trade unions declared themselves satisfied that national sovereignty was being respected.

CHAPTER 4

Removing the obstacles to governability: absence of democracy; indebtedness; financial slippage; power of the major "masters of the world" groups; interference

It would be overly optimistic to believe too readily in "operational-ization" of the development strategies which we have proposed. Regardless of the level at which we consider it – global, regional, or national – governance is only possible if the conditions that ensure governability of the economic, social and political world are met.

In all disciplines, the problem of governance is one of control, a fact well known to the theoreticians of cybernetic systems, who take into consideration the systems that are capable – metaphorically or otherwise – of perceiving their environment and themselves, of deciding on these bases, and at the same time of acting on it and on themselves.[1] No architect would undertake the construction of a new building without first preparing the ground. No economic and social policy, indeed no action aimed at economic and human development, should be undertaken without a prior survey of its possibilities or unless a dialectic of the possible and desirable reveals the extent to which the economic and social system can be controlled.

A society learns by evaluating its structures, institutions, organization and rules, on the basis of criteria adapted to its culture and values, and by reshaping them the better to ensure its power over itself, and, consequently, its reproduction and development. Viewed from this perspective, governability implies collective learning, and since, when all is said and done, politics have the last word, it also implies the programming of major priority objectives capable of maintaining the buoyancy of the economy and the markets, even while conferring pride of place on human development.

A small symposium was held in Villemétrie in 1986 on "Ethics and the ungovernability of the world today".[2] As David recently wrote,[3] "the decomposition and reconstitution of the world are now offering the perspective of paths so open that anything – or almost anything – is imaginable". National, regional and global governability is now on the ebb, whereas it is needed more than ever for a type of development that is both economic and human. In the past, the internationalization of the economy and society brought into play the intervention of national actors whose autonomy remained unthreatened. Today, globalization, albeit far from universally or equally intense, "globalizes" the economy which, under its influence, forms a whole, subject to rules of operation, indeed, "totally" organized to form a "system".

It is not from the demands of human and economic development that the system takes its logic, but from those of rapid return on capital without reference to the people's real needs. The great political options for the world's future are hijacked by tiny interest groups: according to an IMF study, between 30 and 50 banks and a handful of brokerage firms control the key foreign-exchange and currency markets. A report by the United States Federal Reserve Bank reveals that six commercial banks control 90 per cent of derivatives transactions.[4] What should be a movement towards human liberation has turned into submission to destructive disorder. Governability is confronted with a monetary system which, all at once, is becoming autonomous and immune to the real world, constantly transcending new frontiers, spreading and implanting a civilization in which capital is the dominant economic and social category, and money becomes the supreme value.[5]

It is virtually impossible to distil the ethical requirement from such a system as long as the "mechanical" connections established through practices and – as wrote Ladrière[6] – "market mechanisms controlled by money so congeal as to become second nature, which is in fact unregulated sociality". To do so and to introduce the type of governance that is faithful to the strategic choices required for the conjunction of economic development and human development calls for thorough reforms, if not complete breaks with the past.

1. MAKING CIVIL SOCIETY A PARTNER IN DEVELOPMENT

Sachs sees in organized civil society a new partner in development. It is, he says, "one of the major phenomena of the latter half of this century", and one of its fundamental tasks must be to raise awareness of, and monitor respect for, human rights. For Sachs, "development and democracy" as an historical process are one and the same, provided, however, that "democracy" is interpreted not only as the establishment or re-establishment of the rule of law and the democratic institutions of governance, but also as the pursuit of the "never achieved" deepening of "day-to-day" democracy, of citizenship ranging from the local to the planetary, with a view to the universalization and effective exercise of formally proclaimed rights.

In the same vein, the international organizations never tire of repeating that the solution to the problems of sustainable development and the fight against poverty lies in popular participation in the political and decision-making processes and in the attainment of the rule of law. The founding texts of the United Nations are, however, silent on the need for democracy. One General Assembly resolution (20 September 1993) declares that each State has the right to choose and freely develop its political, social and cultural systems, reverting to the old unwritten rule that relations between States pay no heed to the nature of their political regimes. The only condition of membership in the United Nations is that States must be "peaceful", accept the obligations imposed on them by the Charter, and, in the Organization's opinion, be willing and able to do so.

What do the international organizations mean when they speak of "democracy"? First and foremost, the participation of local populations in the preparation and implementation of the authorities' decisions aimed at more efficient development.[7]

That entails recourse to "mechanisms" of expression, the favourites being the ballot box and periodic elections. That is not deemed sufficient: electoral fraud, political interference, corruption and the refusal to tell the electorate the truth all seriously undermine the validity of election results. Surveys conducted in Latin America show that most of the respondents think that their country's elections are flawed by fraud and manipulation. The Indian electorate, after years of electoral democracy, are less inclined to trust their elected representatives than they were in the early 1970s.

Add to this the possibility of inter-ethnic conflicts arising from inadequate representation of minorities where majority voting is the case or the fomenting of rivalries between groups, lured by the prospect of favours in return for votes. The control of such conflicts has induced some countries to structure their electoral systems in such a way that political parties are forced to solicit the support of all the communities (Mauritius) or a more equitable, peace-generating redistribution among them of the dividends of growth (in Malaysia, the progressive redistribution of capital goods in favour of Malays).

When this is the case, democracy is contingent upon more than the polls. An initial response might be to set up actual intermediary organizations with representatives on the decision-making bodies to serve as the mouthpiece of the citizens. Organizations of this kind are already playing a very active role with local and provincial administrations in developing countries where the State does not function properly and where their action is not repressed.[8] If they are to perform fully their task of pinpointing basic needs, they must also have direct contact with the ordinary citizens, the so-called neighbourhood bodies such as associations of farmers, religious groups and even parents.

The major importance of grassroots communities, villages or groups of villages was recognized at an early stage. "Community development"[9] was seen as a process designed to satisfy the people's real basic needs, with their active participation, since it can only yield results if an interested and motivated population is willing to put up with the sacrifices and constraints required for the realization of the objectives it helps define. Community development rests on the Anglo-Saxon-inspired hypothesis of a civic sense deeply rooted in the people, alongside fierce opposition to any "planning" technique. Hence "social" issues tend to override economic considerations, and meetings of the participants assume a para-administrative function, so to speak. The lesson to be learnt from these experiences is that community development can facilitate the execution of an existing "plan", flesh it out, adapt it, enhance coverage of local needs through improvements that make people use their potential wealth more efficiently, and help maintain a balance between the poles of industrial growth created elsewhere and the rural areas.

Mention could be made of many other development experiences relying with greater or lesser success on the "grassroots".[10] Reflection on the role played, and more particularly the role that the associative potential of cultures can play "is only now beginning", as observed by the World Bank experts.[11] The harnessing of that potential must not be seen as a panacea for all ills. Not every element in civil society is always represented; the traditional holders of power and the political factions are generally self-serving in their appropriation of anything that brings citizens together. The diversity of the activities covered by the intermediary organizations and the grassroots associations reflect the heterogeneity of needs and the diversity of preferences at the heart of civil society; there is no guarantee of correctness of every viewpoint or of the full validity of the priorities recommended. If democracy is to progress, recourse must also be had to other means of expression.

These are not lacking: major public debates, consultation mechanisms in fields ranging from economic and social policy to institutional reform (consumer surveys, simplified evaluation sheets, etc. (India, Uganda and Nicaragua), the establishment of specialized boards (educational development), to joint management programmes (water in Kenya, forests in India) and reports emanating from citizens and, therefore, progressing from the bottom up (successive reports on the state of the environment in India during the 1980s).

It is also necessary to create an enabling environment and, thus, resort to decentralization and to horizontal linkages between territorial communities and citizens, non-governmental organizations and private enterprises, while bearing in mind that such a policy runs the risk of deepening the divide between regions in a single country, of submission to the interests of categorial groups and of the central authorities' loss of macroeconomic control.

While we ignore them at our peril, "grassroots" must be used with great care and perseverance; we must not optimistically overestimate their capacity to engender mobilization and initiative. In the scenario of development from the bottom up, a permanent process of transformation and learning about society is launched and penetrates all activities from the base to the apex, both at the local and the national level. Its central themes are culture and its interaction with economics, eco-development, health, the conflict between real needs and the accumulation of wealth, participation and coordination, the most underprivileged groups and the critique of the authorities, while a minor place is assigned to the conditions of growth of the productive forces, which De Bernis regards as "erring on the side of idealism".[12] Democratization is also about recognizing the tasks to be performed at the apex.[13]

The international organizations' pro-democracy stance, the fact that some of them (such as the European Community)[14] confer the right to membership on fledgling democracies and assume the obligation to welcome them, the use of democracy as a weapon to disqualify and undermine opposing political and economic systems[15] all raise doubts about the reliability of those bodies that invoke it as a justification. How can aid or support be given only to "democracies" if one is not oneself a democracy? This function is all the more important since there are those who already speak of the emergence of an "international civil society".[16]

The question is far from simple. Indeed, sovereign rule of equality among States is at odds with equitable representation of the people. No criterion for weighting votes in international bodies is satisfactory, hence equality, including at the United Nations itself, is often "adjusted" if not abandoned.

Many United Nations agencies have, alongside the General Assembly at which all their members are represented, one or more smaller councils whose membership is determined – at least partly – on the basis of a series of procedures in which States' influence in the matters entrusted to the councils is taken into account. Some members of the IMF's Board of Governors represent Member States with the largest shares of subscribed capital, while others are elected under complex procedures based on demographic considerations. During voting at its meetings each State has, in addition to the same number of votes, a supplementary vote for each $ 100,000 in its quota. This means that the Western industrial countries account for approximately 60 per cent of all votes. Hardlly a situation of democracy!

Since 1919, the ILO Member States of chief industrial importance designate 10 of the 28 representatives who sit on its Governing Body. Two representatives are appointed by the most important agricultural countries, the rules for appointment of the latter being established by the Governing Body and implemented by an impartial committee (contribution to the ILO budget, national income, importance of external trade, gainfully employed population). The 14 employers' representatives and the 14 workers' representatives elected by the delegates of the respective electoral colleges at the General Conference of the ILO must each include two representatives from non-European States.

The institutions of the European Community project a different image: alongside the intergovernmental executive there is a decision-making Assembly elected, since 1979, by direct universal suffrage, according to the terms agreed on by each Member State. This Assembly – the European Parliament – has seen its powers enlarged by the Maastricht Treaty.[17] Furthermore, although it plays

only a consultative role, its consultation, mandated by certain provisions of the Maastricht accords, bestows a certain influence on the
Economic and Social Committee composed of representatives of
farmers and industrialists, of artisans and shopkeepers, and of wage
earners and members of the liberal professions.

Could one ask for more?

The non-governmental organizations (NGOs) group together
local organizations with fairly flexible structures, as well as national
federations or international networks. They tackle not only the
problems of the protection of ethnic groups' fundamental rights,
but an entire mosaic of development problems. The World Bank
has greatly developed its co-operation with them, both in respect of
loans and of the general-policy dialogue, inviting NGOs to devise,
prepare, implement and conduct a retrospective evaluation of sub-
projects it finances in connection with operations it supports, and
soliciting their help in securing greater involvement on the part of
the beneficiaries. Some "fora", attended in particular by numerous
NGO representatives, have been held in the margins of more than
one "summit", be it on population (1974, 1984, 1994), the environment (1993) or social issues (1995). Hence at international conferences we find the States' representatives discussing among
themselves, with the NGO representatives doing likewise in a parallel conference.

A representative of an NGO dealing with the rights of the child
(Mrs Onigman) was delighted that at various conferences (on adult
education and higher education) UNESCO had taken the initiative
of allowing those who were in the field – and as such the representatives of civil society – to speak to the political authorities and
to be heard by them. Along the same lines, a report by the
Commission on Global Governance recommends the establishment
of a "civil society forum" prior to each General Assembly of the
United Nations, which would bring together the representatives of
the NGOs accredited, or likely to be accredited, to the Economic
and Social Council.[18] While such linking of intergovernmental
arrangements and civil society in the form of co-operation between
a decision-making and a consultative organ, as Merle observed,[19]
might enhance the former's moral authority, it would have no effect
on the legal weight of its decisions. People today, he notes, have
the right to information and must participate to the best of their
ability in international activities, but they are citizens of a national
State before they are citizens of the world, and that element of society remains essential to the proper functioning of international rela-

tions, the full democratization of which is "mere wishful think-ing".[20]

Kant believed that the purpose of evolution was the constitution of a republican State, that is a State in which human rights would be respected and equality under the law would reign.[21] He saw human progress as a step towards the universal "cosmopolitan state".

The content of democracy is not immutable. It is not a "state" but a "movement". It postulates the popular origin of power, but nothing could be more detrimental to its future than for it to assume in the developing countries the form of some "direct" representation or other fuelled by illusions of "direct" democracy. Nothing could be further from the requirements of human and economic development than to forget that the democracy they call for must be a combination of "governed" democracy, founded on the power of the nation (the people being sovereign because they are the masters of the work accomplished by the State), and of "governing" democracy, dominated by the real will of the people (democracy of struggle owing to the divisions among the people which call for State authority capable of dealing with popular imperatives). If democracy is to advance and if its progress is to be accompanied by achievements, its requirements must be recognized, without illusions or weakness, and, as Burdeau[22] points out, "humankind must know how to remain free, not from outside threats, but from itself".

2. "PILOTAGE" PLANNING AND COLLECTIVE EDUCATION. NEW INDICATORS

In his address during Paul-Marc Henry Day, Berthelot described the "Russian crisis" and the catastrophic damage occasioned by the country's observance of the plethora of recommendations (notably from the IMF in 1995) to implement a rigorous macroeconomic policy that ruled out all financing of the budgetary deficit by printing money or borrowing. He concluded that the main lesson to be learnt was that "it is necessary to implement in the next dozen years or so a plan – merely a plan – that precisely establishes the chronology of the institutional reforms and the pace of privatization and liberalization".

Anxious to propose for Africa an alternative economic strategy relying on the initiative of groups, communities and individuals, Engelhard[23] finds it difficult to obtain convergence of efforts without a shared, intelligent vision of the future of the real economy and the "implementation of open, democratic and strategic planning". It is necessary, he writes, "to reinvent planning," avoiding the snares of bureaucracy and unsound decisions. As a consultation open to all social actors (including the poorest), planning must be a privileged site for the emergence of all social issues. It must not only inform and predict, it must pinpoint priorities and establish follow-up to the path selected; and at the same time it must trust self-organization, aware that a society "learns" and that its ever-complex regulation becomes more so when its economy is open to competition and is subjected to pressure from foreign interests which do not necessarily coincide with national interests.

The World Bank experts themselves still think today that there is nothing better for growth and for workers' improved standard of living than development by the market that encourages businesses and workers to invest in physical capital, new techniques and training.[24] Nevertheless, with regard to infrastructure contributions, they consider that spatial, sectoral and intersectoral "co-ordination and planning" are essential for State activities and that incorporation of the social and environmental implications of projects is vital.[25] For their part, the UNDP experts continue to affirm the need for strong "policies", with commitment and political will – more than resources – as the "main constraints to taking care of economic growth and human development simultaneously;"[26] governments could base their "plans" for the next decade on comprehensive and realistically costed national strategies for human development.[27]

It is quite interesting to compare the positions on evolution found in studies on the developing countries' planning that appear in the journal "Finance and development" which purports to be the mouthpiece of the Bretton Woods institutions. Starting from the "operational" angle, Waterston[28] uses "experiences" to distinguish three types of planning: integral planning (more and more abandoned), informal planning (of no practical importance), indicative planning (concerning first and foremost the rationalization of investment projects and assigning prime importance to interaction of prices and market forces). The type of planning that each country resorts or would resort to depends on the country's social, economic and political structure, development level and size. Nevertheless, Waterston, for whom the main obstacles to the plans' success are their administration and the lack of political will, advocates "partial" planning.[29] Unlike "classical" planning, which progresses from objectives to strategies, projects, instruments and policies, and unlike "optimization" planning, which takes resources as its starting point and attempts to make them perform to the maximum, "partial" planning is geared to problems as they are actually experienced and appears to be a genuinely continuous process. Its purpose is to identify and determine the essence of development problems and find solutions based on the criteria adopted, prevent malfunctions and deviations and correct or alter paths so that development can progress.

There are many who feel that planning – which they equate solely with Soviet-type administrative planning – has been discredited. There are good reasons for that attitude: a future which has become too uncertain, constant transformations in all social dimensions, shrinking distances, widening temporality gaps, increasing volumes of intangible wealth, virtually instantaneous reactions by agents on certain markets made possible by the new information and communication technologies, scattered interventions by the State – calling into question its capacity to define aims – globalization and the ensuing deterioration of national sovereignty. While all that is true, far from banishing all ideas of planning, it makes its renewal and reinvention in a new context all the more necessary.

The opinion of this author is therefore similar to Waterston's. Management of the complexity and uncertainty of the economic and social phenomena necessitates myriad adjustments, gives rise to pragmatic experimentation and demands adaptations that are not determined in advance. Deliberate and ongoing "pilotage" planning should be sought throughout the process, starting with the elaboration of programmes and projects and continuing during their establishment, implementation and monitoring; operational strategies would be aimed at tighter organic links among the various authorities and levels, while the non-traditional strategies would pinpoint the target populations. In other words, from this perspective, the traditional notion of the development "plan" should be replaced by that of "planning process". This would be fully in keeping with the hypotheses of effective perception of the real (constructivist hypothesis) and of mobilization with a view to pursuing the actors' projects (projective or teleological hypothesis) which we will soon make our own.[30]

The disparities between projects and the results can be considerable. The way to reduce them is less through refining techniques, statistical and econometrical instruments, or even simulation models, useful as they are, and more through improving response capabilities of all the actors. Structuring interactions according to the powers assigned to the different levels of responsibility, ensuring that they interlink properly, allowing the districts and regions of a particular country, in agreement with all the economic and social actors concerned, to tackle the problems of development on the basis of experience and to enter into the responsible commitments they can make: these are the keys to the conception of planning as a process.

But yet more is required. It was Tinbergen's view[31] that planning should begin with an estimate of the tasks of long-term development (10-15 years), followed by medium-term and annual estimates, and that due account should be taken of them. Today Gruson,[32] noting both the failure of all the heavy structures (education, research, technology, transport, energy, etc.) to adapt, due to the speed of developments and, above all, the novelty and extent of the prospects of evolution opened up by dynamic factors, recommends a "reasonable, adapted" forecast that "takes the long view". On that basis, it is vital that the planning process should not be limited to establishing coherence among the various public interventions or their coherence with the strategies of private enterprises, nor should it perform a mere surveillance function; rather, it should be a true instrument of collective education, helping civil society to learn, for that is the price of its "progressiveness".[33]

It is not enough to opt for a form of planning. There must also be instruments for calculating and measuring. When *Ramsès* wonders about the continuing possibility of directing the economy, the response is the existence of a veritable "crisis" of indicators, especially in the monetary domain.[34] The Bretton Woods institutions' experts do not restrict their activities to method planning and experience in the subject. As Caire points out,[35] they also study investment criteria and the possible definitions of the costs and gains associated with the projects that concern them; above all, and in line with our thinking, within the framework of the UNDP they concern themselves with identifying advances and regressions in human development.

In 1979, the General Conference of UNESCO invited the Division of Socio-Economic Analysis to study quality of life in terms of quality of the environment and quality of work, with a view to development.[36] In 1990, the UNDP Human Development Report, defining human development as "the process of enlarging people's choices", proposed a new development yardstick no longer limited to income alone, but grouping together three indicators in a composite index: longevity (life expectancy at birth), education (a weighting of two-thirds to the adult literacy rate and one-third to the gross rate of school attendance, all levels taken together), and gross domestic product (GDP) per head (income being presumed to be indicative of standard of living). A minimum global level was established for each of the three components (minimum life expectancy, minimum adult literacy and minimum income per inhabitant). Some desirable maxima or, rather, "adequate" levels, that should be attained were also set. This makes it possible to measure a country's "shortfall" in each of the basic variables, define an average shortfall index (a simple arithmetical mean of the three indicators) and calculate a human development index (HDI) on the basis of non-weighted aggregation.[37]

This indicator is indubitably a more complete measure than income per head. Nevertheless, it is still only a partial measure of development. It attempts to express a very complex reality using imperfect data and leaves room for much refinement: enlargement of the time-frame showing life expectancy world-wide, and blocking of the upper and lower thresholds applied to the country under consideration (25 and 85 years); estimation of educational level by combining the illiteracy rate and the number of years of individuals' schooling, while modifying the former's lower threshold (0 per cent instead of 12 initially) and the latter's upper threshold (15 years instead of 12.3); introduction into the calculation, when possible, of the Gini coefficients used to measure income distribution, and the corresponding correction of income disparities, considered on the basis of a declining scale of income multiples beyond the threshold value (global mean of per capita GDP).[38]

The HDI can be illustrated in several ways.[39] It promotes investigation of sociological disparities between groups, notably between the sexes (gender-related development index (GDI) and the gender empowerment measure). The establishment of distinct HDIs for certain categories of inhabitant or region makes it possible to pinpoint the regions where poverty is concentrated and on which to focus the effects of development.

A capacity shortfall indicator (CSI) was established in 1996, also with three components: the proportion of children under five years of age who are underweight (measure of ability to enjoy a healthy life with adequate nutrition), the proportion of births not supervised by health personnel with ad hoc training (ability to procreate in adequate health and safety conditions), illiteracy rates among women aged 15 and over (ability to read and write and to teach themselves). Human poverty indicators (HPI 1 and 2) followed in 1997 and 1998. These still took into consideration the three essential elements of human life already mentioned in connection with the HDI, but focused on deficiencies. These are, where the developing countries are concerned, the likelihood of dying at a relatively early age (percentage of individuals whose life expectancy is not more than 40 years), exclusion from reading and communication (percentage of illiterate adults), lack of access to decent living conditions (percentage of those with no access to safe drinking water or to health care services, percentage of children under five suffering from malnutrition); and for the industrialized countries: percentage of people whose life expectancy does not exceed 60 years, percentage of illiterates, percentage of people living below the poverty line, established at half the median of available individual income, and percentage of the active population in a situation of long-term unemployment (at least 12 months).

Such indicators have made it possible to update the correlation between economic and human development and to analyse, albeit imperfectly, the conditions for translating economic growth into greater human well-being. The annual national human development Reports would appear to have a real impact in that they help to bring groups together and help build consensus that opens the door to new thinking and policy perspectives.[40] The positive aspect of the effects of public intervention has been clearly established in several countries which, even with a pallid growth rate, are making substantial progress (such as Côte d'Ivoire, Kenya and Senegal).

Despite the very real contribution made by the entire range of indicators originating from the HDI, it is regrettable that excessive attention is paid to measurement of and comments on composite indicators; it would be preferable for more indicators of situations and trends to be used. Country "profiles" could be drawn up to serve as true performance indicators comprising numerous non-aggregated indicators. In addition, quantitative indicators should not be sought out to the detriment of a qualitative evaluation, for, as Sachs affirms,[41] what must be avoided at all cost is to yield to apparent, superficial and often fallacious objectivity. The use of circular charts should provide a more accurate picture of the effective levels of human development. Starting at the centre, the values of the indicators would fan out along lines on a scale of 0 to 100; the further away from the centre the silhouette formed by the lines connecting the ends, the more favourable the situation of the countries concerned.[42] To that end, we have at our disposal data published by UNDP on "North-South disparities",[43] but we can also undertake a direct graphic representation for each country studied, using the banks of indicators that express the rates of human development levels so that the data could be more easily compared.[44]

It is quite remarkable that while the United Nations experts do important work on measuring human development levels, they almost never measure the human costs of the workings and evolution of the economy. For instance, when the World Bank devotes one of its world development Reports to "the world of work",[45] it is quite silent on the human costs of labour, save for a few pages on unemployment; even that is little more than pure description with no analysis on the impact it has on individuals. The ILO has devised some "indicators of human development in the enterprise (HDE), the composition of which – subject to alteration and negotiation – starts from variables relating to recruitment and training practices (HDE 1). To these are successively added other variables covering the non-discriminatory nature of those practices, safety and hygiene at work (HDE 2), equity (HDE 3), and democracy (workers' means of expression, profit-sharing) (HDE 4). While those are all useful indicators, they do not represent the human costs of development or, more important, of labour.[46]

We possess a great deal of information concerning labour "inputs" (hours worked, organization of working time, amount of work corresponding to the products of the various branches, breakdown by socio-professional category or by socio-demographic category) and these we express in working time for social accounting.[47] Efforts are being made to measure the rate at which workers accomplish the tasks they have to perform in the unit of time; since the "standard times" allotted by the enterprise's work-measurement department correspond to "norms" relating to the "standard" effort of a worker with average experience, motivated by his or her wage and related bonuses, the "units of work" the department evaluates in advance are "psycho-physiological quanta" of units of human effort.[48]

An analysis of working conditions furnishes valuable data on existing constraints (physical environment, physical burden, mental burden, psycho-physiological aspects, added to working time, hours of work and work structure). A variety of grading systems is used to evaluate these in order to determine the nature and significance of the defects to be remedied.[49] The constraints are directly measurable using objective indicators by separating physical load (energy expended, cardiac cost) from mental load (behavioural criteria, variability of the task performance, "added task" method, use of physiological and neurophysiological criteria). Although the indicators of the operator's performance or reliability do not directly analyse the load factors, they supplement observation by referring either to work quality and quantity or to worker satisfaction.[50] Sociology contributes to the study of constraints and obligations with its knowledge of the way people function in enterprises and, more generally, in any kind of organization.[51]

Further clarifications are furnished by statistics on work-related accidents and occupational disorders (number, frequency, gravity and ensuing deterioration), by the work of ergonomists and, even more so, that of doctors on the semiology of fatigue and the methods of analysis required,[52] on occupational wear and tear and premature ageing,[53] on the deterioration of health caused by unemployment and by exclusion from working life[54] and on differential mortality.

To the above we should add that an external diagnosis by "experts" is not enough, the diagnosis by the workers themselves being of primary importance since it stems from their own experience. Their own perception of their work and the load factors makes for better scientific determination of the human costs of labour. Hence the proposal of a method consisting of the following: inventorying the possible sources of human costs; the use of "non-directive" interviews concerning working conditions in all their dimensions; ascertaining how workers subjectively perceive the human costs of their labour. The quantification could be based on a scale of grades from zero load to a very high load, possibly arriving at a global mark by attributing weightings to the different load factors according to their recognized relative importance.[55]

All the indicators relating to the human costs – ignored by economic accounting that leaves people out of the equation and is therefore unsuited to controlling the development and employment of human agents – should contribute to partial planning focused jointly on economic development and human development, the object of our desire. Its governability calls for the indicators to be constructed and improved as the investigation of the economic field evolves in that direction, relying in large measure on interdisciplinarity.

Chapter V of the "Programme of action" of the Copenhagen Social Summit provides for the development of statistics and indicators capable of helping the developing countries formulate their strategies. We advocate the same. Mahalanobis, the father of Indian surveys, designed ongoing surveys consisting of "rounds", each round comprising several inquiries, some filling in statistical gaps, others providing the information needed for framing a country's economic policy and plan. He includes specific inquiries in the multipurpose inquiries and general inquiries in local inquiries.[56] An initiative such as that of the fledgling European University of Labour, although on a much more modest scale, follows the same lines: the establishment in the various countries associated with the same research project of task forces with a precise mandate and, among them, partnership networks counting among their members researchers, academics, entrepreneurs, union leaders and public officials; constant monitoring in a limited number of enterprises; development of syntheses; seminars at the various stages followed by a final forum; selection of the survey topics and the desired direction of the work of a pilot research group.[57]

It is not unreasonable to think that such practices would considerably improve economic governability since the samples are selected with care, the surveys are rigorously conducted, interdisciplinarity is systematically applied, and the participation of stakeholders, far from damaging objectivity, strengthens it. Both democracy and the effectiveness of economic policy would gain from it.

Where indicators are concerned, there is one last and, in the circumstances, brief factor. Human development cannot be complete without freedom. The World Conference on Human Rights (Vienna, 1993) put on its agenda the implementation of a system of indicators that would make it possible to evaluate the progress made in the effective exercise of such rights. In the 1980s Charles Humana, referring both to the Universal Declaration of Human Rights and to the two 1966 Covenants, essayed an evaluation of their implementation using 40 indicators and one composite indicator.[58] In an extension of that task, the UNDP experts[59] constructed a human freedom index (HFI) using a different ranking system (binary and, therefore, simple) and updated its 1985 rankings. The attempt fizzled out owing to the differences in democracy throughout the world and to some Asian countries' objection to the underlying "Western" conception of human rights. It also transpired that the HFI could not be satisfactorily integrated into the different HDIs because whatever typical variation it contained did not automatically entail a comparable variation in the HDIs of all the countries in which it occurred.

Sachs takes up the idea but gives it different content. Opposed to a composite indicator, he proposed a totally different approach.

A choice could be made from among human rights, following which surveys would be conducted country by country to reveal the actual situation of the exercise of each of the rights selected, distinguishing between social categories. He observes that the project is an ambitious one but that its adoption would enable national and regional observatories to establish a "citizens' report on the human condition". There is no doubt that, should that occur, the choices to be made in the framework of a strategy organized around human development would emerge more clearly.

3. CANCELLATION OF DEBTS; MEETING CAPITAL NEEDS

Perpetual indebtedness[60] and usury[61]: the indebtedness of developing countries is an "infernal machine".[62] Debt repayment and service of interest makes government difficult and imposes a heavy burden compromising the future of the South, and particularly of the least developed countries. In 1970 the total foreign indebtedness of the developing countries was of the order of $ 100 billion; by 1980 it had reached $ 650 billion and by 1992, $ 1,500 billion. Between 1980 and 1996 the indebtedness of the low-income countries rose from $ 110 billion to $ 435 billion; that of the middle-income countries from $ 435 to $ 1,656 billion, and that for all the countries concerned from $ 603 to $ 2,091 billion – an increase of almost 250 per cent. This increase is partly due to the securing of access to a number of international financial markets and increases in direct foreign investment.[63] In 1995, debt service was taking up 24 per cent of the revenue from exports of goods and services of the countries with average HDIs (as against 20 per cent in 1980) and 26 per cent of that of the countries with low HDIs (11 per cent in 1980). The highest levels were those for Zambia (174 per cent), Guinea-Bissau (67 per cent), Sierra Leone (60 per cent) and Haiti and Peru (45 per cent). In 1995, too, Mozambique devoted 3.3 per cent of its budget to health, 7.9 per cent to education and 35 per cent to debt service; half its population had no access to drinking water and 190,000 children were dying each year before reaching age 5.

A first debt "crisis" occurred in 1982-83. It broke out in Latin America when the United States and other OECD countries raised their interest rates and restricted credit, sucking in capital from Latin America, where, moreover, fears of local instability existed, due to the delicate nature of the transfers of power from military to civilian governments and the almost complete inability of the latter to resort to austerity policies – not to mention the effects of the second oil shock in the region and the effects of increases in military expenditure (Argentina).

Procedures and mechanisms designed to "lighten" the debt burden were established by the international institutions and the principal donor countries. Cancellations, reschedulings and consolidations were granted to countries which undertook energetic reforms under conditions laid down in structural adjustment programmes.[64] New instruments for debt reduction were designed, such as conversion of debt into equity or physical assets[65] and the repurchase by the debtor countries of their foreign debt at a fraction of its face value accompanied by new bond issues. From the mid-1980s onwards, public and private creditors increasingly accepted the fact that in most cases full repayment would not take place. Some banks wrote off "irrecoverable" credits in their accounts or resorted to ingenious arrangements.[66]

In March 1989, with the Brady Plan, the strategy for tackling the debt problem took a radical new turn. For the first time debt reductions were officially proposed as a means of escaping from the difficulties in which the deeply indebted countries were enmeshed. The banks were asked to exempt the debtor countries from part of their debt in exchange for limited guarantees of repayment financed by the World Bank and the IMF; they were also asked to grant new loans to the countries concerned for growth promotion, while the debtor countries were invited to pursue liberal policies facilitating private investment. In Mexico this meant the conversion of old debts, at a discount of 35 per cent of their face value, into new 30-year bonds paying a variable rate of interest; the exchange of debt at face value for bonds paying 6.5 per cent interest annually; and the granting of new loans. The World Bank, the IMF, Japan and Mexico itself took part in the operation with $ 10 billion of guaranteed financing. The country thus seemed to have overcome the debt crisis – for a time, at least.[67]

Throughout the 1990s the Paris Club, which is made up of the governments of the advanced countries (and consequently the creditor countries), concluded debt restructuring and reduction agreements. It increased from 50 per cent to 67 per cent the proportion of foreign debt of the debtor countries which could be cancelled to enable them to "take off" as rapidly as possible. Together with the World Bank and the IMF it put together the HIPC (Highly Indebted

Poor Countries) programme for the benefit of countries for which the burden of debt repayment, or even interest payment, was "unbearable".[68] Six years had to elapse before their applications for relief could be considered; during that period they had to undertake structural reforms in the form of two successive programmes, with the additional requirement that the relief measures should benefit the entire population and not only the ruling classes. According to the World Bank, 41 countries, 33 of them in Africa, could be recognized as "eligible".

The debt problem is still with us. Political will is essential if the HIPC programme is to be credible. The consistent aim is to ensure that the partial or, better, total cancellation of debt does not encourage the debtor country to relax its efforts; hence the continued imposition of "conditions". In 1997 the global financial system came under serious threat; and, under considerable pressure from the United States and the IMF, the G-7 countries reacted to the "Asian" crisis by raising over $ 100 billion, to be advanced in loans, in the space of a few months; while at that time $ 7 billion would have been enough to launch the HIPC programme in some 20 African countries. The countries which had applied to benefit from the programme were gravely disappointed. Uganda, which for ten years had scrupulously complied with the conditions imposed on it by the IMF, had to wait a year before its application was accepted; the same was true of Bolivia. Tanzania is unlikely to meet the necessary conditions before 2002; in the meantime, the proportion of its budget taken up by debt repayment is three times that allocated to primary education and nine times that earmarked for primary health care.

In 1994, in his letter on the preparations for the third millennium, Pope John-Paul II proclaimed the year 2000 to be a "jubilee year" and urged that, as such, the year should be one of charity and active solidarity with the poorest. In the Biblical tradition of cancellation of all debts every 50 years, he called for the cancellation of the public debt of the poorest countries. The theme was immediately taken up by the national Roman Catholic bishoprics, the Christian churches and the organizations related to them. A worldwide mobilization of opinion resulted; a petition, signed by 17 million persons, calling for the cancellation of the debts of the poorest countries was handed to Chancellor Gerhard Schröder at the 25th G-7 summit, held in Cologne in June 1999. Unquestionably the cancellation of debts would free resources for human development and the economic development on which it rests. These debts should be cancelled without any political or economic conditions other than a commitment to introduce reforms guaranteeing transparency in the management and administration of the resources so freed, and without any compulsion on the countries concerned to adopt economic policies conforming with the ideologies of the dominant Powers; the policies adopted should match the needs of their peoples.

Two factors which make debt cancellation on these terms particularly urgent are that, first, the policy of providing new credits to ensure debt service has reached its limits, and, second, that repayment could be achieved only through an inverse transfer of capital contrary in every respect to the principle of fructification of capital in a global context.

Failing cancellation, one solution might be the repayment of the residual debt and outstanding interest on condition that that sum should immediately be reinvested in the country concerned to finance development projects of every kind; this would be the equivalent of giving new purchasing power to the poor countries in the form of transfers from the rich countries. The creditor countries which claim that they are unable to increase their public development aid could include the amounts involved in their official aid figures, thus approaching somewhat the objective of 0.7 per cent of their GNP which has for many years been deemed the necessary minimum. One might also return to the idea of a world-wide Marshall Plan in the form of new long-term (20-year) loans at low rates of interest, with no interest payable during the initial years, but tied to purchases in the creditor countries of capital and intermediate goods essential for the development of the poor countries. This would imply the setting up of a large-scale programme of production and transfer into the productive sector of liquidities likely otherwise to give rise to financial "crises".

The French government proposed to its G-7 partners that a decision be taken at the Cologne summit to the effect that the highly indebted poor countries should not be required to make any further debt-related payments to public institutions in the rich countries and that the resources so released should be transferred directly to the peoples instead of being used for non-productive expenditure (arms) or squandered by the State through mismanagement. President Clinton took up the French proposal at the Afro-American summit meeting held in Washington in March 1999; he considered that the United States should support a cancellation plan designed to reduce more substantially and more rapidly the debts of some 50 developing countries, provided, however, that the countries concerned adopted "sound" economic reform policies.

In fact, the Cologne summit meeting approved an agreement previously reached by the ministers of finance of the G-7 and decided to introduce an unprecedented measure of flexibility into the debt-relief procedures. Within the next few years, $ 65 billion of debt is to be cancelled for the benefit of the poorest countries. Of that total, $ 15 billion will consist of bilateral debt (loans granted by rich countries in the form of development aid) and $ 50 billion of multilateral debt (loans from the IMF and the World Bank) and commercial debt (bank loans). This represents an increase of $ 45 billion over what was previously planned.

The criteria of the HIPC programme were also relaxed. The ratio of debt to exports was reduced to 150 per cent and that of debt to the budget to 250 per cent; the cancellation ceiling (previously 80 per cent) was abolished; and the duration of the procedure providing for compliance with a structural adjustment programme was reduced from 6 to 3 years. The number of countries to benefit from debt cancellation was to increase from 29 to 36.

However, the debt problem has not been finally resolved by these measures. The slow pace of implementation of the HIPC programme has already been mentioned. In addition, no decision has yet been reached on how much of the additional $ 45 billion should be provided by each donor. France has proposed that the countries which have lent most on a bilateral basis should be required to furnish least and has argued in favour of the continuance of public development aid, without which, it claims, no real development will take place in poor countries. The United Kingdom wishes to involve the private sector and is leaning towards the view that the Cologne summit meeting should be considered as marking the end of the era of "bad debts" and "bad governments"; henceforth the poor countries should be left to deal with private banks.

Debt cancellation is one thing; the continuing need of developing countries for capital is another. To turn again to the IMF: that body estimated in 1995[69] that the aggregate external debt of all the developing countries would amount, during the period 1991-2000, to 85.3 per cent of their exports of goods and services, and debt service to 10 per cent (the corresponding percentages for net debtor countries were 95.3 and 11.3). This immediately raises the question of availability of capital, both within developing countries (what is the position regarding domestic savings?) and in the rest of the world. The thesis of insufficiency of saving at global level does not seem to be borne out by the absence of full employment, since flows of employment can adapt *ex post facto* to world-wide investment. The only possible constraints seem to be due, as regards private transfers, to a lack of confidence in the capacities of the recipient countries and, as regards aid, a lack of goodwill on the part of the donor countries.[70]

The question of the consequences of direct foreign investment for growth in developing countries must also be considered. Empirical studies[71] have revealed that the countries in which direct foreign investment has been greatest have known lower growth rates than originally anticipated and that, where there is a positive correlation between the level of investment and the amount of direct foreign investment, the "additional" investment which the latter brings does not contribute to economic growth.

Andreff,[72] for his part, emphasizes the extent to which the establishment of large corporations in developing countries facilitates the implantation of new forms of presence (subcontracting, licensing agreements, management contracts, etc.) which reduce the financial input needed to gain control of certain sectors of production. He argues that as a consequence it is preferable to rely on the complementarity of direct investment and debt rather than the substitution of the one for the other. It is useless to attempt to stimulate an increase in foreign direct investment inputs to launch or relaunch growth; if high levels of indebtedness do not drive away investors, market growth will attract them. A relaxation of the constraints of adjustment will be more favourable to them than the introduction of constraints – which is an additional argument in favour of debt cancellation.

It has also been argued that borrowing abroad is preferable to foreign investment in developing countries because it does not threaten their sovereignty and does not bring with it an automatic transfer of advanced technologies and management techniques into a completely different context, thus permitting utilization of resources in a manner related to local customs and traditions. We had thought to see the key to governance within the framework of the nation-State in the "popular" (informal) sector and small and medium-sized enterprises. Likewise, at the Nairobi[73] tripartite symposium on structural adjustment and employment in Africa, the need to improve the production capacity of the poor – for example, by encouraging them to organize as a means of gaining access to production factors and markets – was emphasized. Technical co-operation projects have been designed to improve the financial management of small enterprises or to promote the income-generating capacity of target groups.[74] In the ILO projects financing is seen as a means and not as an activity as such; thus benefits are generally provided through revolving credits or guarantee funds. The results are positive when the projects are actually implemented. However, it has become apparent that all too often these projects are not sufficiently precise, and that, if the experiment is to continue with chances of success and replication, in-depth reflection on the duration of technical co-operation, repayments and subsidies will be necessary.

On his return from sub-Saharan Africa, Federico Mayor claimed that responsibility for the instability, conflicts and hardship prevalent there were to be attributed to the lack of the necessary aid. He immediately made it clear that by "aid" he did not mean "loans". Once debt had been cancelled the need would become clear for a completely different type of aid, relying less on technical assistance provided by expatriates, less directed towards capturing markets in the countries assisted and more directed towards long-term measures to build up national infrastructures and resources. We said earlier that sharing must be one of the main principles governing the strategy for the achievement of the "new paradigm". Indebtedness and aid are proof of this. As Mayor said, it is not the interests of the "lending" and/or "assisting" countries which have to be served, but those of the countries which need "gifts" and "support".

4. REGULATION AND CONTROL OF CAPITAL MOVEMENTS

The liberalization of capital movements is continuing in parallel with the increase in the volume and instability of international capital flows. The removal of statutory restrictions on capital transactions, the increase in the numbers of commercial lenders, the increase in the volume of financial transactions to hedge against exchange risks and the commercial risks arising from the globalization of trade, the proliferation of new financial techniques and of derivative instruments (swaps, options, term contracts) designed to reduce the exposure of international investors to certain risks (while exposing them to others) and the increased changeability of the attitudes of intermediaries and its effect on conventional methods of providing credit (adjustment to markets of the terms offered by banks) are all combining to make economies money-driven. The trend is being given additional impetus by the changes in information and communication techniques; investors and speculators are informed almost instantaneously of the cost of assets, of differentials in prices and rates, while at the same time the dematerialization of transactions which the new EDP linkages permit makes the identification and control of international capital movements by the public authorities increasingly difficult. Today over 97 per cent of daily transactions are in fact financial transfers unconnected with physical exchanges of goods but which result in substantial gains (or losses) together with substantial transfers of power. Far from being a "regulator", the world capital market is becoming increasingly independent of national and regional economies and is distorting their regulatory and equilibrium-seeking processes, as it is doing in the global economy. The governability of the economy is threatened at three levels.

Before the "Asian" crisis erupted, the primary concern was to adjust "global capitalism" by strengthening the supervision of the financial flows, banking systems and economic policies of emerging countries exercised by the international agencies. But today the question of a radical change in orientation is increasingly coming into discussion. Camdessus has always admitted that temporary exchange controls should be possible in certain cases (short-lived inflows of short-term capital, the need to secure resources required to undertake radical reforms, etc.). The IMF now admits that before exchange liberalization is undertaken the presence of certain important preconditions must be verified.[75] It also recognizes that, owing to the asymmetries in information which are endemic in capital markets, efficiency in allocation has declined sharply and that markets are particularly exposed to drastic reactions by investors and speculators, the formation of "financial bubbles" and the outbreak of financial "crises" when market behaviour becomes irrational. To moderate capital flows it suggests recourse where necessary to instruments such as compulsory deposits on foreign currency investments or short-term borrowings, while insisting on the fact that the objective is only "to prevent excesses and abuses".

One IMF study emphasizes the need to apply, at national level, policies designed to establish a financial system much less dependent on banks and other intermediaries than is at present the case, and shifting more of the burden of direct risk on to the actual investors.[76] This implies that the national authorities will apply strict preventive regulations and supervision: restrictions on the net uncovered foreign currency positions of the banks, taxation of short-term capital inflows, modulation of the percentages of compulsory reserves to be held by the banks according to the residence and the currency in which the deposits are held.[77] These measures should be parallelled by an approach to the function of lender of last resort of central banks of a nature to reduce both the ability of participants in capital markets to take excessive risks and the considerations which might lead them to do so. The same IMF study observes that its member countries are increasingly removing restrictions on capital transfers in order to benefit from the expansion of international financial transactions and capital flows; it advises them to proceed gradually, as a sudden lifting of restrictions can open the door to corruption, insider loans, risky repayment practices and irresponsible behaviour taking advantage of the safety net consisting of bail-outs by the central banks, where such arrangements are possible.

Some doubt is permissible concerning the possibility of implementing a number of these measures, and above all the taxation measures. In this connection de Boissieu[78] imagines a tax of 0.1 per cent on certain exchange transactions and raises a number of questions highlighting the difficulty of applying it. Transactions relating to international trade should be exempt; only purely financial transactions should be taxed: can one distinguish between the two? If so, should all of them be taxed, even those which are not speculative? Can the taxation system be restricted to the G-7 countries only? If not, what steps can be taken to involve the newly-industrialized countries of Asia and Latin America?

In September 1998 the French Minister of Finance sent his European counterparts a memorandum containing 12 proposals designed to make the international financial system function better. The measures included an improvement in the preventive supervision of financial institutions and compliance with international regulations by offshore centres (Bermuda, Cayman Islands, Virgin Islands, etc.[79]). The most original proposal was for the extension to the entire world of article 73 of the Maastricht Treaty, which authorized the introduction of exchange controls for a maximum of six months "when, in exceptional circumstances, movements of capital... cause, or threaten to cause, serious difficulties".

In October 1998 the heads of State of the G-7, concerned at erratic capital movements, approved a series of measures. These included the establishment of a strengthened IMF preventive credit line which could be drawn on in appropriate circumstances by countries implementing IMF programmes, supported where necessary by bilateral financing and suitable commitments from the private sector; a search for greater transparency in the financial transactions of each country and of the international financial institutions, with the adoption of internationally approved codes of conduct; the strengthening of the global financial system by closer supervision of national financial and regulatory systems; a study to be undertaken by the ministers of finance and central bank governors on the strengthening of preventive rules for financial institutions in industrialized countries and the promotion of reliable and lasting capital flows; and an examination of the consequences of the operations of institutions making speculative investments, with the particular aim of encouraging extra-territorial financial centres to adopt and comply with approved international standards.

Good governance demands good governability. It would be mistaken to believe that a system of standards valid for all financial agents – and, for example, to make speculative funds lodged in tax havens subject to greater transparency – could be extended to the whole world. Even so, regulation and supervision must be strengthened. It would be equally mistaken to wish for a more efficient IMF with greater resources and a "government" with the power to act as a lender of last resort, for, since it intervenes only at the request of governments, it is hardly in a position to envisage preventive policies. What is desirable is closer co-operation between the IMF, the World Bank and the Bank of International Settlements (all too often forgotten) and between them and central banks, with recourse (as the IMF proposed after the Mexican crisis of 1994-95) to an early warning system which would be based on carefully selected indicators; greater emphasis on the analysis of trends in international capital markets and, also, of the situations of individual national economies; and, if a crisis threatens, suggestions to the competent authorities concerning ways of averting it or palliating its consequences. Equally desirable are a sharing of tasks between the IMF and the G-7, and reflection on the role the WTO should play vis-à-vis each of them.

Even so, as Camdessus said in relation to Asia, the financial crisis "is not that of a country but of a system". That system is made up of international financial institutions, banks, multinationals and States, all of them subject to a logic in which market mechanisms and opposed powers are intermingled, with conflicts and alliances alternating without any "invisible hand" intervening. In the current state of the global economy, where capital movements are concerned, any governance and any governability is exposed to the "moral risk" that investors will continue with their speculative transactions in the firm belief that if a "crisis" occurs in a particular country, the IMF and the G-7 will certainly intervene to bail them out.

A point of equilibrium must be found between that risk and the need to be able to provide countries in difficulty with resources sufficient to avoid jeopardizing the international financial system as a whole. One can attempt to "improve" the system; but one cannot prevent it from becoming increasingly unstable; that is the inevitable consequence of the extension of international financial integration. Whoever accepts the logic of financial capitalism may consider it the price to be paid for the much greater benefits deriving from that growing integration.[80] One is entitled to hope that the implementation of the radical reforms of the Bretton Woods institutions (which is, in our opinion, necessary, as stated above) will confer on those "benefits" a significance quite different from that of profits destined to remain within the sphere of finance. But that can only be achieved through bitter struggles, for the established interests are powerful.

5. FACING UP TO THE MASTERS OF THE WORLD ECONOMY: THE MULTINATIONAL ENTERPRISES

The world economy is still far from being "globalized", that is to say consisting of a hierarchized network governed by operating rules and composed of centres and peripheries the boundaries of which no longer have the rigidity of State frontiers. In every sphere, the networks of production and exchanges which make up the economy reflect the interplay of strategies resulting from the interventions of firms and State, both of which act as agents of globalization. To the conflicts which oppose them and the alliances which bind them together must be added those between States, and also those between States and regional and world-wide international agencies. From this interplay of forces other obstacles to governability spring at various levels.

Globalization is primarily the outcome of the decisions and strategies of enterprises and groups seeking to derive profit from the opening-up of markets and the opportunities to secure market shares offered by the new technologies. Reflecting on the parallels that can be drawn between military and oligopolistic strategies, Rothschild[81] argues that the theory of oligopoly should take into account Clausewitz's "Principles of War". Chesnais[82] describes "world-wide oligopoly" as "the sphere of rivalry" determined by the relationships of mutual dependency linking the small number of firms and groups of firms that have succeeded – in a particular industry or complex of industries with a common generic technology – in acquiring and maintaining a position of true competition; since each competitor knows its rivals the competition among them is pitiless. Perroux observes the mutual incompatibility of the plans of the major companies and the importance for them to obtain access to the natural resources of the developing countries. Many of these are exploited under conditions which reflect the purposes of the international oligopolies rather than the wishes of the markets, in developed as well as developing countries; this raises the question of the attitude of the States in which those markets are located.[83] Donahue[84] writes that the world has become a huge bazaar; he too expresses concern at the attitudes of governments of developing countries which are forced to "place" their manpower by artificially depressing prices and wages, and to adopt conciliatory attitudes in order to attract foreign direct investment and to avert the flight of capital from excessively burdensome taxes or regulations.

Time and time again the neo-liberals have highlighted the "advantages" which they claim the developing countries enjoy in terms of penetration of new technologies and methods of organization through the transfer of resources effected by the multinationals; time and time again, they have denounced the functional incapacity of the State, which they hold to be the principal source of inefficiencies and disfunctioning. North[85] goes so far as to assert that public institutions are doomed to collapse, since they are victims of the appetites of a bureaucracy concerned exclusively with its own interests and under attack from interest groups seeking to lay hands on the machinery of government; and that, consequently, it is up to private interests to resist those pressures.

Time and time again, too, the theoreticians of dependency have argued that, although capitalism is a powerful stimulant to growth in countries at the centre, it inevitably leads to under-development and poverty[86] in those at the periphery. They therefore recommend the pursuit of policies directed towards the abolition of dependence, even – in the eyes of some[87] – in compliance with the rules of international capitalism.

In 1994, an UNCTAD census found throughout the world 37,000 multinational and similar enterprises, with some 200,000 subsidiaries; they control one third of world production. In 1999 that same UNCTAD identified 60,000 multilateral corporations with over 500,000 foreign subsidiaries; they were the locomotives of the world-wide system of integrated production, accounting for one quarter of its production. The diminishing power of the State in face of international agents of this kind – numerous and power-ful – rivals but capable of forming alliances, is a fact. Their ability to think and act without thought for social and political requirements – except under compulsion – with "their eyes fixed on world mar-kets", is also a fact; the great majority of the men and women who inhabit the world are "invisible to them".[88] When dealing with States these companies follow strategies which vary according to the time and the place but are always coordinated; it is they who decide, sometimes in co-operation with the political authorities, on transfers of techniques, choices of supplier markets, outlets for their products and sites for their distribution centres.[89]

One thing is certain: over-simplification is to be avoided. The relations between the State and the multinationals are much more complex in developing countries than doctrinaire economists and theoreticians make out. Goldstein demonstrates this in a very inter-esting comparative study.[90]

In the Latin America countries, the multinationals invest in the most sophisticated, and nearly always the least competitive, sectors; the State invests in industries producing intermediate goods; and national capitalists invest in niches, where their ability to adapt to local conditions (knowledge of distribution channels, favoured access to the local political class) makes them ideal partners for for-eign enterprises. In Eastern Asia the multinationals are subject to stricter State control, public enterprises play a more dynamic role in the accumulation process, and public policy promotes the for-mation of large-scale diversified groups which have to prove them-selves competitive in international markets instead of contenting themselves with the extra profits accruing from their advantageous position in the home market.

In Eastern Asia the public sector is much more efficient than in Latin America. The principal reasons are certainly the greater inde-pendence of governments vis-à-vis the interests of industrialists, landowners and workers where these clash with government poli-cies, and also the considerable resources devoted to orientating investment. Furthermore, it should not be forgotten that at the end of the Second World War most of the larger firms in Eastern Asia were Japanese. They were nationalized, leaving no room for the formation of a capitalist class with interests of its own; in addition, they were placed under centralized management and subjected to recruitment policies of a nature to isolate the bureaucracy from political pressures. Nor should one forget the strategic locations of certain countries, and the interest of the West in sustaining their development and their regimes. In contrast, the military leaders in Latin America were more interested in combating real or supposed enemies in their own territory and consolidating their dictatorships.

The multinational economic and financial powers have no regard whatsoever for State frontiers. However, today the chorus of denunciation of imperialism is somewhat muted; the belief that it is the State's responsibility to "orchestrate" development is losing ground in Asia, the Middle East and Latin America. States are happy to receive foreign investment; they even compete fiercely to attract it. The multinationals play on the diversity of the policies of States; they exploit taxation or social differences; and they are increasingly concerned with political stability, securing complicity through corruption where necessary. The relinquishment by the State of some of its vital functions – even during structural adjustment programmes – not only jeopardizes human development but also undermines the basis of economic development through the markets, which is claimed to be the road to a solution.

The countries which have remained least open to multinationals, or which have controlled them most strictly, are today the ones best placed to negotiate with them transfers of technology in association with national capital and to create national enterprises on which the government can exert pressure for development purposes. The multinationals remain attracted by the potentialities of numerous markets situated in developing countries and the possibility of obtaining, through their subsidiaries or by subcontracting, results comparable in terms of productivity and quality with those obtained in developed countries, but at a lesser cost in wages, social charges and taxes. Thus the difficulty of ensuring governability, at regional as well as State level, is far from overcome. Consequently a new approach must be devised.

During the 1970s the idea was advanced that the multinationals should comply with the development "plans" still in force in certain host countries at the time. In its third "Report"[91] the Club of Rome expressed the desirability of compliance with a code of conduct which would ensure that they did not "recolonize" but instead would meet the most urgent needs of the peoples of the countries in which they established themselves. The subjects covered by the code were to include issues of ownership and control, financial flows, locally added value, the balance of payments, theoretical and applied research, marketing of techniques, employment and labour standards, consumer protection, competition, taxation, information and also non-interference in the internal affairs of States. The Club of Rome also envisaged the creation of international public enterprises, greater co-operation among the governments of developing countries to counterbalance the power of the enterprises, and supervision of the multinationals' statutes by an international or supranational body, which would also be responsible for taxing their profits.

The multinationals are caught up in a dynamic of internationalization which pressures them into seizing every opportunity to accumulate and enhance the value of their capital (and also to affirm their power); they are "globalizing" themselves in the sense that they are seeking to produce and sell throughout the world.[92] Within their directly global strategies, technology plays an essential role; at the same time, the increasing preponderance of the tertiary sector in economies gives additional impetus to a globalization based on the internationalization of production, but less on exchanges of physical goods, since services cannot be exported in the same way as goods. The margin of manoeuvre of the multinationals vis-à-vis governments has widened. They are still dependent on demand in the markets of the host countries and on the policies of the latter's governments; but their strategy of flexible delocalization and deterritorialization allows them to engage in arbitrages between countries, while the concentration of their efforts on technology, along with the obligation on States not to fall behind and become marginalized, strengthen the multinationals' hand. One might, writes Andreff[93], go so far as to say that the governments of the host countries are set in competition with one another by the multinationals, which themselves remain "footloose" – free as the air.

The conclusion of the Uruguay Round in 1993-94 and the creation of the WTO deferred indefinitely consideration of the idea once put forward that a World Authority should be established within the United Nations to ensure that multinational firms did not resort to monopolistic and restrictive practices, particularly to the detriment of developing countries. The Treaty of Marrakesh (1994) established a disputes-settlement body, to which developing countries seem to have recourse more frequently than they did to the

GATT in earlier years; but, although some of these countries complain that the new WTO is dominated by the G-7 member countries, the problem of the multinationals no longer seems of primary concern. When the United States raised the question of labour standards at the first WTO ministerial conference (Singapore, December 1996), the only reply it received was a commitment from member countries to "observe basic internationally recognized labour standards" at a time when the scandal of the exploitation of labour by American multinationals in Indonesia, the Philippines and the Southern Marianas had broken more than once. The matter was thus referred back, somewhat inelegantly, to ILO. The question as phrased by Andreff thus remains open: is the world economy to be dominated by a few gigantic imperialist trusts (Kautsky, Hilferding) or placed under the rule of a few hundred multinational firms which have become "cosmos societies" (Galbraith)?

6. INTERVENTION – CONTROVERSIAL BUT NECESSARY

Badie[94] observes that national sovereignty is firmly clinging on to life notwithstanding the fact that States increasingly sign treaties, and in so doing undertake by definition to respect their international commitments, even setting them above their own laws. It has perhaps escaped him that although they "sign" international treaties, States are hardly open to any "interference" in their internal affairs precisely because they are "sovereign", and that ratification of a convention is no guarantee of compliance with it.

Throughout the 1980s the idea of "intervention" evoked a widespread response. This was due to the extension of measures for the protection of human rights, the emergence of humanitarian movements unhampered by cumbersome bureaucratic procedures, and the reactions of public opinion (especially in the West), sensitized by the vision of events. The international community has been obliged to admit that the sacrosanct principle of sovereignty must give way to the extension of its competence to include "threats to human life" and "offences to human dignity", whether they arise from natural catastrophes or similar emergency situations (General Assembly Resolution (43) 131 of 8 December 1992) or "threats to peace and international security" (Security Council resolution (43) 794 of 3 December 1992).

It has been claimed that "humanitarianism" is liable to revive the ever-renascent dream of the replacement of politics by morals.[95] It has also been asserted that humanitarian assistance is capable of "invalidating the distinction between sphere of competence and international legal order".[96] The right of intervention is transcending all boundaries; anything concerning the protection of humans (labour, health, education, culture) or the milieu humans live in (environment) – and thus, in the forefront, economic and social affairs – falls within its scope. What concerns us here is the oft-repeated observation that intervention is always a sign of failure and that consequently there is an obligation to prevent rather than attempt to repair – to serve life and to avoid death; for those are the real issues. If governance did not seek that end, it would be a hypocrisy.

Intergovernmental organizations have proliferated; they are constituted and founded by States and directed by representatives of governments with power to act on behalf of those States.[97] Their role in "governance" should be neither overstated nor underestimated, but the reforms already mentioned should expand that role by enabling them to fulfil their functions more effectively.

The functional organizations enjoy sovereign power with regard to the provision of benefits and services falling within the ambit of their constitutional objectives – the provision of credits to developing countries within an economic and technical assistance programme (UNDP), the provision of health equipment and medicines to those countries (WHO), the improvement of their agriculture (FAO), assistance in the educational, scientific and cultural fields (UNESCO) or the establishment of employment policies (ILO). Their decisions are effective against States which consider that they have been unfairly denied the benefit of those services, and there is no right of appeal.

In addition, WHO has genuine regulatory powers in the form of international sanitary regulations issued by it. These come into force without prior acceptance by governments; in such cases the rule of law is established by an international organization on a strictly majority basis. However, States may exempt themselves from such regulations by giving notice to the Director-General, within a specific time-limit, that they accept the regulation with reservations or reject it.

The World Bank and the IMF have much more substantial powers, as was seen earlier when mention was made of the "conditions" they impose on countries seeking assistance and the criticisms to which those conditions give rise.

In the great majority of cases the resolutions or recommendations adopted by specialized international organizations have no
binding effect; nor do any sanctions exist in the event of non-com-
pliance. In this connection the special case of the conventions and
recommendations adopted by the International Labour Conference
deserve examination. They are not the outcome of a diplomatic
negotiation, but the fruit of protracted preparatory work by the
ILO. However, once ratified by a Member State, a convention
acquires the same legal status as any international treaty; recommendations, on the other hand, are designed solely to serve as
"guidelines" for government action and consequently do not constitute international commitments. The conventions are submitted
to national authorities for conversion into domestic legislation or
measures of other kinds, but there is no obligation of subsequent
ratification; their legal "value" is thus weakened, since many States
"fail" to ratify them. The role of the ILO clearly requires redefinition to enable it to intervene preventively and to call for the intervention of other bodies (such as an international labour court or a
specialized section of the International Court of Justice in The
Hague) able not only to conduct investigations but also to take measures ranging from simple pressure to the issue of binding rulings.[98]

Coverage of some fields – such as ecology – is far from satisfactory.

In that field a duty of intervention has been recognized without
the establishment of any international authority with powers to
ensure that the times when "anyone could do anything anywhere"
are past. At the Hague Conference in 1989 the time was considered ripe for such a step. Although the "Charter of the Earth"
established the principle of ecological management of the planet,
the texts drawn up by the Rio Conference either consisted of mere
declarations establishing the responsibilities of producer and consumer countries – without mentioning any monitoring of the South
by the North and relying on the good sense of exporters (of forestry
products, for example); or established a simple moral commitment
on the part of signatory countries without fixing any precise targets
or binding deadlines (e.g., for climate); or granted freedom of
access to the results of research into technologies, transfers and
technical co-operation, but without stipulating any practical measures (relating, for example, to biodiversity).

Since the Rio Conference the subject of the environment has
continued to be governed by the conventional mechanisms of international law within which the binding texts are those negotiated,
signed, ratified and implemented by States. The declarations of

intent on tropical forests and Agenda 21 – a catalogue of non-binding legal recommendations – form a body of "soft law" made up of directives and guidelines in respect of which States merely commit themselves to make efforts in a particular direction.

As for the halting steps taken towards international co-operation on environment policies which seemed to be promised by the protocol concerning the reduction of emissions of greenhouse gases concluded at the Kyoto Summit in 1997, the failure of the 1998 Buenos Aires Conference has highlighted the limitations on that co-operation: after two weeks of tense discussions the 161 participating countries merely adopted a text deferring decisions until the next summit. The United States and the European Union were unable to agree, and the developing countries are waiting for the industrialized countries to begin to reduce their own emissions.

It should also be mentioned that certain international organizations experience a loss of credibility which finds expression in temporary or lasting withdrawals following the formulation of positions – considered by some as "slippage" – that have turned their organs into ideological fortresses. Examples are the withdrawal of the United States from the ILO in 1977 and from UNESCO in 1985, or the withdrawal of the United Kingdom from UNESCO at the same time[99] – but to which it returned in 1997.

When the area of action is not structured in the form of a State, it is not an easy task to be the agent of stable and voluntary co-operation enjoying a broad consensus among States and to bring about an adjustment in national sovereignties that can serve as a basis for international relations. A world (or regional) economic organization governed by law in such a way that partner States observe the same rules and possess the same tools is an efficient one. From this standpoint, without a judge there cannot be genuine globalization, or any possibility of intervention which is in conformity with the interests of all the nations and is not detrimental to some of them. A world-wide law which provides for no constraints or sanctions will inevitably be breached continually or be the subject of endless disputes over interpretation.

It may be that, considered from this standpoint, governability should be envisaged at the "regional" rather than the "world" level. The example of the European Union deserves study in this connection.

It constitutes a legal order in the sense that it has normative powers, through directives, and judicial bodies (for instance, the

European Court of Justice, which serves as a court of first instance) which ensure compliance with the law in the interpretation and enforcement of treaties and of implementing regulations; in addition, in certain cases these judicial bodies may be addressed by enterprises and associations of enterprises or private legal persons as well as by governments or the Commission. Although initially conceived as having a technical role in the harmonization of national legislations, the European Court of Justice, after a period during which the major rulings were issued, has been primarily concerned with contributing to equilibrium in the distribution of tasks between Member States and the Union. It resembles in several respects the Supreme Court in a federal State and has established itself as a major institution by its clear and coherent vision of Community unification, its stands on shortcomings in the decision-making process within States, its work on the formal drafting of principles and its interventions as a supervisory authority over national judges, modifying or correcting their questions, rectifying their reasonings and informing decisions in a more or less imperative fashion.[100]

The European Convention on Human Rights is the only legal instrument, apart from the United Nations Charter, which gives an international body a right of intervention in order to monitor respect for human rights and, where appropriate, to sanction violations thereof. It established the European Court of Human Rights, which is responsible for safeguarding human rights and fundamental freedoms. That Court issues reasoned judgements which are final and binding on Member States; its competence extends to disputes between a private individual and a foreign government, or even the government of the individual's own country. Gradually "European" law is superseding national laws in fields where fundamental principles are at issue. There is an enormous difference between this situation and that resulting from the procedures instituted by the 1966 Covenants on economic, social and cultural rights and on civil and political rights respectively, which are primarily concerned with the settlement of disputes between States. There is, it is true, an optional protocol annexed dealing with the rights of appeal of individuals and designed to facilitate the amicable settlement of disputes between an individual and a foreign State; but there is no provision for recourse against violations by a State of the individual rights of that State's nationals.[101]

Paradoxically, Delmas-Marty[102] alleges that formalization of human rights is at the origin of the disorder; he considers that the vagueness of most of those rights makes it easy for courts and governments to interpret them as they wish in the light of their own value systems. The lack of any universal agreement on the "values" which underlie human rights, and on what their content should be, and the fact that to ensure respect for principles it does not suffice to proclaim them, make for caution. Today the issue is one of complete overhaul of the ranking of standards in international relations. Badie[103] sees in this field a shift from sovereignty towards responsibility. In his view, to avert "slippage" towards the triumph over values of the utilitarian, the technical and above all, of money, responsibility must become the new principle governing the organization of international life.

The emergence of the humanitarian factor has been that of a new ethical conscience and of a form of citizenship transcending State frontiers and the laws which ensure their coexistence with a greater or lesser degree of success.[104] As Sfeir-Younis reminds us: "Underlying any paradigm there is a set of values and a system of beliefs which form its kernel." Francis Blanchard adds that, in a development context, the new paradigm must "rest on the values of justice and freedom enshrined in the Universal Declaration of Human Rights". There can be no governability on either a worldwide or a regional plane without peace, the first pillar of which is justice.

---

[1]R. Vallée: *Cognition et systèmes*, Lyons, L'interdisciplinaire, 1995, p. 23.

[2]*Vers une éthique politique*, Paris, Editions de la Maison des Sciences de l'Homme, 1987.

[3]Cinq ans avant, *Ramsès 96*, Paris, Dounod, 1996, p. 5.

[4]R. Passet: "En amont de la crise financière de l'argent, un système contre nature", *Partage*, December 1998.

[5]B. Perret: *Les nouvelles frontières de l'argent*, Paris, Seuil, 1999.

[6]P. Ladrière, C. Gruson: *Ethique et gouvernabilité*, Paris, PUF, 1992, p. 92.

[7]*The State in a changing world*, op. cit., p. 125 et seq.

[8]In the West Bank and the Gaza Strip some 1,200 non-governmental organizations provide 60 per cent of primary health care and as much as half of secondary and tertiary care, as well as furnishing most agricultural, low-cost housing and micro-credit services.

[9]E.H. Volsan: *Community development programs and rural local government. Comparative case studies of India and the Philippines*, New York, Praeger, 1970. Haq M. Nurul: *Village development in Bangladesh*, Bangladesh Academy for Rural Development, 1973.

L. Pasara, J. Santistevan: "Industrial communities and trade unions in Peru: a preliminary analysis", *International Labour Review*, August-September 1973, p. 127.

[10]For example, in a village in Enugu State in Nigeria, the development committee has a management board whose members represent the entire village. It is responsible for numerous infrastructure and development projects of direct interest to the community. The "Brazilian communities" – composed of some 1,500 out of a total of 6,500 local authorities co-ordinating previously existing and, therefore, low-cost programmes – are also worthy of study.

[11]*The State in a changing world*, *op. cit.*, p. 130.

[12]"De l'existence de points de passage obligatoires pour une politique de développement", *Economies et Sociétés*, Feb. 1983, pp. 247-8.

[13]While digging a well is a local task, water cannot usually be supplied without action at a certain level, and the same is true of the establishment of an properly equipped health centre.

[14]In 1961 Greece had concluded with the Community an agreement stipulating its entry in due time. Then came the dictatorship of the colonels (1967-1974). In 1981, Greece's entry appeared to be the logical consequence of its return to democracy. The same was true of Spain and Portugal once they had rid themselves of their dictatorships.

[15]The clause of the Final Act of the Helsinki Conference (1975) relating to respect for human rights and fundamental freedoms, while tempered by mention of the principle of non-intervention in the internal affairs or external affairs that fall to the competence of another participating State, greatly helped the revolt of democrats in totalitarian States. See M. Merle: *Bilan*, *op. cit.*, p. 86.

[16]R. Leveau: "Vers une société civile internationale?", *Relations internationales*, 1988, N° 54.

[17]With the 1986 Single European Act, everything to do with community "legislation" (directives for the realization of the single market, harmonization of national laws) is subject to procedures that confer a right of amendment on the Parliament; but the European Community Council is unanimous and has the last word. The Maastricht Treaty established joint decision-making. A rule is adopted only if it is not opposed by the Council or the Parliament. What is more, by the proposal of a motion of censure carried by two thirds of the votes expressed, the Parliament can reverse a decision of the Commission. Once the Commission has been formed by the governments, it must be approved by a vote in the Parliament.

[18]*The Global Neighborhood*, New York, Oxford University Press, 1995.

[19]*Op. cit.*, p. 93.

[20]Moreover, how can one distinguish, among the thousands of NGOs, those whose action is really beneficial and those that are merely a façade; or between, on the one hand, those which, recognized by the people, intelligently address their real needs and bring pressure to bear on governments to ensure that their policies and priorities are geared to meeting

those needs and, on the other, those that are less independent of the countries' governments than they claim? Even so, the NGOs' voices should be heard in any dialogue centred on the inhabitants rather that the governments of the developing countries negotiating assistance. cf. *Human Development Report 1993*, Chapter 5.

[21]*Vers la paix perpétuelle, 1795*, Paris, PUF, 1958.

[22]*La démocratie. Essai synthéthique*, Brussels, Office de Publicité, 1956, p. 114.

[23]*Op. cit.*, pp. 16 and 169 et seq.

[24]*World Development Report 1995, op. cit.*, p. 3.

[25]*Ibid.*, 1994, *op. cit.*, p. 84.

[26]*Human Development Report 1995, op. cit*, p. 135.

[27]*Ibid.*, 1991, New York, Oxford, Oxford University Press, p. 10.

[28]A. Waterston: Un approccio operativo alla programmazione dello sviluppo. *Rivista di politica economica*, February 1970.

[29]A. Waterston. *Development planning: lessons of experience*, Baltimore, Johns Hopkins Press, 1965.

[30]See below, p. 181.

[31]J. Tinbergem: *The design of development*, United Nations Economic Development Institute, Baltimore, Johns Hopkins Press, 1958, and *Development planning*, London, World University Library, 1967.

[32]*Op. cit.*, Part 2.

[33]H. Bartoli: *Economie au service de la Vie, op. cit.* pp. 330-331.

[34]*Ramsès 83-84*, Paris, Economica, 1984, p. 120.

[35]"Le FMI et la BIRD, tels qu'ils se voient et tels qu'ils se donnent à voir", *Economie appliquée*, No. 4, pp. 815-816.

[36]"Indicators of Environmental Quality and Quality of Life", *Reports and papers in the social sciences*, UNESCO, Paris, 1979, No. 38.

[37]The various weighting systems tested showed slight differences in the results achieved without weighting, thereby confirming the indicator's soundness.

[38]See the technical notes appearing each year in the *Human Development Report*.

[39]M. Genné, La satisfaction des besoins essentiels des plus pauvres. In *L'Economie : une science pour l'homme et la société. Mélanges en l'honneur d'Henri Bartoli*, Paris, Publications de la Sorbonne, 1998, pp. 307-319.

[40]*Human Development Report*, New York, Oxford, Oxford University Press, 1998, p. 18.

[41]Introduction to the special issue of the *International Social Science Journal* (March 1995) devoted to the measurement and evaluation of development, published for the Copenhagen Social Summit.

[42]*Economie et civilisation*, Paris, Editions ouvrières, 1956, Vol. I, pp. 135-145.

[43]Life expectancy at birth, mortality among children under five, fertility, adult literacy, average number of years of schooling, daily calorie intake, population with access to safe drinking water, real GDP per capita.

[44]Thus greatly enlarging the field of observation without, however, permitting immediate comparison with the developed countries United Nations documents classify as "industrialized".

[45]*World Development Report*, World Bank, Washington, 1995.

[46]G. Standing: *The Human development enterprise; seeking flexibility, security, and efficiency*, ILO, Geneva, 1996.

[47]M. Hollard: *Comptabilités sociales en temps de travail*, Grenoble, Presses universitaires, 1978.

[48]Thus the PUL (percentage utilization of labour) indicator of Smith-Gavin and A.J. Bennett, endorsed by the Department of Employment and the Social Science Research Council, and assisted by the Leicester Polytechnic and the Aston University Management Centre, which, using a large panel of enterprises and over 130,000 wage-earners, calculated the exact number of "standard times" worked by workers in the unit of chronological and analysed variations throughout the 1980s.

[49]As early as 1975 an example of "grid" was furnished by the Aix-en-Provence labour economics and sociology laboratory, in which 16 factors were evaluated on the basis of 75 criteria that reduced them to standardized components that led to exclusively objective measurements. F. Guélaud, M.N. Beauchesne, J. Gautrat, G. Roustang: *Pour une analyse des conditions du travail ouvrier dans l'entreprise*, Paris, A. Colin, 1975.

[50]The risk being that certain departments of the enterprise might appropriate the grids for purposes of integration and use as an additional post weighting system.

[51]A. Exiga, F. Piotet, R. Sainsaulieu: *L'analyse sociologique des conditions du travail*, ANACT, Paris, 1981.

[52]M. Bartoli: *L'intensité du travail*, Université de Grenoble II, Doctoral thesis in economics, 1980, Vol. 2, pp. 537-554.

[53]S. Volkoff: "Le vieillissement de la population au travail : diagnostic et moyens d'action", in *Analyses et documents économiques*, April 1995.

[54]N. Frigul, H. Brélin, L. Aussel, A. Thebaud-Mouy, I. Metenier: "Atteintes à la santé et exclusion professionnelle", in *Travail et emploi*, 1993, No. 56. R. Livraghi: "Effetti della disoccupazione sul benessere individuale e familiare nel breve e nel lungo periodo" in L. Frey (ed.), *La disoccupazione nel lungo periodo*, Bologna, Il Mulino, 1997. See also *Souffrance et précarités au travail, op. cit.*

[55]Dr Martinet: "Recherche d'une méthode de quantification des coûts humains du travail", *Séminaire d'économie du travail*, CNRS and Université de Paris I Panthéon-Sorbonne, May 1972, mimeograph.

[56]P.C. Mahalanobis: *The approach to operational research to planning in India*, London, Asia Publishing House, 1963. Charles Prou: *Etablissement des programmes en économie sous-développée*, Paris, Dunod, 1964.

[57]Initial topics selected: restructuring and transformation of labour; economics without ethics?; health and work; work and integration.

[58]Humana divides his indicators into five groups of rights and freedoms. Six questions deal with the right to "do", 12 with absence of constraints, 10 with freedoms, seven with legally recognized rights and five with individual rights. The scale runs from zero (no rights) to three (rights guaranteed). The findings require interpretation. Cf. *World Guide to Human Rights*, New York, Facts on File, 1986.

[59]*Human Development Report 1991, op. cit.*, pp. 19-21 and 98-99.

[60]H. Bouguinat: *L'économie mondiale à découvert*, Paris, Calmann-Lévy, 1985, p. 165.

[61]M. Byé, G. de Bernis: *Relations économiques internationales*, Paris, Dalloz, 1987, fifth edition, pp. 1145 et seq.

[62]G. De Bernis: "Régulation du développement dans le contexte de la 'mondialisation'", in *Economie et sociétés*, Jan. 1998, p. 156.

[63]See above, pp. 84 f.f.

[64]The purchase by a foreign company of a debt on the secondary market; presentation by the company of the debt at the central bank of the debtor country for repayment in local currency at less than the face value; investment of the amount obtained in the debtor country. The central bank has reduced its dollar liabilities and the foreign company has acquired an asset in the country of the debtor; but there is an increase in the money supply and in domestic indebtedness.

[65]Purchase by international ecological groups of debt at below face value in the financial markets; these groups return the amount of the debt to the government of the debtor country in local currency to be spent on the environment.

[66]At the end of 1987 the J.P. Morgan Bank, with the cooperation of the United States Treasury Department, accepted the exchange of old debt for a new and guaranteed debt. The operation took place in March 1988; $ 3.6 billion were exchanged for $ 2.5 billion (a ratio of 1.43:1).

[67]It was in fact for the time being only. In 1994 the confidence of investors was shaken by public disturbances. This, together with a rise in interest rates in the United States, caused a drain on exchange reserves. Aid in an amount of $ 50 billion was needed – $ 20 billion from the United States, $ 18 billion from the IMF, $ 10 billion from the World Bank and $ 3 billion from various banks in the main industrialized countries. The country fell into severe recession in 1995.

[68]"Unbearable" was assessed in relation to export earnings. Initially a rate of 200-250% was adopted for the debt/exports ratio and a rate of 20-25% for the debt-service/exports ratio. The UNDP and Germany have proposed that the rates be reduced to 100-150% and 10-15% respectively.

[69]IMF: *Economic Outlook*, May 1995.

[70]F. Praussello: "La limitazione del credito internazionale e i finanziamenti esterni nei paesi in via di sviluppo", in *Rivista italiana degli economisti*, 1966, No. 2.

[71]For example, those conducted by I. S. Saltz in 75 developing countries during the 1970s. In his view the explanation is to be found in the

price distortions caused by direct foreign investments and the ensuing mis-allocations of resources. The prices of factors drift away from their "shadow prices" in favour of capital; local manpower is underutilized and consumption falls. The result, combined with the monopoly power of the multinationals, leads to a levelling-off of production. See "The negative correlation between foreign direct investment and economic growth in the Third World: theory and evidence" in *Rivista internazionale di scienze economiche e commerciali*, July 1992.

[72]*Alternative ou complémentarité entre endettement et investissement direct à l'étranger dans des pays en développement*, Paris, ISMEA, Cahiers de recherche, 1987.

[73]Report of the symposium, Geneva, ILO, 1989; B. Balkenhol: "Savings, credit and the poor: what has the ILO to do with the financial sector?", in *International Labour Review*, 1991, No. 6.

[74]Women, refugees, artisans in urban areas, rural promotion, etc.

[75]IMF: *World Economic Outlook*, May 1998.

[76]B. Eichengreen, M. Mussa, G. Delle'Arricia, E. Detragiache, G.M. Milesi-Ferretti, A. Tweedie: *Capital account liberalization: theoretical and practical aspects*, IMF, Washington, 1998.

[77]The *encaje* system practised by Chile since 1991 is often cited as an example. Every investor must deposit with the central bank a sum equiva-lent to a certain percentage of the capital he invests in the country (initially 30%, reduced to 10% in August 1998). The deposit does not bear interest and is returned after one year. It is possible to withdraw from that obliga-tion by paying a tax equivalent to the rate of interest on the sum deposited. The system is inexpensive for a person investing for a considerable period but penalizes a person making short-term deposits and withdrawals.

[78]"Peut-on contrôler les taux de change?", in *Economies et sociétés*, Nov. 1995, p. 141. Tobin considered that the levying of an international tax on spot currency transactions (including currency remitted under term contracts and options) would be a dissuasive factor of a nature to check speculative capital movements as well as a source of revenue for the inter-national agencies; but Camdessus termed it "economically incorrect" on the grounds that it would introduce distortions into capital allocation and reduce the efficiency of international markets. Speech at Amsterdam Free University, 28 November 1995.

[79]It should be noted that the recycling and laundering of drug, prosti-tution, corruption and sect money would be more difficult.

[80]D. Salvatore: *La finanza internazionale sul finire del secolo*, Arezzo, Banca Popolare dell'Etruria e del Lazio, Studi i Ricerche, 1998, p. 148.

[81]"Price Theory and Oligopoly", in *Economic Journal*, Sep. 1947.

[82]*La mondialisation du capital*, Paris, Syros, 1994, pp. 24-25, 71.

[83]"Trois outils pour l'étude du sous-développement", in *Economies et sociétés*, June-July 1978, p. 1252.

[84]The perspective of labour. International labour standards and global economic integration. Proceedings of a symposium, Washington, D.C., July 1994.

[85]"Government and the cost of change in history", in *Journal of Economic History*, 1984, No. 2.

[86]K. Griffin and J. Gurley: "Radical analysis of imperialism, the Third World and the transition of socialism", a survey article, in *Journal of Economic Literature*, 1985, No. 3.

[87]D. Bennett and K. Sharpe: *Transnational corporations versus the State*, Princeton, Princeton University Press, 1985, p. 9.

[88]R. Barnett and J. Cavanagh: *Global dreams: imperial corporations and the New World Order*, New York, Simon and Schuster, 1994, p. 31.

[89]Is it appreciated that transnational and multinational enterprises pay very little in tax? Three quarters of those established in the United States pay no taxes there. American multinationals established abroad resort to accounting devices which enable them to declare their profits in the countries where taxes are lowest and their losses in those where taxes are highest, depriving the United States Treasury of between $ 12 and $ 50 billion in revenue! See J. Shields: *Toward overseas investment*, Foreign Policy in Focus, Washington, D.C., Jan. 1998.

[90]"Stato e mercato nella politica economica dello sviluppo", in *Rivista internazionale di scienza economica e commerciale*, Jan. 1994.

[91]J. Tinbergen (ed.): *Reshaping the International Order*, New York, Dutton and Co., 1976.

[92]W. Andreff: *Les multinationales globales*, Paris, La Découverte, 1996.

[93]"Peut-on empêcher la surenchère des politiques d'attractivité à l'égard des multinationales globales?", Xth GDR-CNRS symposium, *Economie et finances internationales quantitatives*, Pau, Jan. 1998.

[94]*Un monde sans souveraineté. Les Etats entre ruse et responsabilité*, Paris, Fayard, 1999.

[95]P. Moreau-Defarges: *Un monde d'ingérence*, Paris, Presses de Sciences Po, 1998.

[96]P.M. Dupuy: "Un droit nouveau. Urgence pour l'urgent", in *Le Monde des débats*, Jan. 1993.

[97]M. Merle: *Sociologie des relations internationales*, *op. cit.*, pp. 359-384.

[98]The Convention concerning Freedom of Association and Protection of the Right to Organise (9 July 1948, No. 87) is a significant case. Its application involves the submission of reports by governments and the preparation of a comprehensive report submitted to the International Labour Conference each year. A committee of experts makes any comments it considers necessary. Difficult cases are referred to another committee of experts, concerned with the application of standards. It is possible to invoke an appeals procedure enshrined in the Constitution; "complaints" are referred to the Committee on Freedom of Association, which was established to conduct preliminary examinations of cases submitted to the fact-finding and Conciliation Commission on freedom of association and which, unlike the latter before the establishment of the Committee, may investigate complaints without the prior agreement of

the government concerned and may also investigate complaints against countries which have not ratified an ILO convention on the subject.

A system of this kind has led to substantial progress; but violations of freedom of association continue to be referred to the Committee on Freedom of Association, and major political changes are often necessary in the countries concerned before the observations made by the supervisory bodies are heeded. See the special issue of the *International Labour Review*, "Labour rights, human rights", 1998, No. 2.

[99]P. de Senarclens: "La dérive de l'UNESCO", in *Etudes internationales*, Dec. 1985.

[100]*Ramsès 1993, op. cit.*, pp. 386-388.

[101]M. Merle: *Bilan des relations internationales. op. cit.*, pp. 80-81. The North American agreement on cooperation in labour matters of August 1993, which complements the free-trade agreement of August 1992 (NAFTA), also deserves study in this context. It refers to national standards laid down in national labour legislation and contains a commitment on the part of States to promote a series of provisions in domestic legislation. It also provides for trade sanctions under certain conditions in the event of failure to respect some of them (child labour, minimum wages, occupational safety and health). Although neither freedom of association nor collective bargaining are mentioned (significant omissions), there is in those instruments a possible starting-point for further developments.

[102]*Trois défis pour un droit mondial*, Paris, Seuil, 1998.

[103]*Op. cit.*

[104]P. Bouretz: "Entre éthique, juridique et politique; le triomphe humanitaire", in *Esprit*, July 1994, p. 96.

CHAPTER 5

Economic thought renewed and open to changes in knowledge

Throughout its formative stage and in its theoretical orientations as well as in its standard-setting concerns, development economics has been under the influence of economy dynamics studies and growth models. Harrod's "prototype" model (1948) is present in the approaches adopted by Lewis (1954) and Nurkse (1953); and the relationships between growth rates, the propensity to save and the capital coefficient formed the basis of more than one development programme during the 1950s.

Gradually the gap between the two approaches widened and the neo-classical models predominated, in particular the Ramsey (1928)–Solow (1956)–Clark (1917)–Koopmans (1965) model. Technical advance – a "residual" factor identified by empirical research and introduced by Solow into his original model as an exogenous variable, together with capital and labour, in the production function – appeared as a determinant of growth. The basic hypotheses of the neo-classical models, which are becoming increasingly numerous, make their application to countries with the characteristics of developing countries difficult. The idea that technical advance "comes out of the blue"[1] and is freely applicable – with the implication that the growth rates of the different countries should converge – is clearly not in accordance with the facts; furthermore, it leaves little room for manoeuvre in policies seeking to increase the proportion of saving and investment in the national product. The growth theory appears "dead"[2] and the development theory quite inadequate.[3]

The field of research was considerably enriched by the emergence of the new theories (referred to as theories of "endogenous growth") stimulated by the early work of Romer[4] and Lucas.[5] Technical progress, reproduction rates, human capital formation, development research, savings rates and economic policy options were each in turn "endogenized". The principal factors making for growth and capital accumulation were identified, while at the same time it was suggested that the market did not always produce optimum results and that intervention by the State might be necessary and effective.

It is difficult not to be somewhat disconcerted by the banality of all these "discoveries". Taken together, they amount to no more than the "discovery" that any economic and social complex cannot but be multidimensional, with laws and institutions, technology and demography, types and structures of enterprises, distribution of revenue and patrimony, government and a mode of organization of political power, culture and education, etc., each playing its role in the functioning and development of the whole throughout the course of history. One model presupposes a closed economy in order to include public expenditure; another endogenizes the population without taking account of technical advance; still another offers a convex general equilibrium with endogenous growth by human capital accumulation in a public education sector. Yet another is concerned with the impact of fiscal policy on factor allocation, and thereby on endogenous growth, in an economy comprising an "informal" sector. Practically all the definitions of "human capital" take into account only the level of education, ignoring the other dimensions of human development. The element of "sustainability" is not incorporated into the models, and increases in the size of the labour force related to the age pyramid and a high reproduction rate are hardly considered. The automatic assumption that the paths of growth are the paths to complete equilibrium and that those paths are not affected by short-term and medium-term experiments is sufficient to demonstrate the unreality of the proposed theoretical approaches. It reduces them to the status of "parables" capable of throwing some light on the realities of life but not of describing or interpreting them[6]. They certainly cannot provide a basis for the framing of a theory which meets the requirements of development – although, admittedly, certain objectives can be found in models of endogenous growth which form part of those requirements: a narrowing of the gap between the theory of growth and the analysis of the situation in developing countries; an incentive in models to explore problems which, in its initial stages, development economics neglected to study, with the result that adopted policies in line with those models have suffered from multiple errors and shortcomings;[7] and the incorporation of economic policies in growth models to permit evaluation of their effects and to contribute to the definition of the tasks to be assumed by the State within development processes.

But the ambition called for today is completely different. An economy is basically multidimensional and as a consequence complex. The history of economics is made up of periods, each of which has been marked by specific problems and has contained specific challenges. The challenge of the current period in economics, as in the other scientific disciplines, is the issue of complexity.[8]

The entire 1980s was a period of developing awareness of that complexity in life sciences (theories of self-organization of systems), natural sciences (chaos theory), human sciences (theories of knowledge, hermeneutics) and social sciences, even music.[9] In 1987 the United Nations University published "Science et pratique de la complexité".[10] A number of symposia were held in Cerisy, successively covering the subjects of "Self-organization, from physics to politics",[11] "Arguments for a method", based on E. Morin,[12] and "theories of complexity", based on Henri Atlan.[13] In 1998 the first inter-Latin congress on complexity in thought was held in Rio de Janeiro under the auspices of the Association for Complex Thought, UNESCO and the Conjunto Universitario Candido Mendes.[14] Economists joined the movement; in 1982 Nelson and Winter developed an "evolutionary theory of economic change";[15] in 1988 Anderson, Arrow and Pines compiled contributions on "the economy as a complex evolving system";[16] and in France, Aix-Marseilles University III is devoting intense study to the interface between engineering and social sciences (including economics) within a research group on adaptation, systemics and economic complexity (GRASCE).[17]

Applied to the different scientific disciplines, complex thought represents, not the final achievement of scientific advance, but a starting-point for new advances. Similarly, when applied to economics, it does not mean the discarding of the earlier paradigms and of the theories whose construction they have permitted, but instead calls for the construction of an alternative paradigm of a nature to help economic agents to "understand what they are doing and do things which make sense".[18] It refuses to isolate an economy from its environment and from the milieu in which its actions are propagated and thus recognizes its multidimensionality. Parallelling the thinking of the "time" philosophers,[19] it fully accepts the irreversibility of time – that the acts it endeavours to identify and guide inevitably take place in the time context of history.

Aristotle said that when one is seeking the "why" one is in fact seeking why the subject is the attribute of something else.[20] One can also seek to render this mode of production "intelligible". From this standpoint "complex" does not mean "unintelligible" but multiple, tangled, rich in uncertainties and indeterminations, plurivocal and pluridimensional. Intelligence is made for "comprehension" and to "grasp the sense". It renders "explicable" and "comprehensible" that which, on account of its "complexity", is not a priori so. The word "intelligence" comes from the Latin intellegere, which means both "to assemble" and "to choose from among alternatives"; intelligence is the ability to discern the elements of a situation and the relationships interlinking them. As was said earlier, an economy is a "service of life", the true "revealer" of being, of which man, in Heidegger's beautiful image, is "the shepherd". Intelligence must be subordinated to human development.

The world is a world of tasks to be accomplished. What we need is not so much new "theories" to meet the "challenge of complexity" and to "lay a bet without which we lose our raison d'être"[21], as adequate principles of intelligibility.

1. PLURALITY OF CAUSES; ADOPTION OF PRINCIPLES OF INDETERMINATION AND RELATIVITY

Kant considered the principle of causality to be one of the constituent laws of the mind. His position has been challenged, and "a-causality" has been affirmed, the necessary and sufficient condition for science having been judged to be the relative uniformity according to which phenomena are related to one another, which means, consequently, the observation of phenomena. As Duyckaerts says,[22] "we believe in causality because we observe the uniformity of phenomena", i.e., the frequencies relating to a sector of social life, and "because we see a connection between them and what is 'normal'".

Newton saw the universe as a beautifully constructed system obeying a few simple principles: gravitation, attraction, weight. The classical authors tended to accept that the economic "laws" whose existence they affirmed were just as "amoral" as the laws of the physical order. Far from rejecting the notion of causality, they invariably and unconditionally saw in the effect the consequences of the cause. Adam Smith studied the causes of the nature and wealth of nations; Malthus sought those of value or rent. Hume and John Stuart Mill argued that economic "laws" had a causal nature inasmuch as the antecedent (or set of antecedents) was the cause of the phenomenon, either invariably or conditionally.

The gradual shift from causality to legality – the law being considered as the formal expression of the constant relationships of succession or coexistence between interdependent phenomena – leads the probability theory to place the problem of causality and chance at the very centre of the epistemological problems of applied mathematics. In physics, biology and psychology,[23] observation of frequencies is considered as the necessary and sufficient precondition of knowledge, for without that relative uniformity no prediction is possible. The rise in prominence of statistics and the adoption by the burgeoning science of econometrics of the idea that laws are functional relationships between certain empirical facts which cannot be verified once and for all (as would be the case if one accepted the concept of cause while remaining in the field of metaphysical or mathematical *a priori*), but can only be confirmed by certain elements, lead to recognition of the variable and fragmentary nature of the "law"; it is arbitrary, incomplete, invariably approximate, and has only a relative value, since it is confirmed "as a probability".[24]

There is no place for the notion of cause in the theory of general equilibrium propounded by Pareto and Walras. To refer to it would be to sacrifice to subjectivity by choosing one element out of all those which jointly and simultaneously determine one another. Pareto[25] argues that value is expressed neither through cost nor through measurement of satisfaction (what Walras called *ophélimité*), but through the entire set of conditions which must be met for the system to be in equilibrium. For Walras,[26] the "cause" of prices had to be sought within the general problem of equilibrium.

Neither "frequentalist" logic nor the theory of general equilibrium have succeeded in supplanting the notion of "cause" in economics. The world of economics abounds with resonators; it has probably derived benefit from the study of oscillations triggered off and given impetus by erratic shocks, developed into a theory by Frisch,[27] and the writings of Slatsky on the "causal" impact of random phenomena which are the sources of cyclical processes.[28] It also draws strength from observation of coexistence and/or succession correlations and the knowledge of the interactions between variables which we owe to that observation; here the active or operative variable is the one which statistical induction or deduction points to as being capable of explaining the levels and movements of the other variables to which it is correlated.

Wold and Simon actually brought about a revival in causal analysis. Wold observes that, notwithstanding the efforts of certain schools of philosophy to cast doubts on its validity, science cannot do without it, and he sees in the fact that the linkages described in economic theory tend to be "causal" an *a priori* reason to work only on recurrent systems.[29] Simon, for his part, interprets the "causal" relationship as a property of the asymmetry of logico-mathematical structures; the important factor in the "x is the cause of y" relationship being the asymmetry which permits indirect control of y (at least stochastically) by acting on x.

Both in the context of theoretical work on causal imputation and in that of econometric research, the same question arises over and above the difficulties of identifying causal relationships and the deviation caused by the recourse to strictly mathematical notions; namely, how to join to the observations made (duly subjected to criticism on the technical plane) a search for circumstantiated causes (or better, a circumstantiated understanding of causal chains) and a knowledge of the plurivocal nature of the effects.

The order – which statistics and econometrics endeavour, with the utmost difficulty, to distinguish in the meanderings of real life, – is not a "necessary" order; it is the outcome of institutions, rules, behaviour patterns and active agents, all in dependence on the operative attitudes – already constituted or in the process of constitution – of a structure which they themselves organize and develop. If, in concrete terms, one observes more "J" curves than Gauss "bell" curves, this is precisely due to the intervention of social conformity, since the agents are caught up in networks of relationships bearing and receiving unequal information and emitting uncertain anticipations that give rise to the framing of projects. Since all economic and social variables are multidimensional, the linkages which express that dependence give a picture of themselves which leaves in suspense the entity they represent – located where synchrony and diachrony, the system and the process, merge, and able to assume new values and new meanings. No order of size, no relationship is invariable in relation to the milieu, which is a galaxy of "initial data" offering a potential for evolution and transformation, the scale of which varies directly with its degree of openness.

Multidimensionality prohibits the attribution of the origin of any socio-economic process to a single cause. For an economist, "cause" is a highly complex set of positive and negative conditions on which the effect depends or is based, or, better, the set of phenomena which, in shorthand, we may call "effect".[30]

Keynes, who considered the determinist hypothesis "of some slight use", especially in the "moral" sciences (including economics), used the term "probable causes" to designate causes in which there was no implication of necessity and where the antecedents pointed to certain consequences rather than others.[31] In his view, "probability" does not measure a property of the event but a linkage, similar to an implication, which binds that event to the body of knowledge available to the person proposing the probability.[32] This explains the need to relativize all affirmations of causality and to situate them within a conceptual scheme which can throw light on the theoretical and methodological presuppositions of the causal inference.

"History is not determined in a linear fashion", wrote Passet;[33] "the conjunction of the plural, the critical point and the divergence results in unpredictability." This is true; but although it is impossible to "predict" in economics (a fortiori in matters of "development") and the plurality of causes and the plurivocity of effects must be adopted as the first principle of intelligibility, this cannot debar us from trying to "understand".

In this context Moigne comes out in favour of a "new understanding" involving apprehension of the thought in the action and vice versa, i.e., "comprehension" of the action, of its context, of the project inspiring it, of the language and of the other party involved.[34] Morin invites us to accept an "ethic of understanding".[35] We must simultaneously resort to observation of the facts, using the most rigorous scientific methods; to explanation, which relates to an intelligible world in which mind is master; and to comprehension, which presupposes a mutual implication of the subject and the object within a given concrete situation in order to reach a human world. Human beings cannot be confined in a single causal series; they are not "determined" by the material, physical, cultural and moral "data" constituting their existential environment; they are rather "conditioned" by a plurality of determinations and incentives of which they are aware to a greater or lesser extent.

The approach to economics is thus the same as the approach to sociology as understood by Max Weber.[36] Economics is an "interpretative" science the purpose of which is to "understand", through an "interpretative" process, the actions of economic and social agents and to explain their progression and effects "causally". Individuals and groups combine means and ends, evaluate opportunities and determine their roles in the light of their cultures and expectations, motivated by a "meta-rationality" in which the "rational" and the "reasonable" are intermingled. A complex network of interactions develops between the causes and the effects of their actions at both micro- and macro-economic levels. Intelligibility achieved through a search for the cause or causes, for their effect or effects, for their multidirectionality, their exhaustion and their propagation and intelligibility through the senses are complementary. One cannot "understand" without participating, without being "in sympathy" with the subject of study and without mobilizing all one's powers of reasoning and imagination in order to "see" and to "grasp" better.[37]

The second principle of intelligibility required for the renewal of economic thought is that of indetermination. It has incorporated the Newtonian model which, in its final conclusion, raises the human being – the "objective, detached and scientific observer" – to the level of "an omniscient deity who can forecast the future",[38] and accepts that science is inevitably determinist. Economic thought has borrowed the principles of physics and used them in a somewhat ambiguous fashion; it cannot remain trapped within its references when what is known as the "crisis" of determinism has led to recognition of the plurality, multiplicity and relativity of determinisms.[39] Newtonian Man was an observer capable of knowing objective data, of identifying the reasons for things and of offering an explanation of the world, but powerless to influence natural laws. Heisenbergian Man is incapable of forecasting events with certainty or of achieving absolute knowledge; but he does have a genuine power of intervention; he "participates" in the processes of creation and destruction. This is equally true of the agents in economic and social life.

We cannot establish, measure, observe or define with any degree of precision, either a priori or a posteriori, the relationships which link economic magnitudes (price, quantities) with one another and with all the variables characteristic of the environment in which economic and social action are propagated. Thus there exists a logical indetermination which is present in both the spatial coexistence of phenomena and in their development over time and is to be found in both a determinist- and a non-determinist-type universe. It is impossible to circumscribe a socio-economic system in its entirety within our systems of operations, however sophisticated.

There is nothing specific (in the physical sense of the term) in economic realities. One is forced to resort to concepts which are ordered magnitudes rather than measurable parameters. At best, one can in certain cases (when, for instance, errors balance or cancel one another out) establish the degree of logical indetermination by means of probabilities, inasmuch as the latter are calculations of degrees of inexactitude or uncertainty (collective supply and demand can be calculated by means of statistical logic or group theories). It then has to be admitted either that the facts are too numerous to be completely observed (uncertainty of induction) or that, taken in isolation, they cannot be observed with absolute precision (uncertainty of observation). If one refuses to isolate an economy from the universe to which it belongs, the relations between endogeny (the set of economic magnitudes present in any economic system) and exogeny (the variables characterizing the environment in which economic actions are born and propagate themselves) offer a perfect terrain for logical indetermination. It is possible to develop theories concerning the ways in which the latter influence the former in a relatively satisfactory manner, and subject to certain conditions. The same, however, is not true of the reverse.[40]

Contemporary science has exploded the myth of continuity of change over time under the effect of slow and imperceptible transformations. Quantum energy in physics and mutations in biology have swept away determinist evolutionist theories. Economics concerns living beings, who execute and pursue projects in an environment on which they act and to the demands of which they respond, an envrionment which changes and with which they themselves change. The inventive action of human beings becomes manifest in a time-frame which is that of history guiding the evolution of systems in directions which it is practically impossible to predetermine and of which we become aware only after a certain threshold has been crossed, so limited is our awareness.[41] Thus a dynamic indetermination combines with logical indetermination, owing not to the inaccuracy of our observations or the uncertainty of our hypotheses, but to the existence of limits to predictability. Dynamological analysis rightly points to operational projects in all sectors of human activity resting on existing structures, but which could be described as "clusters of aptitudes" stimulating the mind to advance into new areas.[42] From this standpoint, genetic structuralism makes a valuable contribution to knowledge. The introduction

of probabilist notions into the actual conception of economic linkages is not sufficient to reach beyond and remove the logical and
dynamic indetermination which is inevitably related to the fact that
we cannot know all the innumerable variables interacting on one
another and the multiple networks linking them, or to the continual
evolution of human activity, both creative and destructive, at work
in the multidimensional universe of the economy.

An attempt can be made to reduce to a determinist problem one
which is not and seek to use a law of feedback command to correct
observed deviations from an average or desired trajectory; but one
must accept, with Shackle,[43] that an economist must choose
between "rationality" and "time". If he/she chooses the latter,
he/she will have to accept uncertainty and indetermination, and
with them the notion of "non-rational" behaviour as measured
against orthodox criteria, as well as the notion of "potential surprise", which permits the maintenance of a measure of verisimili-
tude and the possibility of obtaining hypothetical results from various conceivable hypotheses. Above all, we must accept Shackle's
assertion that the difficulty in economics is that the future of phenomena "does not have to be discovered... it has to be created".[44]

The entry of the notions of "force" and of contractual "power"
into the theory of contracts highlighted a third form of indetermination – a static one. For many years static indetermination was
treated as a purely academic exercise within the framework of the
theory of prices (bilateral monopoly); but it has found new applications with the presentation of the market economy in terms of
equations when, on account of the degree of the equations, there
are several possible solutions and it is necessary to select those
which are consistent and distinguish them from those which are
purely imaginary. It does not seek to find "the" solution; but it does
permit determination of the boundaries of the space (the "zone of
indetermination") within which the solution will be found. It thus
falls within the province of probabilist and stochastic logic.

Demaria[45], having established the "absolute originality and
unpredictability" of future developments, concludes at the necessity
of introducing into theoretical schematizations a specific "element"
expressing that originality, the structure and substance of which can
only be determined by experience. Perroux, who considers armed
strategy as "a fabric of bets torn to pieces by the event" states cat-
egorically that "economic strategy is no better".[46] A third principle
of intelligibility – that of relativity, an essential complement to the
first two – must be introduced.

Economic and social "facts" are complex, liable to plurivocal or multivocal development, distorted by indeterminations and "constructed" by the economist who observes them; thus they can be identified and explained in a variety of ways. There can be no uniform expression of knowledge of antecedents (save – and not always even then – within a single school of thought); as for the future, its unpredictability leaves plenty of scope for hypotheses on what it will be. In the circumstances, it is not surprising that Boulding[47] writes that the idea of an absolute "truth" in economics is the absurd by-product of an outdated positivism. To a greater degree than in any other scientific discipline, the objective of research in economics cannot be "objective truth" but rather "plausibility" or the "intelligibly possible".

In science, truth is always defined in terms of a search for "reality". Reality is not easy to work with; it offers nothing unless it is explored. Thus, in economics as elsewhere, research begins with a representation of the object which owes a great deal to the imagination, followed by a schematizing reinterpretation which isolates certain aspects deemed significant, certain zones deemed critical, and certain relationships deemed characteristic; the entire investigation is influenced by ideas, analogies, theories and beliefs. Economists "argue" more than they "demonstrate". They go astray when, giving way to the dogmatic tendencies of scientific intelligence, they forget or neglect the task of problem-analysis which the very nature of the research subject demands. In addition, there are the deviations due to ideological contaminations, previously denounced by the sociologists of knowledge[48] and partially forgotten today, and to the fact that, as an applied science and a policy instrument, economics is always impregnated by "values"[49] and is consequently far from neutral.

Only by means of constant switching from theory to practice and vice versa, each throwing light on the other, challenging and enriching one another, can even relative truths be attained in economics. Only by rooting their thinking in experience and through apprenticeship can economists identify constructibility criteria open to advances in knowledge and criteria of forward-looking and action-oriented feasibility. This being the case, the principle of plurality must be accepted, together with that of relativity.

2. THE ORGANIZATIONAL PRINCIPLE
AND THE SYSTEMIC PRINCIPLE

The more complex a situation becomes, the more necessary it is to resort to a global reevaluation and to two new intelligibility principles – the organizational and the systemic principle – which complexity theorists combine.[50]

Intelligent cognitive behaviour patterns are organizational in nature. The dynamics of all socio-economic systems are created through the intermediary of organization. Apart from the writings of Marshall and Knight at the beginning of the 1920s, the economy of "organizations" is a relatively new development; its aim has been practically ignored in conventional thinking. It is applied in connection with economic units which Ménard termed "structured sets"[51]; by analogy with biology, organization is a principle which ensures the unity of complex organisms and is a necessary element thereof on account of their high degree of differentiation and complexification.

Organization offers an instrument for the comparative analysis of economic systems (market economies, planned economies, levels of development) and is usable either by focusing on their "architecture" (i.e., adopting a global standpoint) or by adding to that analysis an additional element in the form of a specific co-ordination procedure.[52] Thus the development of a theory of organizations consists of focusing on the behaviour of the participants, on the structured sets which they make up, on the procedures for making choices and decisions, on rules and conventions and on strategies. Among the followers of this line of thinking a significant movement can be detected from the "organization" to the "system"; as they concentrate on the study of the internal criteria deemed to form the basis of the efficiency of the organization, and thereby its ability to integrate into the global economy, the relationship between the organization and its environment is increasingly pushed into the background.[53]

Le Moigne uses the term "organization" to denote the property of a complex system which permits explanation of both the behaviour of the projective levels attributed to the system and the relationships between those levels without separating them.[54] He sees that concept as one which can replace that of structure as it emerges from analytical modelling and seeks a set of non-variant hypotheses which accepts the irreversibility of phenomena. The present author takes the view that organization is rather a concept and a reality in addition to the concept and reality of structure, for – as Le Moigne agrees – the one cannot exist without the other. Organization is based on structure; and, being a shaper of structure, it modifies that structure – and itself at the same time. At all levels, organization is seen to be a succession and a set of operations manipulating structures, using their "operative genes",[55] criticising them and replacing them by other structures and thus organizing itself in response to its own internal needs and to external stimuli.

Any organization is a "contingent social construction"[56] – a project the design and behaviour of which are the resultant of the interaction of its members (individuals or groups), a coordinating unit with a power structure continually open to receipt of information from both inside and outside the system. Individuals, as Betti and Schianchi say,[57] do not follow the patterns of deductive logic dear to conventional economic models in an optimum fashion; but they do have a tremendous capacity for pattern recognition and for developing inductive rules through the process of learning from experience. Any organization (a household, an enterprise, a trade union) and any set of organizations (a nation, a region) produces, regulates and modifies itself and evolves; it also produces, regulates, maintains and modifies the environment to which it belongs.

In evolutionist biology the term "interdependence" signifies the combination at any given level of organization of the functions performed by what are referred to as the "lower" levels (those which preceded it) and their contributions to the formation of those termed "higher" (i.e., which will succeed it). The sequence is thus from the cell to the organism through the intermediate steps of the organs and the major vital functions; thus there is a chain of "integration plateaux".[58] In the same context, interdependence also covers the adjustment of functions performed by one level to produce the functions of a higher level; the convergence of the developments between one plateau and the succeeding one can be interpreted either in teleonomic terms (as directed by a final cause) or in isolation from all metaphysical considerations as the product of a set of reactions giving rise to a certain "order".[59]

In economics, too, a given level of organization can only be interpreted with a knowledge of the levels which preceded it and of those to the attainment of which it contributes. Those who transpose the theory of evolution into economics propose the creation of a new dynamics which is capable of identifying the observable evolutionary processes and is based on a questioning of the separation between micro and macro, since this may explain global structures and dynamics by reference to an understanding of local behaviour patterns and interactions. The sequence thus runs from the workshop through the factory, the enterprise, the branch and the region to the national economy. The emergence of a stable pattern of organization is seen as the outcome of a process of learning from experience. Attention is focused on information, the acquisition and dissemination of new knowledge and the evolution of the economic behaviour of agents (and thereby of society). "Self-organization" refers to the emergence over time of structures not previously in existence, the processes of self-organization being considered as a subset of evolutionary processes.[60]

When a species evolves (by incorporation or mutation) it modifies the milieu of which it formed part and, in so doing, changes the living opportunities of the other species. This interconnexion finds expression in co-evolution; the "whole", made up of singular elements, evolves either in the light of their evolutionary processes or in that of its own. In this sense, when an economy evolves, develops or regresses there is co-evolution, the "architecture of complexity" (H.A. Simon), which is made up of a "mosaic" of programmes emanating at all levels from the elements which make up the "whole"; some of them are susceptible of change, proposing highly complex solutions, while others, less capable of change, serve to facilitate selection from among the first group; others still control the process of change in older projects and the construction of new ones.

The notion of system is just as essential to complex thinking as that of organization. In very general terms, a system may be defined as a set of elements comprising also their attributes, their relationships and their interactions.[61] A concrete economic system invariably takes the form of a complex set of structures, organizations, institutions, production processes and trade channels, as well as lifestyles reflecting the cultures of the different groups of agents. Its consistency and coherence, and also its dynamics, are the outcome of a multitude of balancing and regulating procedures, in other words, balancing processes into which enter the decisions taken by agents or groups of agents in order to further their projects (which are not in spontaneous harmony), but in a state of dependency vis-à-vis the constraints and solicitations of the milieu. There is no pseudo-"invisible hand" guiding the whole process. In this context the linkages between the organization, the rules, the powers and the balancing/regulations are absolutely essential; the agents do not wait passively for changes to take place – they evaluate the range of possibilities, broadening or narrowing it by their own actions.[62]

The interpretation of economic systems as "self-adjusting" complex systems, and the descriptions thereof given by Betti and Schianchi,[63] are extremely valuable here.

A complex system is open and dynamic. It is made up, not of relationships between things or objects, but of actions or operations.[64] The equilibrium model is incapable of taking this into account. In thermodynamics, in a closed system there are no exchanges of mass/energy with the external environment, and thus equilibrium is the normal state of affairs. In contrast, when a system is open, inflows and outflows of energy may lead to a situation of dynamic disequilibrium consisting of a multiplicity of states, some stable, others chaotic. Crabbé observes that open thermodynamic systems are "self-organizing" inasmuch as, according to the gradient of energy they import, they may develop new structures which break down the energy in a highly efficient manner and then expel it into the environment; hence the name "dissipative structures" invented by Prigogine to designate them[65] and the parallel drawn by Crabbé with the "process of creative destruction" which Schumpeter saw as "the fundamental datum of capitalism".[66]

A complex system is made up of agents, each with its own dynamic; but since they are in interaction with other agents they bring into existence collective dynamics which cannot be treated merely as a "sum". These interactions comply with certain rules (moral codes, law of supply and demand, agreements, etc.). According to Betti and Schianchi, if they are fixed, the system is a "complex" one; if they evolve over time, the system is a "self-adjusting complex" one.

Any complex system is subject to retroactive effects. These may be negative (making for equilibrium) or positive (making for disequilibrium). Effects of the latter type are referred to as "autocatalytic", and systems of this type are referred to as "self-organizing" when new structures emerge from their working.[67] Both at the level of the agents and at that of the multiple networks of relationships interconnecting them, the overall result is not the fruit of rational planning but the resultant of self-organizing activity. As Crabbé observes[68], the greater the complexity of the "whole", the greater "the autocatalytic element in the possible economic fabric".

Betti and Schianchi also identify another characteristic feature of complex systems which is immediately applicable to an economy, namely the existence of what they, together with Gould,[69] refer to as "sporadic points of equilibrium". Evolution, they observe, is not linear; it is in fact made up of "points of equilibrium" separated by long periods of stability during which differences and contradictions accumulate without finding expression in open manifestations. Drawing on the evolutionary games theory,[70] they observe that, where the game is a non-cooperative one, the most currently accepted hypothesis is that of progress towards equilibrium by a process of trial and error. However, the theoreticians of "empiricist" games[71] observe that the principal lesson to be drawn from experiments in this field is that individuals, even assuming complete information, do not behave in the manner predicted by the theory. "There is no doubt", writes Simon (who has in fact serious reservations with regard to the games theory), "that the micro hypothesis of the theory – that of perfect rationality – runs counter to the facts. It is not a question of approximation; there is no chance of its being able one day to describe the process which a man follows when making decisions in complex situations".[72] It is only by seeing in the dialectic of the "rational" and the "reasonable" the manifestation of a "meta-rationality" which emerges from the host of institutions, functions, social roles, spheres of activity, symbols, values, anticipations and projects formed in the minds of individuals, groups and organizations which learn, assimilate, adapt and change that one has any chance of making progress towards understanding of the "points of equilibrium" which "punctuate" the dynamic of complex economic systems.

One further point should be made. There are two types of complex systems.[73] There are the "hard", objective, material systems, mainly developed by engineers responsible for the optimization of a certain objective function; here the mastery of complexity results from a comprehension of the processes of coupling the system of technical operations with the system of command which is able to make selections on the basis of entry parameters. The others – the "soft" systems – are subjective, better adapted to human activities; they apply in systems where the rationality of the agents is limited, the system itself little known, and the choice of reasonably satisfactory solutions preferable to pretentious optimizations. Obviously, economic systems belong to the second category, and models of a nature to help "guide" them at any level (enterprise, nation, region and *a fortiori* the world) can only be simulation models expressing phenomena without fully apprehending them, recording observations as well as possible and contributing to scenarios matching reality. One should have no illusions about their use. Simulation raises fearsome problems of logic[74] and equally fearsome problems of interpretation. The present author is inclined to agree with Lombardini[75], who writes that when resorting to simulation the primary aim should be to seek to establish "theoretico-empirical laws". These laws are more operational than the theoretical laws, because they do not derive from a set of postulates which provide a basis for an axiomatic approach, and they are less contingent than empirical laws, which are derived exclusively from observation of facts. Moreover, these theoretico-empirical laws give rise to the collection of new empirical data; clarify the plans of decision-makers by means of a more concrete exploration of the effects of their strategies; allow a better understanding of the functioning and evolution of real economies and suggest appropriate amendments to theories on the subject; and, finally, permit analysis of the possible effects of changes that may occur at certain stages in the process which cannot be picked up by models with supposedly unchangeable structures, but which can be picked up by complex models that can simulate a variety of scenarios. Simon's proposal[76] to assimilate the methods of systemic modelling and artificial intelligence and to speak of the "simulation of cognitive processes" seems to the present author to follow similar lines.

3. THE PRINCIPLE OF RESPONSIBILITY

One of Marchal's favourite dicta was that, once accepted the fact that there is no fatal determinism, but instead a variety of scientifically probable or possible solutions, a choice is permitted; and with that recognition the "crisis" of science, struggling with uncertainty and indetermination, is aggravated by a "crisis" of conscience.[77] Becattini today observes an "abdication of responsibility" among economists, who claim the right to theorize freely but leave to the politicians the responsibility for the conclusions which may be drawn from their writings; at the same time they refuse, with increasing frequency, to seek responses to questions arising in society because they are badly framed or not susceptible to analytical treatment, thus leaving the field open to incompetent chatterers.[78]

Complexity broadens the range of possibilities. Hirschmann states[79] that to take it into account constitutes a commitment which informs human action more fully than relational calculation or statistical forecasting of the probable. It is a paradox that today there should be so many ethical reflections on life and so few on the economy, which is the support of life! In the economic context, ethics originally consisted of the denunciation of the exploitation of man by man and of the alienation due to objects, money and power. Today, however, it is a call to humans to take in hand their own development and to that end to establish the "pseudo-market society" defined by Clarke[80] for the benefit of a society in which individuals seek to live and develop, as persons and together with others, in the name of shared values.

We are responsible, not only for what has been done, but for the things we are doing. Our responsibility is "in-definite", for it concerns the whole of the condition of human life and the future of humankind. As Riccœur puts it,[81] to act implies, in a sense, a triangular dialectic between perception, knowledge and ethics. An economist cannot but adopt the statement of the principle of responsibility as formulated by Jonas:[82] "Act in such a way that the effects of your action are compatible with the permanency of a genuinely human life on earth ... that they are not destructive of the future possibility of such a life ... Know that the undetermined future, not the contemporary time of your action, is the true horizon of your responsibility – never jeopardize in the choices inherent in your actions the existence or the essence of humankind in its integrality. Every suicidal gamble with our existence is prohibited by a truly categorical imperative". That was already the full significance of the "new paradigm" for development as we have defined it; and that is the sense in which we must return to that paradigm, since responsible discernment is one of the principles of intelligibility which must be affirmed with the utmost energy.

An economy, considered as a working and trading society, increasingly needs to be organized, not in terms of the "mastery" of man over nature, but of a harmony between the two and, above all, with human development as its end. Economic activity would thus be replaced in its context of existence and responsibility; by that very fact, ethics becomes the discipline best placed to help it redefine itself.

It was the aggression of man against nature and the danger which our powers represent for ourselves which caused Jonas such unease; and it is the new awareness of the urgencies of development which are at the origin of the present author's own unease.

Responsibility implies subjection to obligations. The vulnerability of others makes me responsible for them. It is through the discovery of the "face of the Other" that "one's own face" is revealed.

The relationship between Myself and Others is more than a physical face-to-face meeting. It urges us to take into account the plurality of humankind, to wish to see justice, ethics and politics each dependent on the others. Did not Levinas say that "the most fundamental mode of responsibility is the face-to-face approach"?[83]

Themes of this kind have subtended the argument throughout this book.

We have made the cancellation (at best) of Third-World debt, or (at worst) its review, one of the requirements to be met if the "new paradigm" is to be more than a deceitful proclamation. Worms points out that everybody is pretending that the debt can be repaid, whereas in many cases that is clearly not the case, and that the problem of loans to the South falls to some extent within the scope of the Biblical condemnation of loans at interest. In his view, the invention of new regulatory mechanisms with "an essential ethical aspect for that reason" is imperative.[84]

We have made sharing one of the basic elements of development strategies. The definition *par excellence* of poverty, in the words of Sen, is to be deprived of freedom to act, to think, to believe – "never to be able to choose". To be poor is to be in continual contradiction with one's own values and one's spirituality; to live in a manner contrary to one's beliefs; and to experience at first hand the incoherences and shortcomings of society. Naturally, material poverty is an obstacle to the achievement of a fully human existence for oneself and one's family; but it is only one of the many dimensions of exclusion.

Bonvin asserts that poverty cannot be overcome except with a genuine political legitimacy and that the latter requires growth and equity. Jolly, too (and the present writer shares his views), envisages equity as one of the foundations of a development strategy. It is impossible to conceive such a strategy as a by-product of an unconstrained market; it must be envisaged as a basic requirement of any development policy. We belong to the same world as hundreds of millions of poor people; if an economy is to have any meaning it is one of ensuring the human advancement, not only of a privileged minority, but of everyone. In the words of Sfeir-Younis, we must "harmonize economic thinking and policies", and human and spiritual values must occupy a central place in decision-making at all levels.

Horkheimer and Adorno[85] unhesitatingly denounce, in the treatment of human beings according to the allegedly "rational" principle of the "minimum means", a movement similar in nature to fascism, a "commercial totalitarianism" of the same nature as "political totalitarianism". In a note which he describes as "tongue-in-cheek", Summers, a former economist at the World Bank, states that he had always thought that the under-populated countries of Africa were considerably under-polluted and that the calculation of the cost of pollution dangerous to health depended on the profits absorbed by the increase in sickness and mortality, and that, from that standpoint, the economic logic of the argument that toxic wastes should be dumped at the point where wages are lowest was incontrovertible. His "conclusion" was thus that a large-scale migration of polluting industries to the least advanced countries should be encouraged.[86] The absurdity of the pseudo-justifications substituting the yardstick of money for ethical values is obvious here.

To act "reasonably" is to act in accordance with our interest as a member of the human community, which is indissociable from our knowledge, our values, our place in society and our freedom. An economic system is never more than a set of collective means of attaining politically chosen objectives; the technical problem to be solved is that of combining those means and regulating the system as a whole in the search for efficiency, while the ethical problem is that of determining which criteria should govern the choice of those objectives. This the present author has sought to do in defining the "new paradigm" of development which has become necessary today.

When social relationships have taken on the phantasmagoric aspect of relationships between objects and when money has been transmogrified from a useful instrument into an idol, economic activity ceases to be regulated in the service of Life and alienation sets in. Alienation is anti-creation, the major obstacle to the accomplishment of the task of humankind. It is an attack on freedom which freedom must overcome. "The truly free act of a human being", wrote the philosopher Lacroix,[87] "is that by which he chooses what he will be." We do not have to live in dependency on events in the market; we must place our trust in reason and in the freedom of the individual to choose his path by himself. Here the acceptance of the principle of responsibility as one of the salient dimensions of the intelligibility of the economy for purposes of action is not enough; it is essential, in fidelity to the object of economic acts, to also affirm the necessity of an ethical obligation of responsibility.

4. A POLYPHONIC KNOWLEDGE

Any development policy must be based, not on theories (although these are useful for both its framing and its conduct), but on a "thinking" which comprises the principles of intelligibility as defined above. Since that "thinking" seeks to achieve both economic progress and human development, it demands an improvement in the very notion of "economy".[88]

The Greek words *oikonomia* and *oikoumené* have the same root (*oikos*). One designates the administration (*nomos*) of the house (*oikos*); the other refers to the universe, the inhabited Earth. Here we have a reminder not to forget that economic thought is not self-sufficient and that the science of economics cannot isolate itself from the other scientific disciplines. To paraphrase Morin, one might say that the enemy of development economics is the "mutilation" which occurs every time unidimensional or reductive concepts are adopted, and all reality and sense is denied to what is discarded.[89] How, when "rethinking development", can economists speculate on the choices to be made and the tasks to be accomplished in order to improve the well-being of peoples without considering the relationship between the economic factor and the milieu in all its varied aspects? How can they, without disastrous consequences, ignore the history of the civilizations and their cultures, on the basis of which development must make its way?[90] What could be more vain and ridiculous than to forget that Japan is not the United States, that Singapore is neither Taipei nor Mexico, and that the utmost attention should be given to the diversity of socio-economic spaces?

Myrdal recommended that economists in countries "lagging behind in development" should construct a completely new "science" specially designed for the solving of their problems and should mistrust all imported "sciences" which, to a considerable degree, are "only rationalizations of the dominant interests of the industrialized countries promoting them".[91] At the opposite extreme, Bauer and Yamey[92] saw no major reason to withhold from economic "science" absolute competence to pronounce judgement on the "particular case" of "under-development". The experience of the last half-century has taught us that a valid approach to development can be reached only on the basis of knowledge founded on observations and ideas derived from an in-depth exploration of social constants and social changes considered in their multiple aspects and in a spirit of complete freedom vis-à-vis traditional predilections. Such a complex approach to a reality which is in itself highly complex cannot remain the province of economics alone; it involves all the social and human sciences. Its truth resides, not in a "synthesis"[93] of geography, geology, ethnology, demography, sociology, ecology and the more technical disciplines such as agronomy, hydraulics, town planning and administration, but in a dialogue among them all. Likewise, it cannot be grasped if allowance is not made for clashes between powers, themselves highly varied (for they may be political and financial, on the one hand, or social, technical or cultural, on the other).

Brock (quoted by Crabbé)[94] suggests that to obtain a complex dynamic the following elements must be present: economic agents with a high discount rate; rising returns and externalities; incomplete markets; the abandonment of parametric price hypotheses; stability or regression in preferences; technology and equilibrium; the introduction of exogenous forcing techniques directed at the population; and technical advance. Leontiev[95] regrets the relatively superficial level at which eco-empirical analysis currently operates and considers that, to explore in greater depth the foundations of our system of analysis, one must unhesitatingly transcend the boundaries of the field of economic phenomena as they have hitherto been marked out. This is a far more accurate description of the path to be followed than Brock's.

The new awareness of multidimensionality, of complexity and of non-linearity reveals how essential dialogue among the disciplines and the sharing of their gains are to obtain a better knowledge of the economic and social universe and to develop a better critical discernment with a view to better seizing the opportunities for development offered by the present time.

The task is a considerable one. The disputes between specialists in the "scientific" disciplines recall the quarrels between the teachers of philosophy, music, swordsmanship and dancing in Molière's Le Bourgeois gentilhomme, in which each one exalts his own "science" and all four finish up insulting one another and exchanging fisticuffs! The intransigence and hegemonic pretensions of one "team" or another have wrecked more than one attempt at a meeting of minds, however modest. A recent example is the persistence of all the contributors in barricading themselves within their own disciplines when the Interdisciplinary Group for the Understanding of the Food Industry in Montpellier assembled within a single publication contributions from a number of disciplines (macroeconomics, marketing, nutritional science), techniques (statistics, biomimetism, networks of neurones) or methods (uniform and multivariant descriptive, explanatory); but no move towards integration ensued.[96]

Interdisciplinarity presupposes a monodisciplinarity around which dialogue can develop. It cannot yield results unless in both questions and answers there is a desire to obtain what is most advanced and most certain – the two are not incompatible – in each discipline. It must shun the "interstitial" sciences which will not progress beyond the "para" level (parapsychology, parasociology, bio-economics in the manner of Becker) and the pseudo "general sciences" of society, the different disciplines of which are alleged "specifications" that can easily degenerate into idle chatter. It must be capable of detecting those elements in an association of two or more disciplines which promise to open up new fields for the advancement of knowledge (such as biotechnologies). It will require a solid information base; this implies long-term effort, exploratory work, careful attention to the polysemy of concepts, the removal of many ambiguities and caution in the use of analogies and of instruments brought in from outside. It is highly desirable in this connection to set up courses in research and reflection of a multidisciplinary nature open to collective work. In particular, universities should cease to content themselves with the assemblage of a number of diverse elements around a single discipline; they should be more ambitious and organize dialogue within training centres, seminars and symposia.[97]

As Resweber[98] has brilliantly put it, interdisciplinarity must seek a recapitulation in "knowledge" of the "knowledges" which invest in the multiple fields and aspects of reality; for knowledge can only progress by "signifying itself" among the plural elements constituting it. In other words, the aim is not to remove the lines of demarcation between disciplines but to bring several of them together around a single object and to evaluate accurately each of them from two standpoints: awareness of their relativity; and discovery of their radical specificity.

The "new paradigm" for development requires interdisciplinarity. On this score Despouy is right; he believes that the struggle to eliminate extreme poverty, "a scourge as great as all the wars put together" and a state of affairs in which human rights are compromised, is an "interdisciplinary problem" requiring inputs by every ministry in each country and by all the governmental and non-governmental organizations throughout the world. This requirement reminds us of one essential element of interdisciplinarity, namely that knowledge must not be separated from the ethics which should inspire it. As Goldman said[99]: "scientific thought is the ultimate goal for the researcher; but for the social group and for humanity as a whole, is it not merely a means to an end?"

The time has passed when the disciplines could retreat into their shells; the time has now come for free exchanges conducted with the aim of arriving at provisional approximations guided by "project-oriented rationality" and by ethics. Much work has been done – and is still continuing – in this area.[100]

The ISEA (International Social and Economic Analysis) models used in the United States locate the socio-demographic "heart" at a meeting-point of influences coming from the economy, the political system, science and technology, the environment and natural resources. They include "attributes" such as education, employment and public opinion. They take into consideration the effects of values, beliefs, social standing and the feedback among all the elements assembled. They speculate, through information and communication models as well as decision models, on possible changes, and do not leave out of account either certain human costs (crime, delinquency) or certain ecological costs (pollution).[101]

The IDEA project (Interdisciplinary Dimensions of Economic Analysis), directed by Ulf Himmelstrand and supported by the International Social Science Council,[102] proposes a method termed "successive dissection" within which, to achieve a successful outcome, "exogenous" factors must be progressively "introduced" into economic analysis; the linkages between the endogenous and the exogenous, where the latter forms part of other disciplines, are initially identified in abstract terms and subsequently interpreted as "plug-ins", "spillovers" or "mediated feedback". The recognition that in the real world, unlike in the abstract world, agents are engaged in complex games situations (and are themselves *ipso facto* "exogenous" factors) leads the designers of the project to come to the same conclusion: the need for interdisciplinarity and practical application.

How can one ignore the "new economic logic" which Demaria[103] has continuously been working on for over half a century? Dagum,[104] convinced that the interdisciplinary relationships between economics, sociology and political science are at the root of economic science – the "science of action" – considers it the work of a "pioneer".[105] Does not Demaria interpret the multivariate relationships between the components of the economic system (causality, solidarity, reversible or irreversible, uniform or pluridirectional, dialectic, certain or uncertain, probable or random, monovalent or polyvalent) as the concrete expression of the behaviour and actions of the economic agents, conditioned by the active presence of "exogenous" variables (the propagators of action), within which group he includes institutions, law, technology, demography, social classes, ethics, market forms, income distribution, etc.? Does he not also take into account the impact of original events of varying degrees of intensity – and primarily wars – but also major events in every field of activity which disrupt, influence or upset the regulation and evolution of economic systems?

To "rethink development" or to "rethink economics" is to enter the complexity and the tragedy of action. To ensure that development is simultaneously economic and human, intervention is necessary by the philosophers, for it is they who renounce violence; by the jurists, for it is their task to place strength at the service of justice by promoting the Law; by the politicians, for it is their task to ensure respect for the Law and the service of the common good; by the economists, for the economy provides the support for human development, which, as was said earlier, must be ensured at the least instrumental, ecological and human cost; by men and women of culture, for culture is at the origin of every constitution and every institution; and, finally, by the peoples, for only with their acquiescence and the mobilization of their energies will it be possible to form the coalition of all in the service of all.[106]

Only a polyphonic knowledge of societies, their functioning, their changing patterns and their learning processes, animated and orientated by ethics of responsibility, can provide a starting-point and an effective foundation for a policy and a strategy for human development.

---

[1]F. Volpi: "Introduzione, in Crescita endogena e paesi in via di sviluppo", in *Giornale dei economisti*, April-June 1994, p. 186.

[2]F. Hahn: *On Growth Theory*, Quaderni del Dipartamento di Economia politica dell'Università di Siena, 1994, No. 67.

[3]A.O. Hirschmann: *Ascesa e declino dell'economia dello sviluppo*, Turin, Rosenberg & Sellier, 1983.

[4]"Increasing returns and long run growth", in *Journal of Political Economy*, 1986, No. 5, and "Endogenous technological change", in *ibid.*, 1990, No. 5.

[5]"On the mechanics of economic development", in *Journal of Monetary Economics*, 1988, No. 1.

[6]F. Volpi, *art. cit.*, pp. 187-188.

[7]Human capital formation, satisfaction of basic needs, the respective roles of agriculture, foreign trade, income distribution in development, etc.

[8]G.L. Bocchi and M. Cerutti: *La sfida della complessità*, Milan, Feltrinelli, 1985.

[9]P. Purroy-Chicot: La pensée complexe et la musique, M.C.X., La Lettre Chemin faisant, Nov. 1987.

[10]Paris, La Documentation française, 1986. (A record of the proceedings of a seminar held in Montpellier in May 1984.)

[11]Paris, Seuil, 1983.

[12]*Ibid.*, 1990.

[13]*Ibid.*, 1991.

[14]A Chair bearing the name of Edgar Morin has been established in the San Tomas University of Bogota.

[15]*An evolutionary theory of economic change*, Cambridge, The Belknap Press of Harvard University Press.

[16]*Economy as a complex evolving system*, New York, Addison-Wesley, 1988. The author also refers, with apologies, to his own work on the subject, *L'économie multidimensionnelle, op. cit.*

[17]Under the leadership of J.L. Le Moigne.

[18]J.L. Le Moigne: "On theorizing the complexity of economic systems", in *The Journal of Socio-Economics*, No. 3, pp. 479-480.

[19]A. Alexander, H. Bergson, H.W. Carr, B. Croce, A.N. Whitehead.

[20]*Metaphysics*, Z.1: 7, 1041-10.

[21]Hersch (ed.): *Le droit d'être un homme*, Paris, UNESCO, 1968, quoted by Perroux in *L'Economie de la Ressource humaine, op. cit.*, p. 47.

[22]*La notion de normal en psychologie clinique*, Paris, Vrin, 1954, p. 149.

[23]K. Goldstone: *La structure de l'organisme*, Paris, Gallimard, 1992, pp. 332-334.

[24]An excellent presentation of the theses of econometric neopositivism considered from the probability angle is given by G. Demaria in *Materiali per una logica del movimiento economico*, Milan, La Golliardica, 1953, Vol. 1, pp. 76-134.

[25]*Manuel d'économie politique*, Paris, Giard, 1927, chap. III, para. 226.

[26]*Eléments d'économie politique pure*, Lausanne, 1874, pp. 99-105.

[27]"Propagation problems and impulse problems in dynamic economics", in *Economic essays in honour of Gustav Cassel*, London, 1923.

[28]"The summation of random causes as a source of cyclical processes", in *Econometrica*, April 1937.

[29]"Causality and econometrics", in *Econometrica*, April 1954. *Demand analysis*, New York, John Wiley, 1953.

[30]H. Bartoli: *L'Economie multidimensionnelle, op. cit.*, pp. 390-396; G. Demaria: *Trattato di logica economica*, Padua, Cedam, 1962, pp. 21-32.

[31]*The General Theory and After. Defence and Development. The Collected Writings of John Maynard Keynes,* London, Macmillan, Vol. XIV.

[32]Keynes was not a supporter of deductions based on frequency of occurrence. The proponents of that approach only take into consideration repeated tests with the aim of reaching a certain level of uncertainty in uncertain situations by means of a frequency ratio. The proponents of the "logical" approach, of whom Keynes was one, see in probability an expression of a degree of "belief" which, in contrast to the views of the "subjectivists", represents, not a personal feeling, but a logical relationship valid for all. See *Treatise on Probability, The Collected Writings..., op. cit,* Vol. VIII.

[33]"Prévision à long terme et mutation des systèmes", in *Revue d'économie politique,* Sep.-Oct. 1987, p. 539.

[34]*La lettre,* Chemin faisant, Jan. 1999.

[35]*Mes démons,* Paris, Stock, 1994, p. 136.

[36]*Wirtschaft und Gesellschaft,* Tübingen, Mohr, 1922, Part 1, Chap. 1, para. 1.

[37]The words of Touraine : "The sociologist does not watch actors performing a play; he contributes to the discovery of a play which will be written one day because it will first have been acted out. Better still, he works with others so that they all learn together what the issues are..." can equally be applied to the economist. *Pour la sociologie,* Paris, Seuil, 1974, p. 54.

[38]W.A. Weisskopf: "The method is the ideology from a Newtonian to a Heisenbergian paradigm in economics", in *Journal of Economic Issues,* Dec. 1979.

[39]G. Bachelard: *L'activité rationaliste de la physique moderne,* Paris, PUF, 1951, p. 218.

[40]One can theorize *a priori* on the impact of demographic change on an economy, but not, with any chance of success, on the influence of variations in the distribution of the national income on demography.

[41]From this standpoint the concept of "possible awareness" is of the utmost importance for the understanding of human action in any field. It is the necessary complement of "actual awareness". See L. Goldmann: *Sciences humaines et philosophie,* Paris, PUF, 1952, pp. 113-127.

[42]R. Boirel: *Théorie générale de l'invention,* Paris, PUF, 1961, p. 51.

[43]*Expectation in Economics,* Cambridge, Cambridge University Press, 1949.

[44]*Decision, order and time in human affairs, ibid.,* 1961. Also of interest is J.L. Ford: *The dissenting economist's economist,* Aldershot, Edward Elgar, 1994.

[45]"Di un principio di indeterminazione in economia dinamica", in *Rivista italiana di scienze sociali,* 1932, No. 5, pp. 597-636.

[46]*Dialogue des monopoles et des nations,* Grenoble, Presses universitaires, 1982, p. 102.

[47]"What went wrong with economics?" in *The American Economist,* Spring 1986.

[48]J.J. Maquet: *Sociologie de la connaissance*, Louvain, Nauwelaerts, 1945; K. Mannheim: *Ideology and Utopia*, New York, Harcourt, 1936.

[49]S.C. Sufrin and S. Young: "Applied economic analysis. Standards of evaluation", in *Rivista internazionale di scienze economiche e commerciali*, Dec. 1978.

[50]The first "guiding principle for connective thinking" offered by Morin is the "systemic or organizational principle". See *La tête bien faite*, Paris, Seuil, 1999, p. 107.

[51]*L'économie des organisations*, Paris, La Découverte, 1990, p. 5.

[52]*Ibid.*, pp. 14-16.

[53]*Ibid.*, pp. 100-101.

[54]*La modélization des systèmes complexes*, Paris, Dunod, 1990, p. 74.

[55]*Op. cit.*, pp. 51-55.

[56]C. Everaere: "Le constructivisme, chemin marquant de l'approche systèmique?", in *Economies et sociétés*, Oct. 1993, p. 188.

[57]*Previsioni sul BTP Future. Un' esplorazione con reti neurali.* Università degli studi di Parma, Istituto di scienze economiche, WP 3/1998.

[58]J. Ruffié: *De la biologie à la culture*, Paris, Flammarion, 1976, pp. 196 ff.

[59]H. Atlan: *Entre le cristal et la fumée. Essai sur l'organisation du vivant*, Paris, Seuil, 1973.

[60]Lesourne and Orléan (eds.): *Advances in self-organization and evolutionary economics*, Paris, Economica, 1999, p.2.

[61]D. Berlinski: *On systems analysis*, Cambridge, MIT Press, 1976. See also J. Ladrière's article "Système" in *Encyclopaedia Universalis*, Vol. 15, p. 686.

[62]H. Bartoli: *L'économie multidimensionnelle, op. cit.*, pp. 337 and 380.

[63]*Logica ed economia*, Università degli studi di Parma, Istituto di scienze economiche, March 1998, WP 6/1998, pp. 33-34.

[64]J.L. Le Moigne: *On theorizing the complexity, art. cit.*, p. 485.

[65]*Introduction à la thermodynamique des processus irreversibles*, Paris, Dunod, 1968.

[66]P. Crabbé, François Perroux and Ilya Prigogine: "Systèmes complexes et science économique", in *Etudes internationales*, June 1998, pp. 410 ff; and J. Schumpeter: *Capitalism, socialism and democracy*, New York, Harper & Bros., 1942.

[67]We should bear in mind Crabbé's remark (*art. cit.*, p. 414) that economists tend to speak of cumulative effects, mutual-causality processes amplifying deviations, threshold effects and even convexity rather than positive retrospective effects.

[68]*Art. cit.*, p. 418.

[69]"Il darwinismo e l'ampliamento della teoria evoluzionista", in G. Bocchi and M. Cerutti (eds.): *La sfida della complessità, op. cit.*

[70]*Op. cit.*, pp. 25-26.

[71]B. Guerrien: "Théorie des jeux et normativité", in H. Brochier,

R. Frydman, B. Gazier, J. Lallement (eds.): *L'économie normative*, Paris, Economica, 1997, p. 104.

[72]*Models of bounded rationality*, Cambridge, MIT Press, 1982, Vol. 2, p. 490.

[73]P. Checkland and J. Scholes: *Soft systems methodology in action*, New York, Wiley, 1992.

[74]A systemic exploration of the parametric space cannot be undertaken if the number of parameters introduced into the simulation model is very great, for in such cases simulation serves little purpose. If the number is small, however, there is no more complexity, and only a distorted reality is simulated.

[75]"Prolegomena to a theory of economic development", in *Rivista internazionale di scienze economiche e commerciali*, Oct. 1997, pp. 1020-21.

[76]*La science des systèmes*, Paris, Epi, 1974, p. 18.

[77]*Méthode scientifique et science économique*, Paris, de Médicis, 1952, Vol. 1, p. 10.

[78]"Per una critica dell'economia contemporanea. Alcune considerazioni e una proposta", in G. Becattini (ed.): *Il pensiero economico: temi, problemi, e scuole*, Turin, UTET, 1990, p. xxiv.

[79]*La morale secrète de l'économiste, Entretiens*, Paris, Les Belles Lettres, 1997, pp. 96-100.

[80]*Social control of business*, Chicago, University of Chicago Press, 1926.

[81]*Histoire et vérité*, Paris, Seuil, 1955, pp. 107 ff.

[82]*Principe de responsabilité*, Paris, Editions du Cerf, 1990.

[83]"De la phénoménologie à l'éthique. Entretiens avec Emmanuel Levinas", in *Esprit*, July 1997, p. 131.

[84]In addition, Worms evokes other ethical problems, such as those raised by speculative financial operations which sometimes have a negative impact on the general interest and the real economy. See "Pouvoir de l'argent et l'éthique", in *L'Argent*, XXVIIIth Colloque des intellectuels juifs, Paris, Denoël, 1989, pp. 165 ff.

[85]*La dialectique de la raison*, Paris, Gallimard, 1974.

[86]*Courrier international*, 20 Feb. 1992.

[87]*Philosophie de la culpabilité*, Paris, PUF, 1977, pp. 68-69.

[88]F. Perroux: "Trois outils d'analyse pour l'étude du sous-développement", in *Economies et sociétés*, June-July 1978, p. 1256.

[89]*Messie, mais non*. Colloque de Cérisy. Arguments pour une méthode. Autour d'Edgar Morin, Paris, Seuil, 1990.

[90]H. Bartoli, "Progrès et pauvreté, les concepts et leur dialectique dans les civilisations et leurs cultures", in *Poverty, progress and development*, London, UNESCO and Kegan Paul International, 1961.

[91]*Théorie économique et pays non-développés*, Paris, Présence africaine, 1959, p. 118.

[92]*The Economics of Underdeveloped Countries*, Cambridge, Cambridge University Press, 1957.

[93]As J.L. Lebret suggests in "Commentaires", in J. Austruy: *Le scandale du développement*, Paris, Marcel Rivière, 1965, p. 323.

[94]*Art. cit.*, and W.A. Brock: "Non linearity and complex dynamics in economics and finance", in P.W. Anderson, K.J.Arrow, D. Pines (eds.): *The economy as complex and evolving system, op. cit.*

[95]"Theoretical assumptions and non observed facts", in *American Economic Review*, March 1971.

[96]"Pour une étude pluridisciplinaire de la consommation alimentaire", in *Economies et sociétés*, Sep. 1997.

[97]Since 1951 the University of Chicago has been setting an example by organizing seminars on development attended by economists, sociologists, anthropologists and historians. The interdisciplinary seminars of the Collège de France, which were instituted in 1971 as a follow-up to an interdisciplinary symposium organized by the European Collegial Institute in Saclay in 1970, offer another example; a third is the research group on systems analysis and economic calculations in University of Aix-Marseilles III.

[98]*La méthode interdisciplinaire*, Paris, PUF, 1981.

[99]*Sciences humaines et philosophie*, Paris, PUF, 1981.

[100]See H. Bartoli: *L'économie multidimensionnelle, op. cit.*, pp. 85-118.

[101]M.D. Intriligator: "A case study of an integrated approach to economic analysis: the Rockwell Project for integrated social and economic analysis of the United States", in *Information sur les sciences sociales*, Sep. 1985.

[102]Also by the Tricentenary Foundation of the Bank of Sweden and the Maison des Sciences de l'Homme in Paris. See "Introduction: les facteurs exogènes dans l'analyse économique", in *Revue internationale des sciences sociales*, Aug. 1987.

[103]*A new logic of economics*, Padua, Cedam, 1996; A. Agnati: *Critica dei massimi sistemi dell'economia politica*, Padua, Cedam, 1996, Vol. III.

[104]"Idéologie et méthodologie de la recherche", in *Economies et Sociétés*, March 1977, pp. 553 and 582.

[105]"Economic Model, System and Structure. Philosophy of Science and Lakatos' Methodology of Scientific Research Programs", in *Rivista internazionale di scienze economiche e commerciali*, Sep. 1986, p. 882.

[106]This was originally the conclusion of the author's contribution to *Mélanges J.L. Le Moigne* (Paris, PUF, 1999) entitled "Raison d'Etat, raison politique, et éthique".

Conclusion

Keeping our word

In his last lied, Richard Strauss set to music an exquisite poem by Eichendorff entitled "Twilight".

We have walked hand in hand
Through sorrows and joys.
Now we are both at rest
In the silent country…
We are so tired of walking!
Could this perhaps be death?

Seeing the goal of his long journey draw near, the traveler that we are recapitulates. He picks up the book of life, where few pages are left to turn. He questions himself even more than he had all along the journey.

"There are some things", goes an African proverb, "that can be seen only by eyes that have wept." As a child in Lyon, during the Great Depression of the 1930s, I saw long queues of starving unemployed being handed bowls of soup at mobile kitchens. As an adult, in the concentration camp at Drancy, whose wonderful blue sky Louise Jacobson courageously described in her "Letters" to her parents,[1] I saw human beings penned in, humiliated, doomed to be crammed into the sinister train wagons for deportation and for death at the end of the journey. I have seen the destitution of African and Asian slums and of the people of the Fourth World in our affluent countries. Respect for others became an article of faith with me and, with it, the certainty that economics makes no sense unless it is devoted to the service of life.

Death, for an economist with any awareness, is the inability to fix one's gaze on the human community as it travels along; to posit fetishes as criteria for action; to opt for a bogus rationale of means that ignore the end; not to anchor one's work in the objective of a more just society; to be unable to help clear the road for human development; to shut oneself up in an ivory tower and feel no responsibility for the food, health, housing, education, culture or life of human beings. Death, for such an economist, is to fail to put values before structures and systems; not to realize, as Grange[2] wrote, that it is not economics that "sets the standards", but "its purpose, which is to engender values".

Pirandello tells the story of a young man who, working night and day in a sulphur mine, was filled with wonder at his first sight of the moon. It is high time we discover the real turmoil of our era and recognize the urgent need to introduce radical changes in economics, for what is at stake is a preference for the splendour of Life, which far transcends all wonders.

"All of humankind is threatened with being subjected to an all-embracing system of slavery for all. The scale of the coming degradation may well be the greatest in the history of humankind," wrote Bataille shortly before the Second World War[3]. It was he who, in *Internal Experience*, foresaw a total man, without beliefs and without projects, who abandons himself to his own experience, a raw experience entirely exposed to the unknown. The result has been the Shoah, the totalitarian regimes' tens of thousands of "peace-time dead", the drop in average life expectancy in Africa due to AIDS – a poor man's disease –, drug trafficking that accounts for 8 per cent of world trade, environmental insecurity, civil wars (58 between 1989 and 1998!), the ruthless presence of global competition that threatens solidarity – defined by UNDP as the "invisible heart of human development".

Hensahuro Oe[4], winner of the 1994 Nobel Prize for Literature, sees in the bombing of Hiroshima the threefold symbol of the balance of terror born of the cold war, of human suffering and of our inability to escape from the impasse into which our modernization has driven us. He sees it as the forerunner of the "real end of the world", for while things have changed in Europe with the break-up of the Soviet Union, the same cannot be said of the world situation as long as armies have weapons of mass destruction, and acts of war still abound. Philippe Delmas reminds us that while it is healthy to reflect on the eventual sharing of the "peace dividend" that emerges from the first steps towards disarmament, "small wars" have taken a toll of 30 million casualties since 1945, three quarters of them civilians.[5]

The world is being "thrown off balance," asserts Beaud,[6] who describes "the murky stream of which man is the source": increasing poverty in an affluent world; spiralling violence; disdain for the earth and for life; the boomerang effect of inadequate living; ubiquitous war, behind which economic or financial interests hide or from which they profit. Like Oedipus, we cannot face the accusation, "Know that it is you, you, the criminal who sullies this earth"; like him, we cannot bear to see "the spate of new disasters" on the horizon.[7]

With scant hope we have proposed people's effective exercise of their human rights as the subject of development. The universality and indivisibility of those rights still represent the ethical landscape of our times. And yet, there is killing, torture and ethnic cleansing; and recurrent hatreds are not erased from human memory, witnesses to our unceasing propensity to evil, over which good must triumph if humankind is to survive.

Enthusiasm remains a virtue so long as it does not succumb to naiveté. Humanity is still a utopia.[8]

Massive changes must be made in the law, in organizations and in attitudes, if States, nations and peoples are to "work together" – which is a prerequisite for peace – and if human rights are to cease to be a mere myth or an alibi. We are, at the start the third millennium, weighed down with the burdens and disillusions of the century that has just ended, but we also have within our grasp the prospects and opportunities that lie contained in its discoveries in all fields of human activity.

Gorz[9] wrote that we must "seek the demise of this moribund society so that another may rise from its rubble". In gentler terms, Hirschmann[10] takes issue with the convention that continually repeats the same prescription and the same therapy for curing all ills, and endeavours to subject everything to the law of the marketplace, ignoring the real complexity of the situation. Nor is Berthelot more optimistic. For him, no new direction can be given to actions and institutions already in place, unless we all raise our level of awareness. He recalls that when Boutros-Ghali, then Secretary-General of the United Nations, launched the idea of an Agenda for Development encompassing all the interactions that were taken into account in the "new paradigm" we proposed, the initiative stirred no interest whatsoever.

What is needed is to ensure that dialogue triumphs over hatred, to help initiate a shift towards a "plural universalism", which is a thousand times preferable to the "unified" world order that smacks of a dangerous hegemony of civilization and culture, and even of power. We must also affirm the fundamental role of ethics in development and demystify the *lex mercatoria*.

In that regard, it is pertinent that in the spring of 1999 Jean Fabre, Deputy Administrator of UNDP, commenting on a case from Africa, dubbed the average 0.22 per cent of GNP that the rich countries contributed to development assistance a "statistic of shame and stupidity". He declared that "Africa cannot be asked to open up to the world and to competition, to liberalize and privatize its fragile economies, while we turn a blind eye to the ricochet effect and do nothing to attenuate the resulting social damage". Lambasting the two decades of structural adjustment conducted in Africa, the UNDP file found that the policies pursued "had been misguided" and had resulted in scandalous inequality rather than poverty reduction. It is also laudable that the World Bank's Development Committee has since been discussing the effective adoption of general social-policy principles in line with those established at the 1995 Copenhagen Summit: universal access to basic services, respect for fundamental social rights as set out in the ILO conventions, introduction of "safety nets" so that, in the event of a "crisis", the programmes being implemented at the behest of the IMF (which also raised the topic, albeit briefly) should not prevent those requirements from being observed. That approach was endorsed by the vast majority of the G-7 countries' trade unions, and was opposed, for the most part, by the developing countries, which saw it as yet another protectionist ploy prompted, this time, by the rich countries' trade unions.

The important point is that the international organizations that deal with economic and financial affairs no longer systematically consider the human rights debate incongruous, and that a number of them increasingly admit that consideration of labour issues and social questions is just as important as consideration of economic policies viewed solely in terms of economic and financial criteria. For us, it is equally significant that the Nobel Prize for Economics was awarded to Amartya Sen, whose work takes the ethical dimension of economics into account and enjoins us to review our perception of human behaviour on the premise not of an *a priori* approximation, but of empirical observation, and to focus our attention on "capacities", "expressions of individuals' genuine freedom to achieve certain aims"[11]. Similarly to Aristotle, he affirms that economics is in the service of politics, the purpose of which is none other than "truly human well-being".

The communiqé and joint declaration issued by the 25th Summit of the G-7 – which became the G-8 at Cologne and whose debt-alleviation measures were alluded to above – exhorted its members to preserve and augment the beneficial effects of globalization and to strengthen institutional and social infrastructures in order to harmonize globalization. It promised to increase gradually the volume of public development assistance and to concentrate that assistance on the countries best placed to take advantage of it. The appeal to governments, international institutions and civil society to take advantage of globalization in order to boost prosperity and foster social progress while preserving the environment is particularly addressed to the second group: the IMF and the World Bank are invited to support and formulate social protection policies in the developing countries; the WTO is urged to seek a more effective way of reconciling trade and the environment and to promote sustainable development and economic and social prosperity across the globe, and to co-operate "genuinely" with the ILO to that end.

Action, however, must follow, and the conditions for its implementation need to be considered.

Paul-Marc Henry concluded his remarks on "Progress, poverty and development" 13 years ago with the observation that, if an in-depth analysis highlighted the virtual divorce of the constantly pursued aims of technological progress from the satisfaction of humankind's physical and spiritual needs, poverty would no longer be seen as "a chance mishap" or "a mere episode on the long march to humankind's economic and social progress". On the contrary, it would be regarded as the fruit of our contradictions. Vilifying the economic system, he attacked its internal logic and financial requirements, in which he saw a perfect illustration of "our leaders' conceptual myopia."[12]

The failures and weaknesses of previous development strategies are no secret. Neither the "all market" nor the "all State" strategy has been capable of ensuring long-term development. The successes of the developmentalist State in the 1960s and 1970s have been called into question; those of the newly industrialized countries, attributed to their adherence to the market and their required integration into the international division of labour, resulted in the Latin-American and Asian "crises". All too apparent have been the

deleterious effects of an economic system in which, owing to the
virtual monetary and financial explosion, money has supplanted the
scale of social values.

Paul-Marc Henry was right: the logic of the current capitalist system, the only economic and social system that prevails today, must
be challenged. Cracks are beginning to appear in the Washington
consensus:[13] the evidence is there that while some countries'
under-development can be attributed to excessive State control and
to abuse of power which replaces public order with an "organization" that protects the holders of power and, ultimately, cultivates
the mafia model, the excesses of liberalization and the reduction of
the State's role are equally pernicious. One can only be happy to
hear James Wolfensohn, President of the World Bank, champion a
new approach to development, "the global strategic development
framework"; but we must beware of contenting ourselves with
introducing a modicum of social equity in the operation of the system. It is also necessary to lay down new regulations and talk some
sense into the economic and financial powers which are largely
responsible for the failures of human development and sustainable
development. That is the price of "good governance" which presupposes that the problems of governance we have echoed are
being solved.

At the Intergovernmental Conference on Cultural Policies, held
in Stockholm in the spring of 1998, Federico Mayor told the conference that keeping one's word and "facing up to one's commitments (what used to be called "honour") is a compelling and
formidable obligation... Apart from fine words, what has become
of all these gatherings of the international community that have fea-
tured so prominently in the news? We must stop letting people
down. We must keep our word.[14] "What has become of responsibility? Why is there no response? Could it be because human dignity is not quoted on the stock exchanges of Wall Street, London
or Tokyo?" asked an indignant Secretary-General of Amnesty
International at the States General of NGOs, held in Paris on 10
December 1998. Less gently, Justice Bedjaoui, a judge on the
International Court of Justice in the Hague, after denoncing "tri-
umphalism" as the greatest challenge now facing capitalism,
observed that if the current leaders of nations, peoples and groups
did not rise to the situation, they would, sooner or later, be swept
aside by a tide of history they could not hold back.[15]

Responsibility lies with the holders of power, but it also lies with
us, whatever our place in society; this is especially true if, as men

and women of culture, our mission is to shape public opinion and public will in order to ensure that the authorities are in a position to replace outmoded and inadequate structures and institutions with others that can furnish men and women with the means to live as human beings should, and to build an open community.

"Notice was served on everyone," says Hélène Cixous,[16] "and yet no one understood. What purpose did the Flood serve? Can no-one hear death approaching? Deafness is the problem." And Jorge Semprun:[17] "Everything can always be said, but can everything be heard? Will everything ever be heard?"

History speaks to us.

To hear it, we must cultivate a restless mind and the creative faculties that define humankind. We are "fulfilling our destiny"[18] when we transform and contemplate with an end in view, and when we exorcise the false prophets and invented "apocalypses" which abound today and neither hear nor see.

The Greek word apokalypsis does not mean the end of the world, but "revelation" of a hopeful prospect. The "revelation" is that while, after the experience of concentration camps throughout the world, genocides, especially the Shoah, and indifference to those whose basic needs are not met but who are far away, we are forever banned from proclaiming the inhumanity of evil – for evil is "one of the possible projects of the freedom that constitutes man's humanity"[19] – it is also true that there is a human community that is a fraternity: not a mythical "utopia", but the prospect of consciousness.[20] "A person's death," said Dufrenne,[21] "is first of all the extinction of consciousness". Life means "being present", recognizing and creating values.

Value is what should exist, something that transcends achievement and is therefore to be found in the acts that we must accomplish.

Value is anything which, through a task well done and action undertaken, keeps us on course towards the construction of the human community.

Value is anything that projects consciousness and takes us forward with an acute awareness of the relative and the ephemeral, but also of everything that combines into the history we make.

We have learned not to put our trust in the earthly salvation made possible by scientific and technological progress or any revolution; we have also learned that history is not an irreversible march towards a humanity which is fully and definitively reconciled with itself and which controls nature. We are enjoined once more to be creative, to strive to restore objects and people to the vast movement of possible achievements which still constitutes the web of history, and to endeavour to rejoin the river of life of which each of our lives is a tributary, in order to liberate it by ensuring that it focuses on values.[22]

Development is not in the hands of blind destiny. The main issue is still knowing what we are doing and what we will do with our capacity to develop the being inside us and outside us.

In Brazil's literacy schools, texts used for basic education combined technical education with a content of liberation. Lesson 6 reads: "The people are hungry and suffer from many diseases. Why are there so many diseases among the people? The people need houses and food; the people need work; life is hard for the people. Can the people change life? Yes, the people can change life." Further on, in lesson 24, I read: "Popular art is culture. Any man who invents something creates culture, whether it is his home, plantations, shoes, clay ovens. That is creation. The human being is a creator".[23]

Those texts, which have no denominational reference, are an act of faith. Human beings are given a reason for living that is commensurate with what they give to their works. They advance from a situation of virtual death to an accomplishment of life through liberating action. For all that values are resolutely woven into the fabric of collective conduct, they must untiringly be "recovered" and "revived". There are two facets to that enterprise: the one is critical discernment with regard to life, the other a poetics of the opening up of vistas of opportunity and of promotion of the new human being, with no idea what kind of man or woman that will be, or by what means he or she will arrive.[24]

Paris, 1 September 1999

---

[1]*Lettres de Louise Jacobson*, Paris, Robert Laffont, 1997.

[2]"L'ancienne et la nouvelle économie", *Esprit*, October 1956, p. 529.

[3]*L'apprenti sorcier. Textes, lettres, et documents*, Paris, Edit. de la Différence, 1999.

[4]*Century of war. Conflicts and society since 1914*, New York, The New Press, 1994.

[5]*Le bel avenir de la guerre*, Paris, Gallimard, 1995.

[6]*Le basculement du monde*, Paris, La Découverte, 1997.

[7]*Op. cit.*, p. 36.

[8]C. Chalier: *Levinas, l'utopie de l'humain*, Paris, Albin Michel, 1993.

[9]*Misères du présent, Richesse du possible*, Paris, Galilée, 1997, p. 11.

[10]*La morale secrète de l'économiste, op. cit.*, p. 130.

[11]*Ethnique et économie, et autres essais*, Paris, PUF, 1993, p. 218.

[12]*Op. cit.*, pp. 302-303.

[13]An international conference: "Beyond the Washington Consensus: progress report and prospects for a new approach", organized by the *Ecole des Hautes études en sciences sociales (EHESS)*, in co-operation with UNESCO's MOST Programme, UNESCO, Paris, 16-17 June 1999.

[14]Final report of the Conference, Paris, UNESCO, 98/Conf. 210/CLD 19 p. 9.

[15]Aspects of the United Nations system in the framework of the new world order. Development and conception of a "new world order". General report, International meetings of the Aix-en-Provence *Institut d'études politiques*, Paris, Pédone, 1992, and *Towards a New International Economic Order*, UNESCO/Holmes & Meier, 1979.

[16]*La ville parjure ou le réveil des Erinyes*, Paris, Théâtre du Soleil, 1994, p. 155.

[17]*L'écriture ou la vie*, Paris, Gallimard, 1994, p. 23.

[18]P. Ricœur: *Histoire et vérité, op. cit.*, p.86

[19]Jorge Semprun: *op. cit.*, p. 99.

[20]M. David: *Fraternité et Révolution française*, Paris, Aubier, 1987.

[21]*Pour l'homme*, Paris, Seuil, 1968, p. 238.

[22]C. Danzin: "Le caractère universel de la complexité : convergence des observations, nouveaux paradigmes, orientations de la recherche pour la complexité sociale", in *Science et pratique de la complexité*, Paris, La Documentation française, 1986, p. 91.

[23]These quotations were taken from J. Cardonnel: *L'originalité de l'humain*, XIXth Session of "Sainte Baume", September 1964, p. 13.

[24]P. Ricœur: "Que signifie humanisme", *Comprendre*, 1956, No. 15.

Impression : EUROPE MEDIA DUPLICATION S.A.
53110 Lassay-les-Châteaux
N° 7561 - Dépôt légal : Juin 2000